Spiritual Journeys

A Practical Methodology For Accelerated Spiritual Development
And Experiential Exploration

Howard F. Batie

ISBN: 150082318X

ISBN 13: 9781500823184

Library of Congress Control Number: 2014914563

CreateSpace Independent Publishing Platform

North Charleston, South Carolina

monthly SDG meetings), and Guests (those who attend our SDG meetings infrequently due to distance or incompatible schedules).

The SDG Leader should begin by establishing a free DropBox account, or similar Cloud Service that allows them to store files in folders to which access can be granted to specific individuals by the SDG Leader. The SDG Leader will continue to place 'interesting' articles from the Internet and other sources in the current monthly DropBox folder and ensure that all Members and Guests have the link to access the DropBox articles. The file name of each article will begin with the date of the article to allow articles in the DropBox folder to be sorted and listed sequentially by the date of the article. For example, the file name of an article titled 'The Eclipses of October' provided from Archangel Metatron by James Tyberonn on September 26, 2014 might be "2014-09-26 AA Metatron - The Eclipses of October ~ James Tyberonn"

Suggested SDG Activities

Each month, I host a two-hour Spiritual Discussion Group (SDG) of like-minded people who are curious about or interested in learning more about our true spiritual (not religious) nature. Our discussions topics include virtually any spiritually-oriented information or material we trust from the Internet, interesting articles or magazines we've seen, or even just subjects that we're wrestling with and need some help from other perspectives. These individuals initially were Spiritual Journeys clients, energy healing students or hypnotherapy clients who wanted to expand their information and experiences with the spiritual realms.

At each SDG meeting, the Members who volunteered to review a different week's worth of DropBox articles from the previous month will select from these articles one or two topics that could stimulate interesting group discussion and interaction from different perspectives. In addition, during the month between SDG meetings, all Members and Guests are encouraged to read all the DropBox articles and, if there are any questions about the information provided in a DropBox article or any other 'interesting' articles they come across, they are to send a group email to the other Members of the SDG as soon as possible with their questions or requests for additional clarity and/ or discussion using the "Reply All" email function.

At the next SDG meeting, and after the preliminary introductions, each Member who volunteered to review a week's worth of DropBox articles will summarize their week's articles and lead a discussion on the topic or topics they have selected, if no email discussion has taken place. The SDG Leader will also ask for weekly Member volunteers for the next month's DropBox articles before the SDG is concluded.

The SDG Leader will continue to mentor additional clients, students and SDG Members through the Spiritual Journeys processes. As additional SDG Members demonstrate a clear ability to clearly channel information from the Akashic Record, they may be invited to join a Spiritual Research Group which consists of a subset of the SDG Members, as described below.

If you are a Certified Hypnotherapist, you may also find that being listed publicly as a Spiritual Discussion Group Leader brings to you additional people who are searching for such a group in which they can safely share and validate their own experiences. As each new SDG is established, the Leader is encouraged to forward their name, location, e-mail address and website URL to me, and this contact information will be added to the SDG-SRG column in the Spiritual Journeys Practitioners listing, as shown below. As the SDG Leader, I update this "SJList.pdf" file as appropriate and upload it to the "SDG Archive" Folder in my DropBox account and also to the "Spiritual Journeys" page on my website. In addition, I provide all SDG Members with the access link to my DropBox folder, and they are also encouraged to link to the "SJList.pdf" file on my website if they wish.

This "SJList.pdf" file is a MS Word Table that is organized by Location (Country, State/Province, City/Town) so that all SJ Practitioners and SDG Leaders will be able to locate and communicate with any of their counterparts in any area of the world if they choose. This Table, as shown below, is maintained and updated by me as additions and changes are received. It is the responsibility of each Spiritual Journeys Practitioner and SDG Leader to ensure that their information in this table is accurate and up to date. Changes and updates should be provided as they occur to their SDG Leader.

Spiritual Journeys Practitioners

Country-State-City	Name	SDG-SRG	Website	Email
United States				
California				
Santa Barbara	Carolyn Paige, CHt	002-No	www.carolynpaige.com	carolynpaige@cox.net
Oregon				
Portland	Jillian Brown, CHt		www.jillianbrownhypnosis.com	jillianbrown1@gmail.com
Portland	Aymey Sangill, CHt		www.thewisealchemist.com	missangill@gmail.com
Washington				
Chehalis	Howard Batie, CHt	001-001	www.howardbatie.com	howard@howardbatie.com

Puyallup	Ray Zukowski, CHt, CI		www.body mindmentoring.com	ray@bodymindmentoring.com

Suggested SDG Files & Archive Organization

On Your Local Computer:

Local SDG Archive Folder which contains:

Monthly Folders for Archiving items discussed at each previous monthly SDG meeting

Current month's Folder for listing documents to be discussed at next monthly SDG meeting

"Suggested SDG Procedures.pdf"

"SJList.pdf" File: Contact Information of all Spiritual Journeys Practitioners and SDG Leaders

On Your DropBox:

SDG Archive Folder which contains a copy of the "Local SDG Archive" files and folders

How To Manage Your Own Spiritual Discussion Group

1. Organize a monthly Spiritual Discussion Group (SDG) in your local area and introduce the Spiritual Journeys Program to the members of the Group. (Note: The SDG Leader does not need to be a Certified Hypnotherapist; however, a Certified Hypnotist or Hypnotherapist is required to coach students through the Spiritual Journeys Program.)

2. Inform Howard Batie (howard@howardbatie.com) that you have established a SDG and would like to be included in the listing of all SDG Leaders. Provide your Name, Location (City/State/Country), Email address, and your Website URL, if applicable.

3. Create a Folder on your local computer called "Local SDG Archive". Open a sub-folder for "(Year-Month)" [e.g., "2013-05 May" for the May 2013 sub-folder and "2014-10 Oct" for the October 2014 sub-folder]. This naming convention allows the current and all future monthly sub-folders to be automatically sorted and viewed in sequential order by their file name.

4. Download the Spiritual Journeys Practitioners file "SJList.pdf" file and this "Suggested SDG Procedures.pdf" file from the DropBox link provided by Howard Batie and place them in the "Local SDG Archive" folder on your local computer.

5. From the Internet, magazines, books, etc., select articles and other items that may be of interest to discuss at your SDG meetings, and place these articles in the appropriate month's sub-folder to be discussed at the next month's SDG meeting. For example, in the month before the October 2014 meeting, you would place these articles in the "2014-10 Oct" sub-folder within the "Local SDG Archive" folder on your computer.

6. If you have not already done so, open a DropBox account (free for up to several Gb of data) and establish an empty "SDG Archive" folder.

7. Within the "Local SDG Archive" folder on your computer, copy all the folders files, and paste them into the "SDG Archive" folder on your DropBox account. Provide the link to this DropBox folder to all your SDG Members and Guests.

8. As you come across interesting topics or articles during the month, copy them into the current month's sub-folder within the "Local SDG Archive" folder on your computer, and also ensure that they are also copied into the current month's sub-folder in the "SDG Archive" folder on DropBox.

9. After each month's SDG meeting, establish a new sub-folder for the upcoming month and repeat step 8.

10. As new Spiritual Discussion Groups are established, there will be an updated "SJList.pdf" file posted to my "SDG Archive" folder on DropBox to replace the older version in your archives.

Spiritual Research Groups

As you continue your Spiritual Discussion Group (SDG) meetings, and also continue to coach SDG Members through the individual Spiritual Journeys sessions, you will find that, as they move into the optional Personal Spiritual Growth and/or Spiritual Exploration paths, some will be able to easily and clearly access information from the Akashic Record. As a subset of the Spiritual Discussion Group, you may then want to form what I call a **Spiritual Research Group** (SRG) to separately investigate a wide range of topics recorded in the Akashic Record. This separate SRG consists of an SRG Leader who is a qualified Spiritual Journeys Practitioner and Certified Hypnotherapist, and those SDG Members who have been invited to investigate research topics from the Akashic Record.

Once an individual SDG Member has experienced at least Spiritual Journeys 1-3, Journeys 7-10, and successfully channeled spiritual information on any topic from the Akashic Record, he or she may be invited to join my Spiritual Research Group for subsequent individual channeling sessions to investigate any topic that they or our Spiritual Discussion Group may be interested in. And at that point, it is necessary to begin thinking about how to properly store, archive, and share that information so that it is easily accessible by others who are interested in sharing their efforts as well to maintain the spiritual integrity of the communications.

Separate detailed "Suggested Standards And Procedures For Spiritual Research Group Leaders" have been developed and approved by the spiritual beings guiding this Spiritual Journeys Program; these Standards and Procedures provide guidelines for recording, transcribing, and archiving your channeling sessions, as well as for sharing transcribed extracts between Spiritual Research Group Leaders. These suggested standards and procedures will be provided to each Certified Hypnotherapist wishing to establish and lead their own Spiritual Research Group.

As always, helpful comments and suggestions for improving this proposed methodology and its procedures are welcomed. Please send them to howard@howardbatie.com, or after the dedicated Spiritual Journeys website is established, to howard@spiritualjourneying.org.

Thank you.

Made in the USA
San Bernardino, CA
10 October 2016

Dedication

This book is dedicated to each reader who has been drawn to pick it up, read it, and hopefully be inspired to continue your own journey home. May your journey be made easier and quicker, along with a greater understanding and appreciation of the incredible potential within each one of us.

Acknowledgements

I'd like to recognize each person who has contributed to the material in this book. However, since we all learn something from every single person we meet, that would be a bit impractical. Given this, there are a few very special people who have guided me to where I am now, and I would like to publicly acknowledge their patience, kindness, wisdom, special insights, and talents.

I am indeed indebted to my wonderful wife Anita for her untiring encouragement and support during the writing of this book as well as my previous books. August Armstrong first awakened within me the faint stirrings of healing experiences from long ago, and Elaine Griffin introduced me to a very special group of loving and compassionate healers led by my Mentor, Dottie Graham, who opened my mind and heart to what we are capable of as spiritual human beings.

And special thanks go to Patricia Hayes, Marshall Smith and the other wonderful teachers at Delphi University for providing many initial spiritual tools needed to prepare and develop myself as an instrument of healing for others.

Sharon Solomon, the widow of the late Rev. Paul Solomon, has kindly given me permission to adapt Rev. Solomon's "Seven Terraces Meditation" into what I call my "Inner Light Consciousness Meditation". This is not included here, but it has formed the essential foundation for the development of the Spiritual Journeys Program.

My own clients and students have been most helpful in their willingness to experiment and explore their spiritual consciousness and have made significant and substantial contributions to the information documented here. Of special note are Emma and Karen (not their real names), two people with whom I have explored many realms I would not have thought accessible. Emma's Higher Self "Shirella" and Guide "Samantha" and Karen's Higher Self "Anaka" and Guide "Joshua" and others as well have led me into many new worlds of information that are now accessible to seekers of "knowledge not normally available."

And lastly, my sincere thanks and constant gratitude go to my Guide "Michael," to my Higher Self "Artoomid" and to all the wonderful spiritual beings who have lovingly guided my progress to follow this exciting new pathway to a higher and much expanded appreciation of who each of us truly is.

Table of Contents

Preface

It is good to be a Seeker,
But sooner or later you will become a Finder.
And then it is good to give what you have found,
A gift into the world for whoever will accept it.

Richard Bach in
Jonathan Livingston Seagull

In *Awakening The Healer Within* (2000) and *Healing Body, Mind, & Spirit* (2003), both published by Llewellyn Worldwide Publications, I dealt primarily with developing programs and techniques that could be tailored and applied to the specific needs of my clients for physical and emotional healing through the use of several energy healing and hypnotherapeutic modalities. While Reiki and Healing Touch continue to provide the essential foundational energy-based techniques for working with the physical body, hypnotherapeutic techniques work toward successful outcomes for emotional and mental healings, as well as for my early efforts for spiritual exploration.

The more these hypnotherapeutic techniques for dealing with the conscious and subconscious minds were employed, the more apparent it became that something else was needed to effectively complete the spiritual apex of the pyramid of physical, emotional and mental therapies that can be applied to our *total* being. **What was lacking was an effective way for clients to investigate who and what they really are as spiritual beings**. Thus began the initial development of a hypnotherapeutic program that could greatly accelerate both the opening of our consciousness and the development of our ability to recall and experience our spiritual self through the use of self-hypnosis.

After becoming trained and certified as a Hypnotherapist, initially by the American Board of Hypnotherapy in 1996, and more recently by the National Guild of Hypnotists in 2005, I continued to investigate the natural ability of individuals to develop a stronger conscious connection with their Higher Self and with our Creator. In 2006 I began to develop "Spiritual Journeys," a program that can be used by anyone to quickly prepare themselves for many spiritual development and exploration objectives under the guidance and direction of a spiritually oriented Certified Hypnotherapist.

In Washington State (USA), professional practitioners who provide hypnotic techniques for the public (including Stage Hypnosis) are called Hypnotherapists; in other states and countries they may be called Hypnotists. The two terms are used interchangeably in this book.

The primary objective of the Spiritual Journeys program is to provide a suggested hypnotherapeutic methodology for Hypnotherapists that allows their clients to significantly accelerate their own spiritual development, and then to explore in detail their own personal experiences. A secondary objective is to discover and compile additional information regarding the nature of the spiritual realms we come from and to propose a workable method for sharing that information with like-minded individuals. For my initial Spiritual Journeys investigations, I had ample willing volunteers from my own students and my established client base.

In the text that follows, when referring to individuals I have used the feminine gender instead of using "him or her" or "himself or herself" simply because the vast majority of my own clients have been women.

It must be noted here that, although this book is intended to be read by everyone, **the Spiritual Journeys program is designed to be provided to individual clients only by trained and certified Hypnotists or Hypnotherapists**. This book provides a general description of the steps to be taken in providing each Journey to each client, as well as extracts from actual sessions; however, it does not supply a complete step-by-step script for guiding them through that Journey. It provides a suggested process of What To Do, but not the specific details of How To Do It. It is <u>not</u> a "do-it-yourself" program for the layman untrained in hypnotic techniques.

If you are a trained and certified Hypnotherapist, this book will provide an excellent overview of the objectives and general procedures for providing each Spiritual Journeys session to your clients. If you are not a Certified Hypnotist or Certified Hypnotherapist, you may find that this book ignites a deep curiosity and yearning to learn more about your true spiritual nature. If so, take this entire book to a properly trained Certified Hypnotist or Certified Hypnotherapist whom you know and ask them to learn how to guide you into your own conscious knowledge of who and what you are as a spiritual being.

This book is intended to be used as an informational overview of the potential experiences and additional information each Spiritual Journey can provide; however, a DVD or flash drive containing all the necessary support materials for Hypnotherapists to teach an informational workshop for the public, as well as a complete suggested script for each Journey will be provided only to Certified Hypnotherapists when ordered from website (www.howardbatie.com), or at a Spiritual Journeys workshop that is taught by a qualified Spiritual Journeys Teacher. IMPORTANT: A copy of your Certification as a Hypnotherapist must be provided when ordering the Spiritual Journeys Training DVD or when registering for a training workshop from a qualified Spiritual Journeys Teacher.

My experience with the first three Journeys has proven them to be foundational and necessary to support the processes of all subsequent Journeys. Journeys 4-6 focus on developing the personal healing abilities of your clients if they wish to become adept spiritual healing facilitators, Journeys 7-10 focus on developing your clients' personal spiritual awareness and consciousness, and Journeys 11-16 focus on researching and learning about nearly any topic they wish to know more about outside their own personal spiritual growth.

Much new and very interesting material has been received from my clients in Journeys 7-16 while in a state of highly altered conscious awareness. The source of the information in these accounts is the Akashic Record of all of Creation, which also includes all information in the personal soul record of every being in existence. Although each of us is capable of accessing this Akashic Record, not all of us know *how* to access this universal wisdom. Spiritual Journeys provides one proven way to learn how to do just that very quickly with the guidance of a trained Hypnotherapist, thus validating the processes described herein. If the goal of your clients is to develop their spiritual awareness quickly, the Spiritual Journeys Program can save them decades of dedicated meditation.

In an ancient language, the term "Akasha" means "etheric" or "of the ethers" and the term "Akashic Record" was popularized by the early 20th-century psychic Edgar Cayce to mean "the entire record of information and knowledge on all levels in the entire universe"; Psychiatrist Carl Jung called this record of all knowledge the "Collective Unconscious". By whatever name, those who are able to access the Akashic Record reportedly receive a true answer to any question at all.

However, there are some limitations to this process; the first being that not everyone is ready to access and comprehend the information in the Akashic Record, and the second being that there are some limitations on what questions will receive an answer. The Good Book says, "Ask and ye shall receive," but it did not include the fine print. Guidance has been provided, and experience has shown, that the true answer to any question will always be provided IF: (1) you are ready to receive and understand the information, (2) receiving the information will be in the highest and best good of all concerned, and (3) receiving the information will not harm yourself or any other being in any way. If the information will be for the Greater Good of all concerned, the information will be provided as requested.

This book is organized into five chapters. The first Chapter, "Spiritual Foundations," provides the basic objectives of the Spiritual Journeys Program and describes its history and evolution into its current form. Journeys 1-3 discuss the individual hypnotic sessions that will bring a client to their foundational abilities of being able to expand their consciousness into the spiritual awareness of their Higher Self within a few seconds, and then prepare them to begin their investigations in three different and optional paths of interest – Spiritual Healing, personal Spiritual Development, and Spiritual Exploration.

The second Chapter, the "Spiritual Healing" path (Journeys 4-6), provides for the continuing development of the client's spiritual healing abilities, and for interactive communication and dialogue with the Healing Angels and other Spiritual Physicians. Journey 4 and 5 should be taken in that order since Journey 5 is a very advanced form of remote spiritual healing that, when practiced regularly, can significantly accelerate the practitioners ability to step into their own Mastery as a Spiritual Healer. In Journey 4 the White Light Angels are asked to perform the actual healing process; however, in Journey 5 the practitioner dialogues with and directs the Healing Angels to assist her in the preparation of the client's energy field, and then removes all negative energies from the client's aura and provides the higher dimensional healing energies herself to both the client and to Mother Earth. Journey 6, the Violet Flame in the Hall of Transformation, may be taken at any time in any of the three paths.

The third Chapter, the personal Spiritual Growth path, provides a series of individual sessions (Journeys 7-10) that guide your client into progressively earlier experiences that are recorded in their own Personal Akashic Record. These experiences include their earliest memories as a unique and individual soul, the process that some call the "Garden of Eden Experience," and even their earlier "Memories of Oneness," recollections of their existence before their consciousness became individualized as a unique soul essence. Beginning with Journey 7, significant extracts from transcripts of the sessions given to my own clients are also provided, with their permission of course, to illustrate the nature of the information available about their personal physical and spiritual experiences; these extracts also illustrate suggested lines of questioning used to elicit that information.

The fourth Chapter, the Spiritual Exploration path (Journeys 11-16), provides for expanded explorations into the complete Akashic Record which contains the experiences and information of all events and beings that have been, are, and may be in any world within Creation. Journeys 12-14 investigate several general areas of interest such as the Angelic Kingdom, the Plant and Mineral Kingdoms, and the Elemental Kingdom; and Journeys 15 and 16 investigate the spiritual growth of Gaia (the consciousness of Mother Earth) and a potential glimpse of what lies ahead for us to create both as individuals and as the collective Human civilization on Earth. What we can become is a matter of personal choice for how we intend to use all this information that is now available. My hope is that we can, as a civilization, grow into the compassionate wisdom of those who are now helping us from the other side of the thinning veil. As Rev. Paul Solomon wisely stated, "We are all child gods, growing up to be like our Father."

At the risk of restating the obvious, the Journeys included in Chapter 4 only begin to scratch the surface of what is available in the Akashic Record. Additional Journeys to investigate the functions and responsibilities of, for example, the Ascended Masters, the Animal Kingdom, and the Elemental Kingdom could be easily constructed using a process similar to that of the Angelic Kingdom; the topics available within Journey 11 range from how the Giza Pyramid or Stonehenge was built to information about the Galactic Federation or the characteristics and capabilities of other civilizations in this or other Universes – certainly enough to keep the curious explorer busy for a lifetime!

The information retrieved from the Akashic Record and provided in Chapters 3 and 4 certainly illustrates a great depth and breadth of knowledge about a wide range of topics. I have been quite fortunate to have several clients who are able to tap into this spiritual wisdom quite easily using the methodology described herein. However, I recognize that, while we all have this ability and right, not every client may be prepared for such an expansive experience all the way back to the beginning of their spiritual memories and experiences. Therefore, it is suggested that your client's Spiritual Guide be consulted to determine their readiness to access the specific information sought in each Spiritual Journey beginning with SJ-7.

The methodology described in this book, as well as other similar approaches for discovering and collecting information about our spiritual nature as individuals and as a civilization, has the potential for significantly expanding our understanding of where we have been and where we might be going, both individually and as a species. It might appear that what is also needed now is a means of collecting and disseminating all the information that can be discovered. However, I propose that the investigational approach provided in the following chapters implicitly addresses both of these needs: as more inquiries into our history and probable future are undertaken, those inquiries, as well as the information received during them, are automatically recorded in the One Akashic Record and are thus available for all who are ready to access the answers they seek. Similarly, the approach outlined herein describes one method by which anyone who is ready can be guided to significantly accelerate the development of their ability to access the Akashic Record.

So the important catalyst for accelerating both the individual's and humanity's collective enlightenment is not the availability of the knowledge sought, but is instead a greater availability of Certified Hypnotherapists who are trained and experienced in guiding their clients into higher states of awareness, so that each one can be guided to discover their own answers and information that is already recorded and available. The general purpose and mission of the Spiritual Journeys Program is to provide a proven methodology for teaching Certified Hypnotherapists how to guide their clients into their own Spiritual Area, so clients may obtain the spiritual information that is important and relevant to themselves.

I have been advised that the time is right to provide for a wider examination and review of this Spiritual Journeys methodology so that the process can be improved, and either refuted or corroborated by additional qualified spiritually oriented Hypnotherapists, and so that the information that has been retrieved as shown in the example transcripts can also be corroborated or refuted. Therefore, I invite comments and suggestions for improving the methodology from Certified Hypnotherapists; please send them to howard@howardbatie.com. I also invite all spiritually oriented Hypnotherapists to become a Spiritual Journeys Teacher if you are not one already; training details are shown on the Spiritual Journeys page of my website www.howardbatie.com.

Finally, I also invite the public reader to seek out the nearest trained Spiritual Journeys Teacher or Practitioner and begin your own Spiritual Journeys! To view a list of qualified and trained Spiritual Journeys Teachers, go to www.howardbatie.com and view the Spiritual Journeys page.

Howard Batie
Chehalis, WA
August 2014

Introduction

Much of the transcribed information provided in this book has been provided by Emma's Guide, Samantha, by Karen's Guide, Joshua, and by my Guide, Michael. Since they have all been most instrumental in directing my efforts during the development of this methodology, it is only fitting that they provide their perspective on this Project. Their comments speak for themselves.

SAMANTHA: This Project has been long in the making, and of much discussion as to its validity and its usefulness. We would not have allowed you to begin had we not believed and understood its importance at this time. In the ascension of Gaia and the development of the Hu-Mon, it is pockets of spirituality such as you have developed here in your town with your groups that will help support and maintain the transition, and from these pockets to then send forth information and ability for others to begin their own development, their own pockets. It is one method by which we can increase the vibrations, the ascension, and the continued evolution of the Hu-Mon. For consciousness now is the necessary ingredient, awakening to the spiritual, awakening to all that will come, and that process of evolution and transition is the next step.

And so we have asked you to use your variety of personal tools to develop this Project. Its primary purpose is to spread the ability to expand one's awareness and consciousness under the guidance of someone who is trained to work with these processes which allow the Hu-Mon to touch its spiritual Self in a different pathway. The most difficult task at hand is the breaking open of the closed and sleeping consciousness of the individual Hu-Mon. The second task then is to coordinate these various paths into a coherent structure that allows support from the various pockets from the various pathways.

Because of the limitations of language, it is often difficult for Hu-Mons who are spiritually awakened to share or talk about the experience and understand that they are of one mind. We hope with this pathway that a trained person can do as you have done to open consciousness first of all, and then hopefully form more pockets where people can discuss their experiences and understand the commonality of the ascension process.

It is extremely difficult even for the most enlightened of the Hu-Mons to willingly share deeply personal and spiritual experiences. It is hoped that this Project will in some way support these two difficulties – Number One again is to open the awareness and consciousness of the Hu-Mon to the wonders that are beyond their current incarnation and, Number Two, to somehow drop the barriers so that they can then experience the commonality, the understanding that the ascension process does not threaten the loss of their uniqueness. And so perhaps by sharing experiences in small discussion groups, the ascension can continue.

We are with you in the creation of the Project, and we will guide its growth and its dissemination once it leaves you. We are not uncertain of the outcome; however, we are not yet sure of the path this will take. We have already deemed it will be successful in, as you say, the long run, but because of the unpredictability of the Hu-Mon and its ego experience, it will be our part in the Project to guide the results as needed.

You asked about dissemination. We understand your need for some direction in that area, but this is not information that you need at this point because it will come as they see how the Project develops. You are not to worry about that.

Howard, we believe that this Project will make a significant difference, and we offer you that as incentive and encouragement.

Michael: From the beginning of Gaia and Earth, and the development of the New Hu-Mon, we knew that at this point in its history it would be difficult to raise and open the (individual) consciousness. As Samantha has said, there is a need to not only open the consciousness of many to bring awake those who are still sleeping, but to help them move beyond the ego identity that has locked so many into the duality currently known on Earth and in its societies. We are hoping, and we are sure that with time, projects such as this will both awaken and help nurture a common understanding and sharing and support. There is an awakening happening, but it is difficult to organize it in such a fashion that different experiences can be shared and seen as the same experience.

We see lights coming on all across Earth, but they appear more as pinprick lights, small groups, small lights here and there, and some very close to each other, but still separated. It is time for these individual lights to move together and share and support, and for someone such as yourself to reach out as you have done in not only enlightening, but also in offering support to those who are beginning to understand these experiences and what they mean. Discussion groups such as yours help those wandering and attempting to support themselves to feel some companionship, some coherence. It may not be within the scope of what you are writing currently, the sharing and the support, but it is a part of the Project that we are seeing as an outcome that was designed into the Project, and it may be a suggestion.

Yes, that is what we are seeing as a suggestion for those who are wishing to help the spiritually enlightened come into community. So coming together in small groups might help to share their experiences, or just to be in the Light helps strengthen the resolve to continue. Your methodology is sound, and your plan and organization we believe is, as you say, on the right track. We will be here as needed for guidance, and when it is ready, we will work with its dissemination. But that piece, Howard, at this point in time, is beyond our discussion.

We would like to honor you again for the work that you are doing. We thank you most sincerely for your willingness to take such a task on so joyfully. It is good to share time and space with you again. You are my brother, Howard, in spirit, as well you know.

Joshua: You are on the right path. You need to make it electronically available so more people will read it. There are those out there that need to hear, they are waiting for it, and you will be so surprised how your audience will expand. There are many people waiting for it, and once this information gets out there, people will begin to find ways to access it themselves, but they need your first steps to start. Eventually, because they will learn from your beginnings and other's beginnings, they will feel comfortable going into that space, and asking the questions themselves. But they can't do it without your start. In the beginning they need your help to start. Then eventually, as enlightenment grows, they will learn more and more that it's safe and to begin to ask the questions, say in a meditation space, themselves. Thank you for being our scribe, Howard.

one

Spiritual Foundations

Objectives and Methodology.
Although this book is for everyone to read, it is for actual use only by Certified Hypnotists or Hypnotherapists since it describes to the reader one method of teaching their clients how to bring themselves very quickly into a highly altered state of awareness through a process of self-hypnosis. The Certified Hypnotherapist can then guide his or her clients through their own spiritual discoveries.

The specific objectives of the Spiritual Journeys Program are (1) to instruct the Certified Hypnotist or Hypnotherapist in how to teach a 2-hour informational workshop for the general public that describes what each student will learn in each one-on-one Spiritual Journeys session once they become your client, and (2) to provide suggested procedures for establishing a local Spiritual Discussion Group for sharing spiritual information, first among your local clients, and then among other Groups regionally, nationally and internationally. All the necessary support materials, including complete suggested scripts and narrated PowerPoint presentations for public informational workshops, are provided on a single Windows data Training DVD.

The specific Spiritual Journeys processes described in this book provide the Certified Hypnotherapist with a proven methodology for safely and consistently coaching their clients into a spiritual state of awareness that, for want of a better term, I just call their "Spiritual Area," to then establish a conscious two-way dialogue with specific spiritual beings, beginning with the client's own Higher Self and Spiritual Guide, and then to explore the spiritual realms and guide your clients to discover new insights about who they really are and the many spiritual sojourns and experiences they have had.

Once these basic capabilities of conscious dialoguing with their Higher Self and Spirit Guide are achieved by the client, the spiritual realms can then be further explored along three specific yet complementary paths of investigation and discovery described in Chapter 2 (Spiritual Healing), Chapter 3 (Personal Spiritual Growth), and Chapter 4 (Spiritual Exploration). The expanded spiritual awareness that results from pursuing any or all of these individual paths ultimately leads one to a more accurate understanding of her own spiritual purpose, history and her path ahead, and also strongly reinforces the conscious <u>knowledge</u>, not merely belief, that there is a constant and infinite amount of help and support available to assist each person on his or her own path.

Background.

While I was in Virginia Beach, VA from 1995 to 1998, I was introduced to the very vibrant and active metaphysical sub-culture that offered a wide variety of techniques such as astrologic and psychic readers, and alternative and complementary healing therapies. One of the energy healing techniques I was introduced to was called RoHun, a process of systematically clearing all the major emotional issues and limiting past life issues, and balancing and opening all the major chakras while the client was in a state of hypnosis. This initial hypnotic experience was used in 2006 to form the initial Spiritual Journeys Program.

In addition, many workshops were available to teach one how to meditate effectively; however, none of them 'worked' for me until I came across the Seven Terraces Meditation which was originated by the late Rev. Paul Solomon and then taught by Rev. Thomas Keller. Instead of asking me to empty my mind to the grandeur of the universe, the Seven Terraces Meditation is a fast-paced guided visualization filled with much emotive imagery that stimulates the inner counterparts to our five senses, and then clears, balances, and guides the meditator up their energetic mountain (chakra system) to their inner temple for several very profound experiences in a greatly expanded self-hypnotic state of awareness.

Once in my inner temple, I was invited to become familiar with the Healing Room where spiritual healings are conducted by Archangel Raphael, to the Hall of Records where I learned how to read my own past life experiences without the help of a psychic, and to the Meditation Room for a very deep meditation experience. One day another room appeared – The Learning Room or The Library where all information of the universe was available. This was, of course, a metaphor for the Akashic Records. Because of this addition and change in the original format, I renamed the entire meditation technique as The Inner Light Consciousness (ILC) Meditation Technique after the Church of The Inner Light Consciousness in Virginia Beach which was led at the time by Rev. Thomas Keller.

Subsequently, with the permission of Ms. Sharon Solomon, Rev. Paul Solomon's widow, I have made available the ILC Meditation containing both the original imagery of Rev. Paul Solomon, as well as the addition of The Learning Room. The ILC Meditation is the one meditation technique that was effective for me after trying countless others, and I have adapted it to form the central foundation of additional spiritual experiences that have grown and evolved into the current Spiritual Journeys Program.

The Spiritual Journeys Program begins with three separate one-on-one hypnotherapy sessions to initially develop the natural metaphysical abilities of a person. This allows them to develop a much closer connection and conscious awareness of the spiritual essence that is their core, sometimes called their own Higher Self. In addition, it establishes a firm connection for two-way communication with their own personal Guide. The Spiritual Journeys program offers a practical and effective method for teaching a person how to achieve these goals in weeks instead of decades of deep, purposeful meditation.

As the Spiritual Journeys program began to evolve, the students and clients who volunteered to help structure an effective program found that building step by step on the success and abilities of the session before was the most effective way to allow them to rapidly grow into an even greater and more expanded state of personal spiritual awareness. Certain abilities would be required at one step before proceeding to the next step, and so on.

Each Spiritual Journeys session described in this Chapter represents a separate hypnotic session that must be taken in the order described. When appropriate, the client is instructed how to practice the techniques and processes of that session at home before the next hypnosis session. Each client begins by mastering the self-hypnosis process of Journey 1, and practicing the self-hypnosis technique at home until they come back for their second Spiritual Journeys session, usually the following week. A second CD is then provided for their practice at home until they come for their third session.

Journey 1 is a foundational Journey which is <u>not optional</u> for the Spiritual Journeys program; it introduces clients to the feeling of the state of deep hypnosis if they have never experienced that before, and reinforces that feeling if they have. Journey 1 also teaches them how to take themselves into very deep self-hypnosis on their own very quickly, usually in only a few seconds using a special ideomotor cue; they will also be able to specify the length of time that they remain in this state. This ability will not only prepare them for all subsequent Spiritual Journeys sessions, but will also provide them with a very useful life-long ability to, for example, meditate deeply for 20 minutes, to take a 10 minute 'Power Nap' in the middle of the afternoon, or to prepare for a good 8 hours' sleep at night.

The very deep state of hypnosis required in this program ensures that there is absolutely no conscious interference and that the powerful post-hypnotic suggestions provided to the client in that state will be recorded permanently by the client's subconscious mind. Post-hypnotic suggestions given in moderate states of hypnosis (upper Theta brain wave activity) may work temporarily, but to become a permanent tool to use for the rest of their life, a very deep hypnotic state (lower Theta brain wave activity) has been shown to be necessary. After practicing daily self-hypnosis for at least a week with the CD provided, the post-hypnotic suggestions are strongly reinforced, and the client is prepared for the second Journey.

The second Spiritual Journeys session begins with the client taking themselves into very deep self-hypnosis in only a few seconds using the ideomotor cue taught in the first Journey. The Hypnotherapist will then provide additional instructions to the client's Subconscious Mind that teaches them a second ideomotor cue which signals their Subconscious Mind to execute a different set of instructions to move from a state of full conscious awareness into the greatly expanded state of awareness in their "Spiritual Area," for lack of a better term. This is a state of consciousness where their awareness is that of their own Higher Self in the spiritual realms. The client is then provided with another CD that reinforces the instructions for safely and quickly moving from full conscious awareness "up" into their Spiritual Area, and also for safely and quickly moving them from their Spiritual Area back to full conscious awareness.

In the third Spiritual Journeys session, the client will be able to establish a conversational two-way dialogue with their own Higher Self, and also with their Spirit Guide. This process can also be extended to converse with their Guardian Angel or virtually any other spiritual being they choose.

Pacing of the individual sessions is a matter for the hypnotherapist and client to discuss. Some clients will be ready to explore another intuitive ability or experience different areas in their spiritual realm before others will. However, an interval of a week or two between sessions has been shown to provide the client sufficient time to thoroughly integrate the information they have received during a session. After practicing contacting their Higher Self and Spirit Guide daily for at least a week, the client is then ready to decide if they want to continue their Spiritual Journeys experience, and if so, which path or paths they prefer: Spiritual Healing, Spiritual Growth or Spiritual Exploration.

Some clients may wish to move to the Spiritual Healing path of Journeys 4-6. Journey 4 must be experienced before moving on to the much more advanced spiritual healing techniques of Journey 5; however Journey 6 may be taken at any time after the basic processes of Journeys 1-3 are mastered.

Other clients may prefer to continue their personal Spiritual Growth through Journeys 7-10, which should always be taken sequentially since each Journey lays an essential foundation for the next Journey. The client may also elect to experience Journey 7 (Past Earth Lifetime) several times, since each visit will guide the client to recall a different Past Life experience.

As the Hypnotherapist takes clients through Journeys 7-10, they may recognize a specific individual who is particularly able to easily access information from her own soul record, and would be willing to explore additional information recorded in the universal Akashic Record where all experiences of all created beings and their experiences are recorded. The Spiritual Exploration path of Journeys 11-16 explores the Akashic Record information in many diverse areas of investigation and can significantly broaden the client's spiritual awareness of themselves and of their Universe.

Hypnosis Foundations.

The session discussions and processes for the Spiritual Journeys Program assume that, through your own training and experience as a professional Hypnotherapist, you will have developed procedures and techniques that work well for you. In addition, suggestions for appropriate techniques will be made to assist you in developing your own "best practices" for this program. The process description or outline for each separate Spiritual Journeys session has been used to develop a separate set of scripts that are available on the Spiritual Journeys Training DVD that is available from the author's website www.howardbatie.com.

Relevant to the introduction of the Spiritual Journeys Program to a new client, it is assumed that you, the Hypnotherapist, have developed a practical routine for introducing a person unfamiliar with hypnosis to the concepts, requirements and language that will be used during their hypnosis sessions. Usually, in addition to a detailed client intake interview, you will have developed one or more fairly consistent introductions to what hypnosis is and what it isn't, eliminating hypnosis fears, pre-induction exercises to determine their ability and willingness to become hypnotized, informing them what is required of them, and a general familiarization with how your sessions will proceed. If the client has never been hypnotized before, this may then be followed by an initial hypnotic induction into only a medium depth of hypnotic relaxation to allow the client to feel what hypnosis feels like and to then return to full conscious awareness.

Although the outlines provided for each Journey have proven to be successful in achieving the objectives of each session, there may also be improvements that can be made to them. This can only become apparent through experimentation with a fairly large number of clients to arrive at an "optimum" process for you; subsequent collaboration with other Hypnotherapists investigating and using these techniques can also facilitate this process.

Note that each session usually begins with the client relaxed into the deepest level of relaxation that they are able to enjoy that day. The important thing is to test the client to make sure they are very deeply relaxed both physically and mentally; this will ensure that subsequent instructions given to the client while in hypnosis will be effective and that post-hypnotic suggestions are long-lasting.

Once a very deep state of relaxation has been attained and confirmed through muscle testing, and the subconscious mind has accepted the instruction on how to return to that very deeply relaxed state nearly instantly, the client is emerged to demonstrate that they are able to successfully move into deep self-hypnosis and emerge themselves without external assistance. A Deepening CD is provided for the client to repeatedly practice moving themselves to this deep hypnotic state and safely emerging themselves on their own. This not only provides a useful tool that they can use whenever they desire, it also allows all subsequent hypnotic sessions to begin immediately after the client relaxes in your recliner – the "most comfortable recliner in *this* galaxy".

For the second session that teaches the client how to enter into a "higher" state of greatly expanded awareness, a different set of instructions is provided to the subconscious mind. By providing separate instructions and a different ideomotor cue, the subconscious mind can automatically respond with a different sequence of events ('rising' into their Spiritual Area and emerging, instead of only going into very deep relaxation and then emerging) without the conscious mind getting involved, which would possibly raise the client above the necessary state of very deep self-hypnosis.

In his book, "*Instant Rapport*," Michael Brooks provides a simple questionnaire of 30 statements or questions, each of which has three possible answers – A if the person is primarily Visual, B if the person is primarily Auditory, and C if the person is primarily Kinesthetic. The total number of A, B, and C answers will provide a relative V-A-K profile for that person, and I have found these relative scores quite useful for guiding my own wording while the client is in trance. For instance, if the person has a relatively low Visual score of 6 or below but has a relatively high Kinesthetic score of 13 or more, I would not want to ask them to "see" or "look at" a particular object. Rather, they should be asked what they "notice" or "become aware of," without specifying what physical or inner sense should be used. People low on their visual score are usually well above average on their kinesthetic score, and in my experience, the only people who are primarily auditory have been professional musicians. Both primarily Visual and primarily Kinesthetic clients have responded very well to the hypnotic processes described herein when using the suggested scripts on the Training DVD.

Spiritual Journey 1 – Learning Self-Hypnosis.

The Spiritual Journeys program is primarily intended to be a personal program for development of the ability to experience deep states of relaxation, from which an individual may pursue several further spiritual activities under the guidance and direction of a trained and qualified hypnotherapist. To be useful, practical, and successful, the individual must be instructed in how to induce within themselves a very deep state of self-hypnosis (lower Theta brain wave activity) without the aid of the hypnotherapist.

Since this ability will be required for all subsequent individual Spiritual Journeys sessions, self-hypnosis is the foundation technique to be taught to all Spiritual Journeys students. The process described below includes having the client set their intention for a specific result to occur, to use the simple ideomotor cue that allows them to quickly relax into a very deep state of hypnosis for a chosen length of time, and then to emerge themselves completely from self-hypnosis. The self-actuated ideomotor cue is also ideal for significantly shortening the time required for hypnotic induction during future Spiritual Journeys hypnotic sessions.

After the Self-Hypnosis session of Journey 1, the client is provided a Self-Hypnosis Deepening CD for use at home to reinforce and strengthen the ideomotor cues and suggestions given during the session with the hypnotist. Repeated use of the Deepening CD conditions the client to reach successively deeper states of hypnotic relaxation each time it is used. After practicing with the Self-Hypnosis Deepening CD once or more a day for a week or so, the client may be ready for additional training that begins with reawakening and further developing their natural, latent intuitive (psychic) ability to experience higher states of awareness.

Process:
1. Induce a state of deep hypnosis (upper Theta brain wave activity) in the client using whatever technique you are comfortable with.
2. Ensure that the client can use their fingers and thumb while in very deep hypnosis to answer Yes, No, or I Don't Know questions.
3. Deepen client to very deep hypnosis (lower Theta brain wave activity).
4. Provide programming instructions for quickly returning to very deep self-hypnosis from full conscious awareness.
5. Anchor the very deep state of hypnosis with the physical sensation of an ideomotor cue.
6. Provide programming instructions for quickly returning from very deep self-hypnosis to full conscious awareness.
6. Emerge the client and have them practice the entire sequence as appropriate.
7. Provide a CD for the client's use at home to reinforce the programming instructions.
8. Provide written instructions for the client's use of the CD.

Spiritual Journey 2 - Accessing The Spirit Realms.

The initial starting place is with the client in a very deep, self-induced hypnotic state (lower Theta brain wave activity) following an ideomotor cue; when in very deep self-hypnosis, you will provide an additional set of instructions that, with the use of a different physical ideomotor cue, will take the client to the same very deep state of self-hypnotic relaxation learned in SJ-1, but will additionally allow the client's higher consciousness to safely rise into an expanded state of conscious awareness of the true Spiritual Self. By using different ideomotor cues, the client's subconscious mind can be specifically guided to execute a different set of instructions for expanding into the awareness of the superconscious mind.

At this point, we need to consider terminology and the nature of the experience of the client while participating in Spiritual Journey 2, as well as subsequent Journeys whose purpose is to move the client beyond the intuitive level. Several terms exist in both common and technical expression referring to this "higher level of consciousness," which is in itself one of these terms. They include but are not limited to: spiritual realms, an expanded state of awareness/consciousness, and the Superconscious Mind. I use all these terms interchangeably to prevent repetition; however, you may also wish to discuss with your client whether or not certain terms trigger a specific emotional reaction that would interfere with the experience. For example, the terms "God" and "angel" have highly defined meanings to some, and either or both can create equally strong negative or positive reactions in some clients. Sometimes just the discussion of these terms is enough to remove any adverse reactions to them.

In order to move into and operate within the spiritual realms – the "higher dimensions," an expanded state of awareness, the superconscious mind, or whatever it is called – the client's conscious and subconscious minds must first be reassured that it is possible and safe to do so. Believing that you *can* do something because of what someone else tells you is much different than actually *experiencing* those higher states of love, oneness and complete unity with all life everywhere. And to be meaningful, the experiences while in the higher states of awareness must be able to be recalled and deeply felt after returning to normal conscious awareness. This is *knowing* that it is possible because you've experienced it before, and translates into a feeling of confidence.

This wonderful process begins by moving down into a very deep state of self-hypnosis using the new ideomotor cue. After testing to make sure that state really has been achieved, the client begins to focus inwardly on their breath, and with each out-breath, begins to create a cocoon of golden light all around their resting body – a visual and kinesthetic metaphor for peace and safety. This intentional metaphor provides assurance to the subconscious mind that it is safe to separate a part of its awareness (the superconscious mind), allow that part to dissociate from their physical awareness while knowing that their physical body is safe and protected from harm, and then rise up into the higher dimensions.

The initial attempts to develop a reliable process for the client to rise into their Spiritual Area did not include the cocoon metaphor and simply relied on counting them up into higher states of awareness; however, this process was not always successful. Additionally, one woman easily achieved very deep self-hypnotic relaxation and could create a cocoon of protection, but would not rise into the higher dimensions of love and light. After emerging her, a separate regression session uncovered that her husband had died two years before and that she was still grieving. She stated that she had loved her husband so much that she promised God that she would never love anything or anyone else again. She did not understand that, to her subconscious mind, that meant that she would not love even herself! Therefore, she was not able to experience the love of her own Spiritual Area. After releasing this unintentional contract, she was easily able to rise into her Spiritual Area in a subsequent Spiritual Journeys session. As a result, the cocoon process has been included to specifically identify those who might benefit from separate emotional hypnotherapeutic work prior to subsequent Spiritual Journeys.

When the client's awareness has risen higher and become more expanded under the guidance and visual imagery provided by the hypnotherapist, the client begins to experientially sense and feel the freedom, grandeur, and unconditional love that is everywhere in their Spiritual Area, that part of the higher dimensions of which they are now aware.

It is also of interest that, although clients begin in the very deep state of self-hypnosis where they are unable to move a muscle or to use their voice, once they rise into their Spiritual State of awareness, without any such suggestions being made, they are easily able to use their voice and describe what they are aware of and how they feel, and can answer the hypnotherapist's questions in a normal, conversational voice and tone. They are able to communicate from a level of awareness not normally available through non-hypnotic states. Therefore, beginning with Spiritual Journey 2, it is advisable to keep a digital voice recorder handy in case they spontaneously begin to provide information from that level of awareness.

And since the client may not have consciously experienced her Spiritual Area before, additional steps are taken to ensure that only positive events are experienced there. The three things that must always be done each time the client comes up into her Special Area are:

- To surround herself with Creator's Light and Love,
- To ask that a clear channel of communication *now* be established between herself and the highest levels of love and wisdom, and
- To state her conscious intention that all information she gains while in this higher state of awareness be used only for the Greater Good of all concerned.

Once in her Spiritual Area, the client is asked to FEEL the wonderful energies of love, light, happiness, and joy here and to anchor that feeling to this state of expanded awareness. Once anchored, the client is coached how to return to full conscious awareness by placing her attention on her physical body resting safely in her cocoon 'below', reintegrating her higher spiritual awareness completely with the physical body and conscious mind, and then emerging completely from self-hypnosis by themselves.

Process: 1. Client moves into very deep self-hypnosis using the new ideomotor cue.
2. Client is guided to create a cocoon of golden light around her physical body and conscious mind.
3. Additional kinesthetic cues are anchored into client's subconscious mind to ensure that a part of their consciousness dissociates from her physical being only when they FEEL complete safety and unconditional love within her cocoon.
4. Client's consciousness is guided into higher and higher states of expanded awareness through three specific levels or dimensions of mind to her "Spiritual Area".

5. When in her Spiritual Area, the Client's Higher Self (CHS) does the three things it must do each time it arrives in their Spiritual Area.
6. CHS is instructed in how to emerge themselves from this state of awareness without assistance.
7. Client practices taking herself into her Spiritual Area and then emerging herself completely while under the guidance of the Hypnotherapist.
8. Client is provided a practice CD to use at home to reinforce the instructions for safely rising into her Spiritual Area and emerging on her own.

Journey 3 – Meeting Your Higher Self and Spiritual Guide.

After practicing moving into her Spiritual Area and emerging herself from Self-hypnosis for about a week, the third session teaches your client how to meet and establish a two-way dialogue with two very important spiritual beings: her own Higher Self and her own primary Spiritual Guide. This session also provides very important information about how to safely allow only positive spiritual beings to approach and remain in her presence, and also how to detect and banish negative beings from her presence.

The client's first experience in this state of higher awareness is to move in front of her Spiritual Mirror and observe her own true appearance here in the spiritual realms -- she will see what she needs to see and what she is ready to see. She is then taught how to interact with the appearance in her Spiritual Mirror to obtain reliable information from her Higher Self, beginning with her own spiritual name.

A similar procedure used to show the client how to meet and interact with her primary Spirit Guide or other spiritual beings. For her Spirit Guide, it is only necessary that she ask her guide to come into her presence and make themselves known in a form by which she can easily recall and recognize them. The client can then dialogue with her Guide as desired; answers to questions will always be given if it is in the client's best interest to consciously know the answer at that time.

When meeting any spiritual being other than your own Higher Self, the very first thing you must establish is whether or not they are working with the forces of Light, and the second thing you need to know is whether or not the being that you are aware of is actually the one you have called into your presence. The final step in Spiritual Journey 3 is to teach the client how to emerge themselves safely from her Special Area and return to normal awareness.

It should be noted here that many beings in the spiritual realms are capable of assuming any form they wish, and sometimes the initial form presented is just a metaphor for some aspect that the client's Higher Self may expect to see. For instance, some clients have initially seen Jesus as their Guide, some have initially seen their totem animal, and one client who was very connected energetically to the Cetaceans (whales and dolphins) initially saw her Guide as a pod of Orca whales; we then asked for a representative or leader of the pod to present itself, and the pod morphed into a single Orca. We then asked the Orca to assume a humanoid shape so we could be more comfortable conversing with the Guide, and in the client's inner vision, it again morphed into an old woman who looked very wise and felt very loving and compassionate. The old woman then readily provided the name she wished us to call her.

Names are another interesting topic. Humans seem to need names to understand a thing or individual, so we have a name called 'table', one for 'pencil', one for 'Sally' and one for 'Thomas'. But in the spiritual dimensions, beings are not known to each other by a name, but by the vibratory nature of their energies. However, they are always more than willing to assume any shape needed for us to recognize them, and will respond to any name we call them because they are really responding to the energy of our intentions and the thought-form that calls for them.

Also, be prepared for a wide variety of names for either their Higher Self or for their Guide. One client's Higher Self said that her 'name' was the sound of a tinkling bell, so we called her Tinkling Bell throughout the remainder of the session. Another's name was totally unpronounceable, so we asked if we could call him Bob, and he readily agreed to that. You will surely meet beings who are neither male nor female, but an androgynous melding of the two genders. And no, I have never met a being from this Universe that had more than two genders, although I'm open to that as well.

Be prepared to record this and all subsequent Spiritual Journeys sessions to preserve the information provided during the session. The easiest way to do that is to use a Digital Voice Recorder (DVR) that records and saves files in the mp3 format that can be 'read' by any Windows or Apple computer or mp3 player (I prefer the Olympus DVRs widely available at Staples, WalMart, etc.). The mp3 file of each session can easily be transferred to your computer desktop using the USB connecting cable provided with the DVR, and then transferred again to a thumb drive or flash drive. Alternatively, the mp3 file can be burned directly to a CD if you have a CD Burning application on your computer.

Process:
1. Client moves into her Spiritual Area, and does the three things she must always do.
2. Client's Higher Self (CHS) moves in front of a large Spiritual Mirror standing beside her, and observes and describes how she appears here in the Spiritual Realms.
3. CHS asks her Spiritual Mirror to know what her own spiritual name would sound like here if it could be spoken in the spiritual realms.
4. CHS calls for the presence of her Spiritual Guide to come forth and present itself in a recognizable form.
5. CHS challenges the form that appears and establishes whether or not it is working with the forces of Light.
6. CHS is taught how to banish negative beings not in Service to the Light.
7. If necessary, CHS requests that Guide assume a humanoid form.
8. CHS confirms that the being is in fact the one called, and converses with it to obtain a message or specific information as appropriate.
19. CHS asks to know what name she should call the Guide.
10. CHS thanks and releases the Guide.
11. CHS returns to her cocoon, reintegrates her awareness with her physical body and conscious mind, clearly remembering all information provided.
12. Client emerges self from self-hypnosis.

The processes described in the first three Spiritual Journeys sessions with the Hypnotherapist establish a positive and fundamental ability that will be necessary for successfully taking additional Journeys if the client wishes. This basic ability to hold a two-way conversation with – not just talk to – both the Higher Self and Guide provide a powerful ability to ask questions and get truthful and beneficial answers from her 'inner guidance system' throughout the remainder of her lifetime. For some people, this will be all she wishes to have; however, for many others who wish to explore this new and expanded reality, many additional options are available to them now that they are fully prepared to go exploring under the continuing guidance of her Hypnotherapist.

Depending on the previous experiences of each client, she may be drawn to significantly enhance her energy healing skills for both herself and others. Some may be drawn to explore their own development as a soul from the time when they were first created as a spiritual essence. And others may wish to use their new spiritual abilities to investigate and research areas and topics which have remained outside the realm of so-called scientific knowledge and experience. All these and more are readily available to the spiritual explorer who has established this initial three-session foundation and is now fully prepared to investigate the inner "final frontier" to "go where no man or woman thinks they have gone before."

two

Spiritual Healing

Spiritual Journey 4 – The Temple of Healing.

The Temple of Healing is the first of several "places" in the client's Spiritual Area that can be accessed for different activities including, but not limited to, healing themselves or, with their permission, someone else. In the Healing Room of the Inner Light Consciousness Meditation technique, upon which this Journey is based, Archangel Raphael, the Archangel of Healing, is present and is asked to heal who is on the Healing Table there. This Journey incorporates the experience of the White Light Angels to assist in the healing process instead of Archangel Raphael.

After rising into her Special Area, the client will be guided to her Temple of Healing and call on her Angelic helpers for healing energies. She will learn how to conduct a true spiritual healing for herself and, with another person's permission, for that person as well. The person on the Healing Table may actually be located anywhere at all in the world, since when you are in the conscious awareness of your Higher Self, there is complete freedom from the limitations of space and time, which are characteristics only of our third dimensional physical world.

In this Journey, the White Light Angels assist in the healing process by preparing the client's energy field for the healing energies that will be provided by the White Light Angels. This initial preparation includes removing any negative entities or beings that may have become attached to or embedded in the client's energy field; many capable spiritual healers and energy healers are not ready or trained to deal directly with such negative entities, so this is done instead by the Angels. They also remove any negative devices, monitors or implants, and also any negative or limiting thought-forms from the client's energy field prior to requesting the Healing Angels to provide the healing energies to the client's Higher Self on the Healing Table. The White Light Angel process for removal of negative energies described below are adapted with permission from Greg McHugh's 2010 book, ***"The New Regression Therapy."***

Process:
1. Client moves into her Spiritual Area and does the three things she must always do.
2. Client's Higher Self (CHS) is guided to the Temple of Healing in her Spiritual Area.
3. CHS calls for her Healing Angels to come and to prepare her energy field
4. CHS requests the Healing Angels to provide healing energies to themselves or, with their permission, to someone else.
5. CHS asks the White Light Angels for a personal message.

6. CHS thanks and releases the White Light Angels.
7. CHS returns to her Spiritual Area, and is released.
8. Client returns to her cocoon below and reintegrates her awareness with her physical body and conscious mind.
9. Client emerges from self- hypnosis.

Spiritual Journey 5 – Trans-Scalar Healing.

Trans-Scalar Healing is an advanced energy healing technique that uses higher-dimensional Quantum Scalar energies that, according to the physical and emotional results reported by many clients, are very effective in addressing a broad range of conditions. This technique allows healing facilitators to step into their Mastery as a spiritual healing instrument by allowing them to provide the healing functions that the White Light Angels were requested to perform in Spiritual Journey 4, and to bring healing energies to Mother Earth as well. This healing technique builds upon the concepts provided in SJ-4, the Temple of Healing process, so it is most appropriate for those with previous experience with energetic healing techniques such as Reiki, Healing Touch, Polarity Therapy, Theta Healing, Reconnective Healing, etc.

Trans-Scalar Healing (TSH) was developed separately from Spiritual Journeys, but since TSH perfectly augments the healing path of the Spiritual Journeys Program, it has been included here. Significant contributions of the TSH technique are rapid development of the practitioner's clairvoyance, clairaudience and clairsentience – the ability to 'see,' 'hear,' or 'feel or know' energetic information about your client, regardless of where they are. With TSH, remote healings become the norm, and the practitioner rapidly enhances her natural intuition and her ability to consciously communicate with the Healing Angels and the Higher Self of her client. TSH has proven itself to be extremely effective in successfully addressing not only physical conditions, but also the emotional, mental and spiritual aspects of clients with remarkable accuracy.

Trans-Scalar Healing is also a spiritually-guided technique, in that I have been directly guided to include into the natural flow of each session several individual sub-processes, such as Archangel Michael's Infinity Breath Meditation, the Brotherhood of Light's set of energetic practitioner preparation procedures, and a very special Planetary Healing Process using St. Germain's Violet Flame of Transmutation.

For further information about the Trans-Scalar Healing technique, and the availability of training materials, see http://www.howardbatie.com and navigate to the Trans-Scalar Healing page.

The following steps are taken by the Practitioner:

Process:
1. Request the presence and assistance of the One Infinite Creator, the Brotherhood of Light, and the White Light Angels during the healing session.
2. Ground and clear your own energy meridians using the Circle of Grace process given by the Brotherhood of Light.
3. Open and balance your Chakra System by spinning colored light into each Chakra.
4. Reconstitute the colored light in all balanced chakras back into pure white light.
5. Connect the white chakra column up to the 8th chakra above the head.
6. Begin the Infinity Breath as given by Archangel Michael.
7. Establish higher-dimensional Scalar energies within your energy field.
8. Issue the Self-Healing Decree.
9. Elevate your awareness into that of your Higher Self in your Spiritual Area and do the three things you must always do.
10. Call on your client's Higher Self to come forward.
11. Challenge whoever or whatever appears; banish if a Deceiver or Intruder.

12. Get the true spiritual name of your client's Higher Self; call it by this name throughout the session.
13. Ask if it would like to come to the Temple of Healing with you.
14. As you approach, have the client describe it to you or send an image to your mind.
15. Enter the Temple of Healing and locate the Healing Room.
16. Enter the Healing Room and rest on the Healing Table there.
17. Remind client's Higher Self that it must call the White Light Angels to come and assist in the healing that you will provide.
20. Thank each Angel for coming. How many are there? How are they arranged?
21. Draw a net of golden white light through client's energy field to locate and remove any negative entities or beings who are embedded in the client's energy field.
22. Dialogue with Angels to determine where the negative entities were released from and what they were there to do.
23. Inform captured entities they have only 2 choices: to return to the lower realms where they came from or to go to the Light. What is their choice?
24. Direct the Angels to escort them to the place of their choice.
25. Draw a second net of golden white light through client's aura to locate and identify any other beings who may have been consciously or unconsciously *invited* to become attached to or embedded in their energies.
26. Dialogue with located beings and determine how they can be released to the Light.
27. Request the Angels to escort the released being(s) to the Light.
28. Draw a third net of golden white light through client's energy field to locate and remove any negative devices, monitors, or implants that have been left behind by any other beings.
29. Ask the Angels to cleanse and heal these objects and return them to whomever left them behind in the client's aura.
30. Draw a fourth net of golden white light through client's aura to locate and remove any negative or limiting beliefs, ideas, thought-forms, habits or patterns that were given to them by others and are not their own.
31. Ask the Angels to cleanse and heal these thought-forms and return their energy to the ones who originated those negative thought-forms.
32. Ask the Angels to move out into all the places and all the spaces in all the dimensions of all the universes to locate and retrieve all soul fragments or energies that the client may have left behind throughout all the eons of its existence, and to present them to you for your inspection.
33. Note the shape and quantity of recovered energies; ask the Angels to cleanse and heal them all, then reintegrate them into client's aura, making them energetically whole and complete once more with all of only their own energies.
34. Ask the Angels to seal all client's own energies within their aura.
35. Ask the Angels what energy healing technique you are trained in that would be most beneficial for the client.
36. Provide that healing energy until you know that it is complete.
37. Issue the Healing Decree in the Name of the One Infinite Creator.
38. Witness whether or not the healing has been accepted by the client's Higher Self.
39. Ask the Angels whether or not any subsequent reinforcing sessions would be needed, and if so, when and what type of healing session.

40. Ask the Angels if they have a message for the client.
41. Ask the client's Higher Self if she would like to assist you in a special Planetary Healing Process.
42. Establish another channel of highest dimensional healing energies from Source to the center of Mother Earth.
43. Visualize the Violet Flame of St. Germain cascading down the healing column transmuting all negativity in its path.
44. Chant the Mantra of St. Germain nine times, the number of completion.
45. Thank and release the White Light Angels.
46. Exit the Temple of Healing with client's Higher Self and return to your Spiritual Area.
47. Thank client's Higher Self for coming today and release them as well.
48. Return to full conscious awareness and document the entire session.
49. Provide a detailed written description of what you did and the result that you observed in your (usually remote) client.

A sampling of testimonials as to the effectiveness of this remarkable technique is provided below:

I just love your manual for 'Trans-Scalar Healing'. You write beautifully. Your writing is intelligent, easy to read, understand and very inspiring... actually brings to me excitement and hope. The information puts together all the snippets of beliefs and understanding which have come my way. Now there is clarity. I believe that this is the path which I have been searching for, and with the guidance of my Angels and support team, I am excited to finally be on track! Warmly, with love and appreciation,

K. C., Victoria, BC

Your workshops always exceed my expectations. Today was another example of your incredible knowledge and sincere desire to share that knowledge with us all. Thank you so much for another jam packed day of (Remote Trans-Scalar Healing) exploration and enlightenment!

S.D., Vancouver, WA

Wow, that was an interesting (Remote Trans-Scalar Healing) session! A lot of my physical sensations correlated with your report. I was struck by the little unborn boy you found in my heart. I had an abortion that really broke my heart and I felt sure it was a boy. It was so traumatic for me emotionally, (and) I'm glad he was able to return to the light where he belongs. I found it fascinating that (on the Healing Table) I morphed into a Samurai warrior! I'm 3rd generation Japanese, and I always wanted to be one!!:-)

M.P., Toulon, France

Thank you for a day that I will never forget! The big difference is that I no longer have the chronic pain of a displaced vertebrae or the chronic ache in my mid-back. I feel like I sit up straighter, and it's easier to sit upright. I have also traveled since the (Remote Trans-Scalar Healing) session and travel usually includes a very stiff, sore, achy back. Between the discomfort of long sitting, airplane sitting, and sleeping in a different bed with a different pillow I would have increased back pain. None of that has happened. Overall, I feel like I'm just barely touching the tip of the iceberg on this topic. But, the amazing thing is that almost every day has been pain free. Even now as I type this I feel like I'm sitting upright, erect and without the ache and pain that I had every day.

N.B., Olympia, WA

I found my (Remote Trans-Scalar Healing) session to be a very positive experience overall, with the greatest impact on my development spiritually and professionally. I am very grateful for the experience and want to thank you for the healing session!

T.I., Santa Barbara, CA

I have not had ANY pain since my TSH (Remote Trans-Scalar Healing) with you!

D.R., Santa Barbara, CA

Howard, thank you again so much for that profound (Remote) Trans-Scalar Healing yesterday! My vibration was noticeably higher yesterday and I felt bright light all around me as though the high beings from the session had never left. It was as if one of them stayed behind to oversee my energy field, or something like that! (Your report) is really fascinating and I will read it several times and meditate on it. It certainly resonates with all the bright light and radiant beings I experienced and I am not surprised that some dark energy had to be cleared because I felt an immediate uplift and light as a feather all day! Again, eternal gratitude for your angelic services! Many blessings,

D.S., Medford, OR

Thank you for sharing your (Remote Trans-Scalar Healing) gifts. This was hugely insightful. I will meditate on this message. I truly feel this is my key to freedom into the light for me.

K.L. - Santa Barbara, CA

I am blown away by what I have read on many, many levels. This (Remote Trans-Scalar Healing) is profound. It is beyond words. I wept as I read this. I will continue to read it over and over again. Bless you for this work that you do. I will never be the same again.

T.E., Beaverton, OR

Thank you Howard! I am awestruck by the work done in the Healing Room with the White Light Angels under your inspired (Remote Trans-Scalar Healing) facilitation. I take in this new information in all its fullness, and with heartfelt gratitude. Thank you, thank you, thank you!

K.M., Olympia, WA

I managed to go grocery shopping after my (Remote Trans-Scalar Healing session) yesterday. In fact I went to three stores! Usually I'm starting to have pain and a real lack of energy. I didn't need to take pain medication that I've had to take since late summer. I woke early this morning and was able to cook and get ready for the day by 8:00 which is highly unusual! Most days I can't seem to get up until after 9:30 or so and experience pain upon arising. Today not so much! I feel good, lighter and energized! Dr. Batie, I just can't thank you enough for your healing and love.

H. D., Galeta, CA

What a wonderful (Remote Trans-Scalar Healing) session! I am almost disappointed that I don't need another one! I can finally move forward into who I truly am. Thank you Howard. Many, many blessings to you from my heart to yours.

C.T., Owasso, OK

Spiritual Journey 6 - The Hall of Transformation.

In the spiritual activities described in Journeys 4 and 5, the client is taught how to awaken and develop their natural abilities to bring healing energies to themselves and to others. The real purpose and goal of this activity is to have the client slowly and steadily build within themselves a deep personal knowledge of a great Secret – the 'secret' that we are indeed made in the image of our Creator, and that, like our Creator, we also have within ourselves the ability to create whatever we wish – the power of manifestation.

While our consciousness is in the spiritual realms of higher vibration, this ability to manifest whatever we want – to create the reality we perceive – is heightened and focused to a very high degree. During this Spiritual Journey, all our attention is focused on the Violet Flame of Transmutation that burns forever in the higher consciousness of your spiritual being – that spiritual Self that has been manifested by The Creator. With this ability of manifestation we, His/Her children, are all co-creators of our own reality. Regardless of what we desire or can imagine, we have the ability to create that for ourselves. But there is a catch – we must *want* to create it in order for it to happen and then we must consciously give it enough energy to *make* it happen here in our physical world. Our intention must be to bring that desired object or idea into the physical world so that we can experience it in our life and grow from that experience.

So what should we want to create for the Greater Good of all mankind, of all living beings on this earth? The greatest gift we can all give each other is pure unconditional love, total peace, acceptance without judgement, and a sense of loving helpfulness and good will to all men and women everywhere so that humankind may prosper and flourish as caring stewards of each other and of the world we live in.

And why was that not already given to us by the Creator? Actually, it was! The only thing preventing us from manifesting peace and love in our world is the negativity we have individually and collectively created. The Violet Flame of Transformation is an energy that we can call upon to remove negativity of all kinds and to replace that negativity with unconditional love, kindness, caring for ourselves, for each other, and for our world. This Violet Flame burns forever in a sacred, inner place in the consciousness of each of us, metaphorically called the Hall of Transformation.

To move into this sacred area, the client first sets their intention to go into her Hall of Transformation, and then moves into her Spiritual Area using the Thumb Drop technique. After rising into the awareness of her Higher Self, she moves through her Spiritual Area directly to her Hall of Transformation, and then merges with the Violet Flame to remove any residual negativity she may have brought with her.

After her personal purification, the client is instructed how to bring the transforming and transmuting energies of the Violet Flame to other beings and to Mother Earth herself. Following further purification and transformation of herself, her surroundings and Mother Earth, our Galaxy and the Universe itself, she is gently guided back to her Spiritual Area, and then 'descends' again into the physical reality of her body, and emerges herself from hypnosis.

After the client is emerged and aware, she is provided with a CD that allows her to practice this guided meditation at home.

Procedure:
1. Client rises into her Spiritual Area and does the three things she must always do.
2. Client's Higher Self (CHS) chooses to visit her Hall of Transformation .
3. CHS is taught how to use the Violet Flame to remove any form of negativity within herself.
4. CHS is taught how to bring the Violet Flame to others.
5. CHS is taught how to bring the Violet Flame to Mother Earth, to the Milky Way Galaxy, and to the Universe.
6. CHS exits the Hall of Transformation and returns to her Spiritual Area.
7. CHS returns to her cocoon, reintegrates her higher consciousness with her physical body and conscious mind.
8. Client emerges herself from self-hypnosis.
9. Client is provided with the 'Violet Flame Meditation' CD and instructions for its use as desired.

three

Spiritual Growth

The client's individual soul experiences from a previous lifetime back to the instant she was created as an individual soul are explored in Journeys 7-10. In Journey 7, the client is introduced to a past life by her Guide; it could be a recent previous lifetime, or one in her distant past. Following this session, Journey 8 allows them to re-experience her very first incarnation on Earth. In Journey 9, she recalls her initial memories and feelings at the instant she became an individual soul essence. Journey 10 completes the investigation into her own personal and spiritual experiences by allowing her to recall and actually re-experience the oneness and unity of consciousness within the energy of Creator before the personal consciousness individuates and becomes energetically 'separated' from Creator. Therefore, it is important that these four Journeys be taken in the order described since each Journey builds on the success and information of the previous one.

Anonymous extracts of actual Spiritual Journeys sessions of various clients are provided, always with the client's permission, for you to review, beginning with SJ-7. This allows the reader to notice the wide variability of information provided from different individuals' personal experiences – different individuals each have different experiences in our physical lives, as well as in our spiritual existences.

In addition to noting these subtle nuances in the information presented by different clients, it has also been very interesting to note the variability in the voice pitch while different entities are 'speaking'. For instance, when Emma's Higher Self (Shirella) is speaking, Emma's voice rises above Emma's own natural conversational pitch, but when her Guide (Samantha) speaks, Emma's voice pitch becomes lower than her normal pitch. This gives me a good clue as to who is providing information when we have a three-way or more dialogue; however, not all clients exhibit this interesting characteristic.

Spiritual Journey 7 – Past Earth Lifetime.

In this Journey, you as the client will be introduced to a portion of the Akashic Record where the experiences of all of Creation are stored. You will learn how to read your own personal Akashic Record of past lives, and receive firsthand conscious knowledge of previous physical existences without having to rely on the variable abilities and the personality filters of a psychic – you will be taught how to become your own best psychic! After all, you don't need someone else to tell you what you've already done! Instead of hearing or reading about someone else's impressions of what they think you did, you actually re-live the experience yourself, complete with all the feelings and emotions you felt at that time.

Among the possible lines of inquiry for this Journey are:
What part of the world did this take place in?
When did this happen?
Are you a man or a woman?
What culture and community are you a part of?
How old are you at each stage of progression in that lifetime?
What is your occupation? What skills and abilities do you have?
Do you have a family? What are the names of each person? How many children?
At the end of that lifetime, was it a good life? Hard life? What did you learn?

Process:
1. Client moves into her Spiritual Area and does the three things she must always do when rising into her Spiritual Area.
2. Client's Higher Self (CHS) calls for and verifies the presence of her Guide.
3. CHS asks her Guide if it is permissible to visit the Akashic Record to obtain personal information about her own previous lifetimes.
4. If permitted, the Guide leads the CHS to the appropriate previous Earth lifetime, and the CHS "reads" the information there.
5. CHS returns to her cocoon below, reintegrates her higher awareness with her physical body and conscious mind.
6. Client emerges from self-hypnosis and returns to full conscious awareness.

Case Study 1:

SJ-07: Past Earth Lifetime   June 27, 2014 – Directed by Howard Batie
Subject: "Sandy"   Subject's Higher Self: "Carlosha"   Subject's Guide: "Kwana"

Howard:	Now, Kwana, is it permissible for Carlosha to visit her own Akashic Records, her records of her own personal lifetimes here on Earth to investigate a comfortable, peaceful lifetime so that we can learn what that lifetime was all about, and so she can feel what it's like to re-experience what she's already done and been before? Kwana, is it permissible? *(Pause)*
Kwana:	Yes.
Howard:	Good. Now Kwana, I'd like to work with you. I'd like you to investigate the entire lifetime records of Carlosha while incarnated on Earth, and I want you to guide Carlosha to a very pleasant lifetime, one that is very enjoyable and that will also have meaning for her in her current lifetime today. So just guide her to that lifetime, and Carlosha,

when you're aware of that lifetime, any motion, any movement or sensation at all, just let me know.

Carlosha: OK.

Howard: Good. Now where are you, and what are you doing?

Carlosha: I see a prehistoric setting, in animal clothing like animal skins, like cave-man type setting, and long brown hair, raggedy, and walking barefoot across the plains. I'm a woman.

Howard: Walking barefoot across the plains. And what part of Earth as we know it today, what part of Earth as that in?

Carlosha: I don't know, but it's mountainous, not high jaggedy peak mountains, but lower like maybe the Southwest (of what is now the) United States. I have a large club or stick in my hand, and I seem to be looking back over my shoulder. Something's coming at me, and I kind of feel afraid. I'm making my way to a cave, and I get inside and there's other family members, there's children. They're not my children – they're my sister's children. And she's feeding them, and there's a fire, and they're laughing. There are some men sitting around, but there's not one that I'm attached to.

Howard: Good. How many people altogether are here in this cave?

Carlosha: There's two other men and my sister, and I think one's a baby, but there's three other children.

Howard: OK. Do you have a family anywhere?

Carlosha: I think I did, but they're gone, and I only have my sister. I have the feeling that something terrible happened to my family.

Howard: That's all right. Just let them go, and focus on the children that are laughing. Your sister, safety, the fire, it's good to be around the fire here.

Carlosha: I feel hot. It's too hot in here. I like to be outside.

Howard: Well, just step outside the cave there for a minute – it's safe here, there are no animals around, and tell me what the temperature's like here – is it a lot cooler or a little cooler?

Carlosha: It's a lot cooler than in the cave. And there's stars, and there's a breeze blowing in the trees, I kind of think I see palm trees, and Yuccas, sand.

Howard: OK. What does this family eat?

Carlosha: Meat that the men catch and kill. Wild pigs, and there's fruits from the cactus, and other berries and things that they find.

Howard: Is there enough to eat?

Carlosha: It hard sometimes, hard to find enough.

Howard: And when the men go away hunting, are they away for a short time or for a long time?

Carlosha: Sometimes longer and sometimes shorter – depends on what they find close by, or else they have to look further.

Howard: OK. Are they ever gone more than a day?

Carlosha: Um-hmm. Sometimes for many days.

Howard: Just to find food. And then when they find food, how do they bring it back?

Carlosha: On a stick. They tie the feet to a stick and carry it between them. Sometimes there's antelope, and we take their fur and make our clothes.

Howard: Good. And when they come back with an antelope, do they bring the whole antelope back, or do they kill it and skin it where they are?

Carlosha: No. They bring the whole antelope. And it's our job to skin it and take care of the meat and fry it over a fire.

Howard: Good. And what do you do with the fur?

Carlosha: We scrape the flesh off of it, and tan it in the sun, rubbing it with the minerals and things that we find in the earth. We dig in the earth for the minerals and clay to make our things out of. There's a small stream near by the cave that we use for water, and we bring the water to the cave in skins from the animals.

Howard: Good. And you said that you make pottery, too. Is that right?

Carlosha: Um-hmm. We make our bowls and mortars and pestles – I like doing that... I like using the clay. Feeling the earth in my hands and being able to shape it the way I want. Sometimes we make small figurines of animals and people, and it hardens in the sun and the children play with them. They look like horses and bears, just simple shapes, they're not very exact, and the children use their imagination to decide what they are. I think I have no children. I think my husband was killed somehow. I don't want to remember that, I don't know why.

Howard: Are you aware of any other families in the area?

Carlosha: There's people in other.... not villages, but their own encampments. It seems like we get together and visit with them and share things like food, when there's enough meat to share with everyone, when there's enough to share, and the women get together and go pick berries and do things like that together, and have their own little women society things.

Howard: Very good. Now there in that cave with these two men and your sister and these children, I want you to come forward in that lifetime to a very pleasant event, come forward and be there right *now*, and tell me what's happening here?

Carlosha: Dancing and singing. We're celebrating the sun and the moon. We do this every year on a certain day, Life day. It's to thank the Sun for the warmth and the energy.

Howard: OK. How do you know that this is the right day to celebrate that? Is it the longest day, or the shortest day, or something special about that day?

Carlosha: I want to say it's like Summer Solstice. The seasons are important to our people.

Howard: Tell me about the seasons – how they change.

Carlosha: There's a time of coldness and snow at the higher elevations, and that's when we go back down to the lowlands in the fall after gathering things. The cave is more in the lowlands. Summer's the time for gathering and growing things. We didn't grow things.

Howard: You pick things like berries, right?

Carlosha: Um-hmm. Dig roots by the river, mash them into flour and make them into cakes that we bake on the hot rocks in the fire. We dig the roots of the cattails, and we pull them – they're hard to pull – and we use digging tools that we make from rocks – the men do that – and dig the roots and dry them a little and then... in the rocks like an indentation in a rock, beat it with another rock until it's powdery, and then you can mix it with water and with herbs and things that we find. Then we form it into a ball and flatten it out and cook it on the rocks by the fire.

Howard: Good. And does everybody like them?

Carlosha: Um-hmm, except for the baby, we mush that cake up with some water.

Howard: Very good. And how old are you here now?

Carlosha: I think I'm in my thirties.

Howard: OK. Have you taken a mate?

Carlosha: I did – my husband was killed....

Howard: After he was killed, did you take another mate?

Carlosha:	No. There are not as many men. There are more women than men in our gathering-place.
Howard:	You have this gathering-place that's separate from your cave? Tell me about it. Is it a long walk from your cave?
Carlosha:	It's not too far. I don't know – maybe fifty paces, and everyone gathers there from different caves for celebrations and to just be together to sing and listen and talk and share food and stories about relatives that have passed on, special ways they have handed down of how we do things.
Howard:	And how many people are there altogether in your gathering-place when everybody comes?
Carlosha:	I don't know. There's not so many as there used to be, maybe thirty, thirty-five. They all have different places where they sleep – they're not all caves. Some are small huts made of sticks and branches, and there's pinion trees, and the branches are kind of flexible and they use that and hides and whatever they can find. I see one under a pinion tree where the branches have kind of come down to the ground, and they have reinforced that with some hides and have made a really nice little place to live in there.
Howard:	Good! That's very creative! What other tools do they have?
Carlosha:	Brooms that they have made – the women have made brooms – with straw-like branches they have attached with sinew from the animals. And like a cutting tool with a rock, rock head on it attached to a branch for cutting meat and wood for cutting to burn for the fires. I see sharp-edged rocks used to flense meat from the hide.
Howard:	And what kind of tools do the women use for cooking and making foods?
Carlosha:	Stones that have been pounded out, hides that have been made into pouches for water and liquids. I don't see a lot – very basic...
Howard:	OK. What do the men use for hunting? What kind of tools do they have?
Carlosha:	Bow and arrow, spears.
Howard:	They have bow and arrow! Good. Who makes the bows?
Carlosha:	The men make their own bows. It's special that they make their own; it's important that they do their own, then they can only rely on what they have done.
Howard:	And the spears – they have spears? What are the spears tipped with?
Carlosha:	Obsidian brought from another area, traded with other tribes.
Howard:	Very good. Are the animal bones used for anything, or are they just discarded?
Carlosha:	No, everything has a purpose. Everything is used. Needles for sewing the hides together are made from bone. Some are used for decorative purposes on shields and hair ornaments.
Howard:	And you say there's about thirty people altogether in your group? Does your group ever come across other groups?
Carlosha:	Um-hmm. It's a happy time. Sometimes, if they come and we don't know them already, then it can be kind of fearful until we make sure that everybody's going to get along. The men always go first. And when it is safe, we sit around a campfire, and sometimes the languages are not the same, and so they try to communicate with sign language and gesturing, imitating like a hunt, but they all seem to be able to relate to each other.
Howard:	Good. Are there any ceremonies?
Carlosha:	Yes.
Howard:	What do the people celebrate in ceremony?
Carlosha:	Holy Spirit, Great Spirit. They celebrate the times of the seasons changing.
Howard:	Tell me about their ceremonies with Spirit.

Carlosha:	Very sacred. Everyone believes that there's a Great Spirit in the sky that hands down wisdom, and it is to be revered. We ask for Great Spirit to bring us good luck hunting, and to make the crops, the berries all be plentiful, and for healing.
Howard:	Tell me about the healing.
Carlosha:	When someone is ill, they find herbs; there's a healer – he's an old man, and he knows the herbs and the things to do. He pretty much keeps the knowledge to himself. He's the only one that knows. In other groups there are sometimes a woman, but mostly a man. People know what to use. If their stomach is upset, they know what leaves to boil and make a tea out of. Grandmothers especially are very knowledgeable about these things; they help with birthing of the babies.
Howard:	Good. And what happens when somebody dies?
Carlosha:	There is a great ceremony for that because they don't actually die; they just go on to another spirit world.
Howard:	What do you know about the spirit world?
Carlosha:	Only that it is a good place to go, and that that person's life is welcomed to that spirit world with everybody dancing around. It's not a sad thing.
Howard:	Good. Now, Carlosha, I'd like you to just rest for a moment while I talk with Kwana. Kwana, if it was possible to find out how many years ago in Earth time this particular lifetime was, what would be the approximate answer?
Kwana:	Two hundred years ago.
Howard:	About two hundred years ago?
Kwana:	Um-hmm.
Howard:	All right. Thank you.
Kwana:	You're welcome.
Howard:	Carlosha, is there anything else that you'd like to know about this lifetime?
Carlosha:	Where did all the people go?
Howard:	And what's the answer?
Carlosha:	Things happened. Groups split up. Weather changed things. It wasn't a good place any more, and we moved on. Storms, dust storms. Drought. The river dried up.
Howard:	And where did you move to?
Carlosha:	More towards the mountains; there was water up there.
Howard:	Water is very important. And here, when you moved to the mountains, how old were you?
Carlosha:	Forty-eight.
Howard:	And did you find another place that could support life?
Carlosha:	Yes. It was colder, higher, more trees, rocky.
Howard:	Did you have enough clothing to keep warm?
Carlosha:	Um-hmm. There were more animals up there. It was much better up there. More for the animals to eat, so there were more animals and water.
Howard:	Good. All right, Carlosha, I'd like you to come to the very last day of that lifetime, and I want you to tell me where you are and what you're doing.
Carlosha:	I'm walking by a stream, and it's hard to walk because of the rocks, and I FALL! Down a steep ravine, and it hurts, but not for long, and then I'm done.
Howard:	OK. Just rise above that scene now, rise above the body. There's no more hurt – you're FREE! Free to lift and rise, and as you continue to lift and rise, is there anyone you want to move to to say Goodbye?

Carlosha:	My husband from long ago.
Howard:	Move to him now, and let him know, let him feel your presence. Good. Is he aware of your presence too? *(Pause)* Yes! Good! I want you to continue lifting and rising now, and notice that as you rise, you're met by a beautiful Angel, a wonderful Angel who takes you to a beautiful garden here. And just tell me what your beautiful garden's like, how it feels.
Carlosha:	There's beautiful flowers everywhere, and water and trees, and a lake, and around the edges there are many frogs and turtles.
Howard:	Wonderful! And as you continue moving through your garden, notice that there's a place for you to rest there, so just sit down and rest. And as you do, your Angel comes over and just enfolds you with her love and light, just feel that! And your Angel now invites you to move to a wonderful Healing Table here in the center of the garden. And as you rest on its soft, comfortable cushions, ask that the Angel heal whatever needs to be healed, whatever negativity needs to be released from that past lifetime, let that happen *now*. And as the Angel works, it is happening *now* in that lifetime, in the physical, and in this lifetime as well – anything that needs to be let go of is easily released and you can just move beyond that. And thank your Angel for her love and tenderness, her caring. *(Pause)* Now Carlosha, it's time to return. Thank your Angel there, and let her know that you can come back here any time that you want, and your Angel will always be there. *(Pause)* So Carlosha, come with me now back with Kwana, coming back now, and take a deep breath, and place your awareness on your physical body resting very safely in the comfortable chair there in the present time, the present place, the present YOU. And I'm going to count from five up to one, and at the count of one and not before, I want you to take a deep breath, and you'll automatically emerge from hypnosis. Five ...Four ... Three ... Two and... One – open your eyes and emerge from hypnosis. Welcome back!
Sandy:	Whoa! That just so bizarre and fun and mmmm! Wow!
Howard:	There might be a reason you have a connection with the American Indians! A lot of Southwestern United States there, or what was before the United States.
Sandy:	Yeah! Boy! A lot to process! Fun though!

* * *

Case Study 2:
SJ-07: Past Earth Incarnation June 6, 2013 – Directed by Howard Batie
Subject: "Karen"   Subject's Higher Self: "Anaka"   Subject's Guide: "Joshua"

(Note: Although this condensed transcript is of one of Karen's earlier Past Life Regression sessions, it is typical of the type of information retrieved through a Spiritual Journey session from the Akashic Record)

| Howard: | And as your senses begin to quickly adjust to this other time, other place, other you, do you find yourself indoors or outdoors? |
| Anaka: | Outdoors. |

Howard:	Good. Is it hot or cold or moderate?
Anaka:	It's summer, and everything is green, and it's cool, but not cold.
Howard:	Good. I want you to look down at your hands, there in that lifetime, and tell me if those are the hands of a man or a woman?
Anaka:	A woman.
Howard:	OK. And as you examine your hands and your arms, get a sense of how old you are here in that lifetime, how old are you here?
Anaka:	Thirty, maybe?
Howard:	And what are you wearing, how are you dressed?
Anaka:	It's not exactly like a robe, it's almost like Grecian, and a light-colored cloth cord tied around my waist to hold it all. It's tied and wrapped around and tucked in.
Howard:	Very good. Now as your senses begin to be completely acclimated and adjusted to this other time, other place, other you, become aware of what else is around you here. You said that everything was green and you're outdoors. Are there other people around?
Anaka:	Yes.
Howard:	Are there just a few, or many, how many...
Anaka:	It's a few, like a village.
Howard:	OK. Are you in the village, or on the outskirts of it, or what?
Anaka:	I'm in it, but it's dark, it has trees all around.
Howard:	All right. A small village?
Anaka:	Yes.
Howard:	OK. Good. Now begin moving through the village, and tell me what you're aware of, who you see, or what you are aware of there.
Anaka:	People in their yards, working and cooking, sharpening tools, and ...
Howard:	Good. What kind of tools do they have?
Anaka:	Swords, clothes, butter churns, things like that.
Howard:	Good. Now are there any buildings around in this village, or is it individual houses?
Anaka:	Individual houses, and they're huts like tents...
Howard:	Kind of like tents?
Anaka:	Yes. There are some wood buildings, too.
Howard:	Are there? OK. About how many people do you think that there are in this village?
Anaka:	Two hundred.
Howard:	Good. As you continue moving through the village, is there a particular place that you're drawn to?
Anaka:	A central gathering area that's like a fire pit.
Howard:	And what do they do here at the fire pit?
Anaka:	That's where the ceremonies for the village are.
Howard:	What kind of ceremonies do they hold here?
Anaka:	Like harvest festivals and religious festivals.
Howard:	Good. Now I want you to just become aware of the country that you're in.
Anaka:	I don't know, but I think it's in the Middle East or North Africa. Near there.
Howard:	OK. And about what year is it, as we would gauge years?
Anaka:	I don't know. Long before B.C., a couple thousand years, maybe a thousand years.
Howard:	Great! Now are there others that you regularly meet with here?
Anaka:	Everyone here – just like me. People in the village, I don't know if they... if I help them or what.

Howard:	Do you have a husband?
Anaka:	No. No, I take care of others' children.
Howard:	All right. And I want you to look down at your hands again, and tell me what color is the skin on your hands?
Anaka:	Warm, brownish, not like a black person. More like a native...
Howard:	Good. Now as you continue to move through this village, just tell me what else you're aware of.
Anaka:	The men seem to be like soldiers, and some have armor. And they look at me when I pass, and they're suspicious of me. I don't think they trust the women.
Howard:	Are there other types of men around?
Anaka:	Um-hmm. There are farmers and workers, and men that take care of the animals.
Howard:	Good. And when you pass the farmers, do they look at you the same way that the soldiers do?
Anaka:	No. They like me.
Howard:	Good. Now, is there a particular farmer that you know?
Anaka:	Um-hmm. I think so.
Howard:	Good. What's this farmer's name? What do you call him?
Anaka:	I think it's Mark or something like that.
Howard:	Mark? OK, good. And since you know Mark, he knows you, too, doesn't he? When he calls you by name, what name does he call you?
Anaka:	Sarah. Maybe Sarah, sounds like Sarah.
Howard:	Good. Thank you. Now, Sarah, I want you to come forward in that lifetime, to a very important event in that lifetime, come forward very quickly right NOW, and be there right now. And how old are you here?
Anaka:	Fifty years or sixty.
Howard:	Fifty to Sixty – OK. And what's happening here?
Anaka:	I'm dressed in dark clothes now, and I have a shawl over my head and it's cold like winter.
Howard:	Do you have enough clothing to keep you warm?
Anaka:	Yes.
Howard:	Good. And what are you doing here? What activities are you doing?
Anaka:	I'm gathering the children.
Howard:	OK. Are you still looking after the children in the village?
Anaka:	I think so, yeah. Oh! Oh!
Howard:	What's happening here?
Anaka:	Oh! We're being attacked!
Howard:	Who is attacking you?
Anaka:	Soldiers. *(Sobbing)*
Howard:	All right. I want you to just rise above this scene so that you're not in it, but you're just observing it, and just observe it.
Anaka:	*(Sobbing)* The children are dying! *(Crying)* I can't stop them!
Howard:	All right. Are there any other adults around?
Anaka:	No, I have them all by myself. *(Sobbing)*
Howard:	OK. Now continue just rising above, and as you look down, what's happening below now?
Anaka:	They're all around us and they're pointing spears at us.

Howard: OK. Now I want you to just observe everything that's happening without any pain or discomfort. Just tell me what happens, what happens next?

Anaka: They're moving 'round back... I don't know... It's like they stopped.

Howard: They stopped attacking?

Anaka: Yeah, they're around me and I'm talking to them. Their leader comes to me. He says I can leave with the children.

Howard: Thank the leader, thank him for that.

Anaka: Thank you! Thank you!

Howard: Now I want you to safely lead the children away, lead them away to safety, move them away from the soldiers.

Anaka: I move them to a cave that I know.

Howard: All right. Good. And what are the soldiers doing?

Anaka: They take our village, and they take all of our animals, and they burn all of our crops.

Howard: OK. It'll take a lot of effort to get that village reconstructed again, won't it? And what about the men in the village?

Anaka: They all got killed.

Howard: OK. So what do you do with the children now? Once the soldiers leave, they take your animals and what else they want.

Anaka: We go back and find what's left and gather the things that are still good, and move into the houses that are still OK, and start over.

Howard: OK. How old are the children?

Anaka: They're from teen-agers on down. They killed pretty much all the adults but me.

Howard: So it's really up to you to lead these children into adulthood, isn't it?

Anaka: Um-hmm.

Howard: All right. Now, I want you to come forward in that lifetime, come forward to a very important event, right NOW and be there! And tell me how old are you here?

Anaka: It's not much later. They're starting to have babies, and I'm helping them.

Howard: Very good. And there are homes built for the families?

Anaka: Um-hmm. We're all OK again.

Howard: Do the young men hunt successfully? Are their crops planted?

Anaka: We do both. They don't hunt big things, but they hunt rabbits, and small things...

Howard: Do you have farm animals?

Anaka: We have cows and goats and just a couple horses.

Howard: Good. But there's enough to sustain you, isn't there?

Anaka: Yes.

Howard: How many children... How many people are there in your entire village at this point?

Anaka: Maybe fifty.

Howard: And the young adults – what do they think of you?

Anaka: They all think of me as a Grandmother.

Howard: Are there any other adults that have found your village, that might have come wandering through?

Anaka: Um-hmm. Sometimes they come through, but none have stayed.

Howard: OK. Now I want you to just relax and become comfortable again, and I want you to move even more forward in time, I want you to move to a point in this previous lifetime just prior to leaving the physical, just prior to moving into the spiritual realm, and just be there right NOW. And tell me, how old are you here?

Anaka:	Near seventy-five.
Howard:	OK. And what are you doing here?
Anaka:	I'm on a bed, and I'm dying. There's a fire nearby to keep me warm.
Howard:	Good. And what are you dying from?
Anaka:	Just being old, I guess.
Howard:	Just worn out. It's been a tough life, hasn't it? Keeping track of all those children, and seeing them safely growing up. I want you to reflect on the highlights of that lifetime. As you look back on that lifetime, just let me know what was most important to you in that lifetime.
Anaka:	That I saved the kids. That they weren't alone.
Howard:	And what do you feel was your purpose for that lifetime?
Anaka:	That was it!
Howard:	What else did you learn in that lifetime?
Anaka:	That you can survive.
Howard:	What special abilities, very special abilities did you have in that lifetime?
Anaka:	Leadership with the kids, calmness, strength to deal with the soldiers.
Howard:	You did each one admirably, didn't you? You did very well. All right. Now, it's time to move on from that physical existence, and in a moment I want you to just let the physical go and move through transition, move into the spiritual realm. In just a moment, you'll leave the physical behind, and quickly move into the spiritual. When I count to three, you'll move from the physical realm, and BE entirely in the spiritual realm. One, beginning to leave the physical realm now.... Two, going through the transition between the physical and spiritual realms .... And Three, now completely back home in the spiritual realm. Just relax and feel how good it is to be back here again. How does it feel differently here, than in the physical?
Anaka:	It feels light, white light, everything's lighter, and I feel calm about everything.
Howard:	Good. And now, let's move to an even higher level of consciousness. We're going to go to a very special place in the spiritual plane, a very special garden, an absolutely beautiful spiritual garden. And as you move into this beautiful garden you're astonished by the colors, the brightness of the light here, many shades and hues that aren't even possible on Earth. So tell me how your garden appears to you.
Anaka:	It's like everything is made of crystals, and it's colorful, and it's bright, and you don't have to eat the plants, you just get the energy from them.
Howard:	Wonderful! It's an incredible, beautiful garden, and that's because this is the Garden of the White Light Angels. As you continue to move through your garden, you're greeted by the Angels of the Light. And as they move closer and lovingly encircle you, just FEEL their total unconditional love and light. Here, there's no judgement – there's just completely loving acceptance of who you are, just as you are. And describe to me how your Angels appear to you, and how many there are with you now.
Anaka:	Six, seven, and they are all very light-filled, they all glow. They're smiling, and they're all projecting love to me.
Howard:	Thank them for their love.
Anaka:	Thank you! Thank you!
Howard:	And open your heart, and radiate gratitude and love back. And feel them returning even more love, as you radiate back even deeper gratitude and thanks.... And now notice that they gently guide you to a wonderful Healing Table right there in the garden. Notice

	that it's a beautiful Healing Table made entirely of shimmering, shining white light! A wonderful table! And as you rest on this marvelous Healing Table made of white light, just feel its infinitely high vibration beginning to move through you in pleasant, comforting waves of the highest vibrations of healing energies. And ask your White Light Angels to rejuvenate you, and heal you on all levels of your being with these very high vibrations. And let me know when they've done that.
Anaka:	They have.
Howard:	Great. Now as your Healing Angels work on your energy field, FEEL that surge of energy returning to all levels of your being, bringing harmony and balance, and a very deep knowing of who and what you really are – an eternal spirit created in the Light and the Love of the One Infinite Creator. And pause for a moment, and ask to receive from your Angels whatever it is that you may need most, whatever you need for your physical well-being, for your emotional well-being, mental happiness, and for your spiritual well-being. Whatever it is, ask for that NOW, and it's happening NOW in the spiritual realms and in the physical plane, it's happening right NOW! And know that these healing energies will continue to flow into your life, day after day, after day throughout the rest of your lifetime and beyond. And as you begin to move from your Garden of Angels, begin to detach more and more from that past lifetime and move back to the bottom of the stairs, bringing all the thoughts, feelings and knowledge and insights back with you so you can consciously remember them. And now you're at the bottom of the stairs that lead back up to the present time, the present place, and your present body. And in a moment I'll count from Five up to One, with each number that I count, you'll move up the stairway one step at a time. Beginning now – Five, Four, Three, Two, and ... One! Take a deep breath, open your eyes, and emerge from hypnosis.
Karen:	(Laughs) Wow! That's great!

Spiritual Journey 8 – First Earth Lifetime.

The process for this Journey is similar to that of Journey 7, except that, instead the Client's Higher Self simply asks her Guide if she has permission to visit her own entire personal Akashic Record, specifically for the information concerning her very first incarnation on Planet Earth. If permission is granted, she is then guided by the Hypnotherapist to investigate what area of Earth this was in, the culture she was a part of, whether she was male or female, the lifetime experiences she had as a member of a clan or group, etc.

Among the possible lines of inquiry for this lifetime are:

How did you first become aware of the existence of Earth? Who told you?

What is your purpose/mission for coming specifically to an Earth lifetime?

How does what you feel begin to change as you approach Earth's atmosphere?

What part of the world are you drawn to?

What life forms are available for you to incarnate into?

What life form do you choose to incarnate into? Male? Female?

What country/culture/community do you choose to experience? Why?

How many years ago was this lifetime? (May need help from your Guide here)

What did you eat? How was it prepared?

Did you have a family? Children? How many? Names?

What is the average age for a lifespan in this culture at that time?

Process:
1. Client moves into their Spiritual Area and does the three things they must always do when coming up to her Spiritual Area.
2. Client's Higher Self (CHS) calls for her Guide and challenges him/her.
3. CHS asks her Guide if permission is granted to visit her personal Akashic Record for the purpose of investigating the experiences of her very first physical incarnation on Earth.
4. If permission is granted, record all the details of that first Earth lifetime.
5. CHS returns to the physical planes, reintegrates her Higher Awareness with her physical body and conscious mind.
6. Client emerges herself from self-hypnosis.

Case Study 1:
SJ-08: First Earth Lifetime   April 15, 2014 – Directed by Howard Batie
Subject: "Emma"   Subject's HS: "Shirella"   Subject's Guide: "Samantha"

Howard: Now, Shirella, I'd like you to move to the Akashic Record that contains all of your experiences on this Planet Earth, and from this Akashic Record of all of your experiences, move to the beginning of that record now, to the time and place that your soul essence first became aware of the existence of Planet Earth. *(Pause)* How did you first become aware of the existence of Planet Earth?

Shirella: From the stories told by those who wanted to change humankind, to introduce Light and Love. There's such a potential for a beautiful planet through life seeds that would change Earth and humankind. It was known that without the Light and the Love, life there would be meaningless, brutal, and without substance.

Howard: And when the Light and Love was introduced, were there already physical beings on the Earth?

Shirella: Some beginnings. That's how they knew.

Howard: What form of life was represented by these life forms? Was it animal life?

Shirella: Muck. *(Note: After emerging from hypnosis, "Muck" was later defined by Emma to be the unorganized primordial soup of amino acids from which the organized cells of amoeba formed.)* It was a beginning of life with energy, but not of Light. It was MUCK! Muckish. It was before bigger life grew. It was in the beginning. Life came to Earth, but was not of the Light and Love. It was energy gone awry. It was created early, before its time, and would not have developed properly. It was natural creation, but gone awry. It did not have soul.

Howard: Did these very early life forms... were they created through a natural chemical process?

Shirella: Yes, but the potential was there for meaningful life, and for a beautiful planet that would help the Universe. But it lacked the Light and Love at first.

Howard: And where did this Light and Love come from, this seeding process?

Shirella: Other beings of Light and love, the High Masters, the One That Is All, decided to create this Eden, this planet for spirit growth, and they decided to create seeds that would survive and flourish and evolve into beings of Light and Love.

Howard: Wonderful! Who are these Masters?

Shirella: The Elohim. They have the knowledge of what must be done. They are Creators for The One That Is All. They have the power of creation in defining forms as needed. They would know ... they would learn from other beings sent to Earth what was needed.

Howard: And when these beings went to Earth, what did they find, and what information were they looking for?

Shirella: How life needed to be created to survive, what needed to be in the seeds to allow life to survive, the conditions of Earth at that time, and to grow and to prosper.

Howard: So these representatives visited Earth to bring back the information about the environment of Earth? Is that correct?

Shirella: Yes, and of what was already begun as mindless energy that would not grow into meaningful life because of a deformation.

Howard: How were they deformed?

Shirella: Something was missing, so they decided... the Elohim, The One That Is All... that Earth would be a good place to build an Eden, to create a planet for separation life development. To build a planet where life would grow with the Light and Love, but not always aware of that, that would start as a basic life form and grow into their awareness and intelligence. It would be an evolving life.

Howard: At this point, did the life form have a physical form that was humanoid?

Shirella: No. No, that's too big, too far. This muck held the potential for life, but not what it needed to develop into meaningful life.

Howard: And this muck had developed just through chemical means?

Shirella: Yes. Unexpectedly. Unexpectedly it had developed.

Howard: Really! How did it develop unexpectedly?

Shirella: To other beings, it was not a known process, not known that chemistry would create life. Gaia had an evolutionary soul in the beginning, but not consciousness. And although one understood that there was a life force there, but not for meaningful life, it needed help, and it would be a good place for Gaia to raise herself and life. I can say that Earth was meant for a journey that was different from other planets in the area... in the galaxy. Earth had a different purpose to evolve from less developed energy, for life to take its course with free will.

Howard: You mean the development cycle on Earth serves a different purpose?

Shirella: It allows the beings who wish to translate here to Earth a different growth experience. It is high duty soul work here, and while it is difficult, it rewards heavily, we would say.

Howard: Excellent. Now let's return to the seeding process, the initial seeding process for Love and Light on Planet Earth. Where did these seeds come from?

Shirella: They are treated with Light, energy, spark by The Elohim based on what is needed for survival and development. The Elohim translate pure energy, love and light into form.

Howard: Are there examples or templates on other existing worlds that The Elohim use to create forms for a specific world?

Shirella: Sometimes, yes. Do not reinvent the wheel! Ha!

Howard: And what were some of the very early life forms?

Shirella: Amoeba. Some believe that the evolutionary life form and life process does not create viable beings of light and love – conscious. It takes so long and it has more opportunity to go awry, as we know happened in Earth's history. Many beings of the Universe did not think that developmental life could be viable in the long run, as you say – consciousness-raising, vibration raising would not happen. But we are now knowing that CAN happen with patience and guidance.

Howard: What changed? How did you become aware that...

Shirella: By watching and by helping Earth realign with the light. Once it was disconnected by the negative, light beings survived. It was a great debate whether to start the Earth Experiment and whether or not it would grow to the point and allow other beings to grow to the point of Gaia raising her consciousness.

Howard: And in this great debate that was going on, who were the beings debating?

Shirella: From other known worlds. They felt it was the waste of a good planet. It was not known in the Universe among sentient beings whether life could develop from the very most simple form, from the amoeba and before. The muck and the seed. So Earth became an experiment, and it was allowed because it was needed to fulfill the Oneness, to balance, and to have a place where other sentient beings could go through this growth process.

Howard: Thank you. (Pause) Now let's return to the time when the initial seeding began, the seeding of light and love energies as a composite template from many worlds. As that energy was given to Earth, was it given to Earth AND Gaia or just to Earth?

Shirella: Gaia participated willingly... Gaia is a part of that process. Gaia is the life energy of the planet, and as such, as a life form in and of herself, the life energy grows and changes, and part of her growth is to help sustain other life forms on the Earth. So the seeding allowed her to continue her path.

Howard: Thank you. Now as time went on, plant life began on Earth, and then animal life developed. Out of that animal life, early humanoid types evolved. Is that an accurate statement?

Shirella: Yes.

Howard: During this time in Earth's history, were you 'visiting' or had you physically incarnated?

Shirella: I had chosen to help with the seeding and then chose to incarnate, to go through the evolutionary and growth process.

Howard: OK. Thank you. So when you first decided to incarnate, into what part of the world as it existed then did you incarnate fully?

Shirella: In the Southern regions, the bottom of the planet in Africa.

Howard: And what kind of a climate was there that you first experienced physically?

Shirella: Hot, humid.

Howard: Good. And were there many others like you that were nearby, or were you the only being that incarnated fully?

Shirella: No. My incarnation started not long after the planting, and I was in a tribe eventually. The dark time, the darkness of evolution to consciousness is unknown, the dark time of animal instinct and growing.

Howard: And what was the type of humanoid life form that you first incarnated into?

Shirella: I think you call it Neanderthal. All human life, once evolved to a certain conscious-ness level, has an incarnated soul. Human life was seen to have the potential for more complex mental processes early on, and therefore, it was decided to allow off-world souls and some new souls to incarnate into human life forms as a means of guiding and directing human development. My essence is not of a formed nature, so it was difficult to understand life in a formed nature.

Howard: I see. Well, when you first incarnated fully into that Earthly life form...

Shirella: That was so I could expand my understanding of life by living as a formed being.

Howard: Thank you. At that time when you first incarnated, did you also retain the conscious knowledge of what you had been as a pure spiritual being?

Shirella: No, because that would have influenced my experience.

Howard: Now at that point where you decided to incarnate, why did you want to incarnate on Earth?

Shirella: It is the nature of all life to want to explore, to grow to its widest possible self, and to meet that need. Incarnation, despite it looking as if I went backwards, would give me the greatest opportunity to understand, to grow by taking my opposite. All life in all beings must grow, and consciousness allows that by return learning. It is a driven, it is a need, it is a requirement. We seek experiences that expand us. As the Universe expands, we expand with it. And Earth was formed to help with that experience for many forms of life and previous existence. So many beings, souls, many souls as you say who had been beings in other places also wanted to experi-ence Earth because it would be unique, as is all experience, but Earth provided new challenges.

Howard: When you first incarnated into physical life form in that area in Africa, tell me what the other people in your clan or group did... how did they survive and exist?

Shirella: Hunting, gathering, and staying close for protection. Learning how to do something better. It was a struggle at first because for humans, there is safety in staying the same – that is their biggest downfall, as a species, as individuals, clinging to the safety of the same.

Howard: But you needed that initially for your survival?

Shirella: Initially, but there is the driving life force in all beings to learn and grow, and there were those who listened and found new and better ways to do things, and so it began.

Howard: What were some of the new ways of doing things that you learned and experienced in that early incarnation?

Shirella: Foods to eat, not eat.

Howard:	And when you incarnated into that humanoid life form for the first time, approximately what was the life span in years, as we now measure them? What was the lifespan of that humanoid life form?
Shirella:	Maybe twenty.
Howard:	All right. And why was it that short?
Shirella:	Very harsh life, and a need for the species to progress more rapidly.
Howard:	And at the end of those twenty years, what do you recall doing, what happened at the end of the twenty years' lifespan?
Shirella:	I had made a commitment to stay on Earth through the entire developmental process, and so I, to use your term, 'rotated' into another human life after a brief rest.
Howard:	And in Earth terms, what was the approximate length of that resting period?
Shirella:	Maybe a hundred, a thousand... it is hard to know because those early years went fast. It has been the later years that have been the slower.
Howard:	All right. Now in your first incarnation into a humanoid life form, were you a man or a woman, male or female?
Shirella:	I was female, and I gave birth.
Howard:	How many children did you have in that lifetime?
Shirella:	Two.
Howard:	Now as time passed, and several incarnations later, did you always incarnate in the same general area of the land mass, or ....
Shirella:	No. We moved, we travelled to the very North, to the very cold, to experience it. Each of my incarnations follows the human development, although I may have chosen different segments of the planet. Some were for energy support reasons from Gaia, some were for learning experience, some were for helping Earth, helping Gaia.
Howard:	Good. How did you receive energy support from Gaia by choosing a specific location?
Shirella:	She has portals so that some of us who are in essence pure energy can reconnect, plug ourselves in.
Howard:	And some of the energy beings who are of a higher nature, do they incarnate as well, such as The Elohim?
Shirella:	Not The Elohim.
Howard:	What other forms of conscious energy do incarnate?
Shirella:	From other planets – they leave those bodies and go to Earth. If one is moving at a higher dimensional level and chooses to go to Earth in its density, it is an adjustment, but not as severe as one like myself who has never been confined to a form, whose energy is meant to flow. It is very fatiguing, and as we get closer to Gaia changing vibrational levels, I feel the fatigue of the years behind me.
Howard:	Tell me more about the changing vibrational levels of Gaia. What's causing the change and...
Shirella:	Gaia is naturally growing, as does all life, and it is time for her to raise the density level of the planet so that she can continue to grow. There is no other way for Gaia to survive. She is like all life in the Universe, meant to grow. And so, it is part of her natural evolution, and those of us who have been here from the beginning, especially, are rejoicing and are doing our best to assist and encourage the change, for her sake as well... for her sake first, and for ourselves as well.
Howard:	Wonderful. Now in that record of all your experiences while incarnated into a fully sentient human being, I want you to review that entire record, and I want you to select

from that record the lifetime you've lived that was the most memorable, that gave you the strongest feelings of satisfaction that you had achieved your purpose very well, that you had made strong, positive progress in your own spiritual development as a soul. So just take your time and review them all, and select the one that gave you the most satisfaction, and in a moment we'll review the high points of that lifetime. So just let me know when you're ready to proceed. *(Pause)*

Shirella: It would be this lifetime.

Howard: Good. And as you review the entire record of this lifetime, just move to the most memorable event, the event that caused you to select this lifetime as the most memorable.

Shirella: It is the growing. It is the combination of a body with a good mental capacity, with an innate desire to grow, and to live in a time on Gaia when I am not so confined. I can rejoice openly with others about the changes, the growing, the energy, the Love and the Light, and having a strong enough personality that my human self can carry this through. It did not start this way in this lifetime. This lifetime was a struggle, a darkness, and a closing, but the Universe is rejoicing in Gaia's birthing into a new energy level, and it is a great time to be here, to be able to add my special essence energy to that process. In all of my incarnations, I have tried to let Light and Love be seen or known in even the smallest of ways – it is my nature. And there were times it was needed, but never so much as now.

Howard: That's beautiful! Thank you. Thank you very much, Shirella, for all of this very interesting and very important information. Now is there anything else that you'd like to relate or to discuss before we conclude?

Shirella: Only that it is hard to find ways to express what I know, and I am confined to your language and your symbols and your other constructs. It is an expansive place, it is unknown to humans, the sense of freedom and joy beyond this life, and I am ready to return to it. I have done my work, and I am honored to be here at this time, but I am ready to go home. And it has helped, Howard, that you have let me touch there, and that you have taken me on these Journeys. It gives me strength, and so I say Thank You.

Howard: Thank you, Shirella! Thank you very much.

* * *

Case Study 2:
SJ-08: First Earth Lifetime   July 23, 2014 - Directed by Howard Batie
Client: "Dee"   Client's Higher Self: "Ileka"   Client's Guide: "Saywanda"

Howard: Welcome Home, Ileka! Have you asked for Creator's light and love to surround you, established a clear channel of communication between yourself and the highest levels of love and wisdom, and asked that all information you receive be only for the Greater Good of all concerned?

Ileka: Yes.

Howard: Good. Now I want you to ask Saywanda if it's appropriate for you at this time to visit your Akashic Record to learn the details of the very first lifetime that you lived on Planet Earth. And what does Saywanda say?

Ileka:	Yes.
Howard:	Excellent. Now, Ileka, I want you to move to your Akashic Record that contains all of your experiences related to Planet Earth, and from this Akashic Record of all your Earth experiences, move to the beginning of that record – to the time and place that your soul essence first became aware of the existence of Planet Earth. How did you become aware of Earth's existence?
Ileka:	It was shown to me by a higher essence. I don't know them. I see a visual, but I'm familiar with them.
Howard:	Call this being to come forward and challenge them: "Being – are you in service to the love and light of the One Infinite Creator – Yes or No?"
Ileka:	Yes.
Howard:	Say, "Being, please share with me who you are? Who are you who first told me of the existence of Planet Earth?"
Ileka:	He's a Guide. He's not my soul Guide, but he's a Guide that travels with you when you go from place to place and helps to integrate into that place.
Howard:	All right. Well, thank you for coming anyway. Now at this point when you first heard about the existence of Planet Earth, what did you know about Earth?
Ileka:	All I have is a visual. I'm seeing the planet from afar, and it's the blues and the greens and the wispiness of the atmosphere.
Howard:	Are you aware of any specific purpose that you have for visiting Earth or are you just curious?
Ileka:	To start the path of my infinite soul's journey on this planet.
Howard:	Good. And as you gaze at that planet off in the distance, describe your feelings.
Ileka:	Right now I'm kind of excited to go there and find out about it; it looks appealing to me.
Howard:	And as you approach closer and closer to Earth and begin interacting with the energies of the atmosphere – the physical plane – for the very first time, how do you feel then?
Ileka:	Heavier and heavier, I'm being pulled down.
Howard:	And as you descend more and more through Earth's atmosphere, how does it begin to feel differently here than in the spiritual realms?
Ileka:	I'm starting to become aware of temperatures and sounds and smells and all the aliveness of this Earth.
Howard:	And you didn't have that in the spiritual world?
Ileka:	It was different; the spiritual world was more like peaceful, light, softness, and goodness compared to this aliveness.
Howard:	Good. How does that make you feel – to touch into that life energy?
Ileka:	Alive!
Howard:	Yes! Now the very first time that you visited this planet, did you come fully into a physical body for a time, or did you enter the body and then move back out into the spiritual realm, to become accustomed to physicality?
Ileka:	I don't see myself in a physical body yet. It's more like I'm in an energy form.
Howard:	Good. Keep approaching closer and closer, and what are you aware of below?
Ileka:	I would say small flying... species? Birds?
Howard:	Good. Are there any animals or life forms that walk on the ground?
Ileka:	There's a lot of scurrying, small... scurrying and they're close to the ground.
Howard:	All right. Do they look interesting?

Ileka:	Being alive is!
Howard:	Good. Keep moving across the landscape, and do you encounter any other life forms, any more advanced life forms?
Ileka:	I don't.
Howard:	Just lift back up and move to a different area, and begin to explore and investigate the various areas here, and where are you drawn?
Ileka:	To the coldness, the upper coldness – what would be our North.
Howard:	Good. Are there life energies there?
Ileka:	In the water.
Howard:	Can you move through the water and look at those life forms and notice them?
Ileka:	Moving like fish.
Howard:	Good. And now come back up, up out of the water, back up into the atmosphere and in the air, and just move to another part of the world. Let's explore this area! Where are you drawn to now?
Ileka:	The mesas – the sandy mesas. I saw a palm tree or what I think would be a palm tree.
Howard:	On the sandy mesas?
Ileka:	Um-hmm. Like on a table top – from far away like a table top look with different step levels that just also look kinda flat. I see water, and there's a cave...
Howard:	A cave? Can you move into the cave? What's in the cave?
Ileka:	People!
Howard:	Yes! Good. How many people are there in this cave?
Ileka:	About seven or eight. I'm supposed to go there.
Howard:	Good. Is there a specific individual that you're supposed to go to?
Ileka:	There's a woman with a baby that's under one year. She's holding it, and just bathing her.
Howard:	What do you feel about this woman holding the baby?
Ileka:	I feel like we're not strangers, but I really don't know about a connection with her. But I'm supposed to be there.
Howard:	Can you move into one of these beings?
Ileka:	The baby.
Howard:	Move into the baby and just feel its energies.... And how does that feel?
Ileka:	Comforting. I'm being held and loved and cared for. That's a nice feeling.
Howard:	And what else are you aware of as the baby?
Ileka:	I have a lot to learn!
Howard:	Do you think it will be easy to learn or hard to learn?
Ileka:	I think it will be an unknown experience, and I'm excited to travel it and find out.
Howard:	Good. Now, this woman holding the baby – what does she call her baby?
Ileka:	Mm-tata.
Howard:	All right. Mm-tata, tell me what else you're aware of.
Ileka:	Just that it's dry in the cave and warm – not overly warm, but warm. I don't see a fire going; I see where there was fire. I don't understand that; that's what it is. I see about three men and two women and the baby and a couple of children.
Howard:	Good. Now, Mm-tata, as the baby, I want you to grow a few years older and tell me – what's happening now, where are you here and what are you doing?
Ileka:	We're still at the cave, and I'm just playing with some rocks. It looks like I'm a girl.

Howard:	Good. Now I want you to grow even older, about ten or eleven. And what are you doing now, Mm-tata?
Ileka:	I'm with other children and we're trying to find the water. There's an area where the water is, and we're going to it.
Howard:	How do you get the water back to the cave?
Ileka:	A type of basket.
Howard:	All right. What keeps the water from falling out?
Ileka:	Leaves, woven well with a reed type of plant. My Mom did it.
Howard:	Your Mother made it? She's very talented! Is she teaching you to do things like that?
Ileka:	Um-hmm.
Howard:	What else can you make or do?
Ileka:	Not very much.
Howard:	Yes, that's mostly for the grown-ups. Well, let's just get a little bit older now. Let's come forward to about eighteen or nineteen years old now – you're a grown woman! And what are you doing here now?
Ileka:	I have a mate. His name is hard to pronounce. Ah-lah-lu or something like that.
Howard:	What do you feel for Ah-lah-lu?
Ileka:	I care for him and he takes care of me by providing for me. He protects me; I don't know what from at this point.
Howard:	OK. Are there any animals that you need to be protected from?
Ileka:	All I saw was a big huge... I guess it would be a saber-toothed tiger because they can mark (?) in that area.
Howard:	And how do Ah-lah-lu and the others protect you from the tiger?
Ileka:	They have a type of stone on a long pole, it's like a spear.
Howard:	So they can keep the tigers away with the spear – that's good. Do they have any other protecting tools?
Ileka:	No.
Howard:	OK. When he provides food for you, what kind of food does he provide?
Ileka:	Small animals – I don't know names.
Howard:	Where do you sleep?
Ileka:	In the back area of the cave. It has other chambers and expands out into the hillside. We're together for protection.
Howard:	Are there other groups nearby that might live in other caves? Do you ever run across other people?
Ileka:	No.
Howard:	Now what do you do when Ah-lah-lu brings back small animals?
Ileka:	I take the fur off to be used and then we eat the animal.
Howard:	Do you use fire?
Ileka:	Sometimes; sometimes not.
Howard:	Do you eat anything besides the animals? Do you have fruits or other...
Ileka:	We eat the grasses and that kind of stuff. We don't eat any kind of fruit or anything like that. It's too desolate.
Howard:	And what part of the world are you in, if we could call it like today's continents?
Ileka:	Somewhere maybe in the African area.
Howard:	All right. Do you and Ah-lah-lu have a good life together?

Ileka:	Um-hmm. We're happy.
Howard:	Good. Is there enough to eat?
Ileka:	Not all the time, but there's plenty of water. We don't know that we could go to other places, so we just stay by the cave.
Howard:	When the men leave the cave and go on a hunting party have they ever found other caves or other people?
Ileka:	For some reason, it's a Yes and a No, and that doesn't make sense. I think it means they have, but they don't tell us. So I think that's my understanding. The men want to keep us from them.
Howard:	Oh, I see. All right. Now I want you to come forward in time and get a little older now. Mm-tata, I want you to come up to your mid-twenties, and tell me what you're doing now, and where you are and who is with you.
Ileka:	I have a baby in my lap – it's a girl – and a little one about two or three, a boy. I'm just sitting there with my legs crossed in front of a dead fire pit, meaning there's no fire right now. Ah-lah-lu is right beside me. Everybody's doing their thing, their projects – sharpening sticks, the weaving still, and trying to find a way to use the furs.
Howard:	OK. What do you use the furs for?
Ileka:	Protection. What I was seeing was on the feet, like for moccasins or shoes, but leaving the fur, like not tanning it, that's all we know.
Howard:	All right. And what other clothes do you have?
Ileka:	Not much.
Howard:	OK. Well, how are your clothes made?
Ileka:	Grasses and bits of fur. Grasses are like the reed grasses.
Howard:	Now as you look at other people there with you in and near the cave, how old is the oldest person there?
Ileka:	Has white hair. We don't count ages.
Howard:	How many summers have they seen?
Ileka:	Forty. A woman.
Howard:	How many people are there in the cave now?
Ileka:	Twelve to fifteen. There are more babies, more children.
Howard:	Now, around this fire pit or somewhere close to the cave, are there ever any ceremonies conducted?
Ileka:	Um-hmm.
Howard:	And what do you celebrate?
Ileka:	We celebrate the moon every time it becomes really bright. We celebrate the sun, too.
Howard:	Now what do you know about the sun?
Ileka:	It keeps us warm, and it's cold when it's gone.
Howard:	Good. Now I want you to look over to that old woman, the oldest person there. What will happen when she dies?
Ileka:	The next one in line will take her place.
Howard:	OK. Well, what will happen to her, the one that dies?
Ileka:	They just take her outside and leave her. They know that she will disappear.
Howard:	All right. Now when you were mated to Ah-lah-lu, was there a ceremony for that?
Ileka:	I just put my hand on top of his. I accepted him.
Howard:	All right. Are there any ceremonies or any celebrations when a baby is born?

Ileka: The baby is held high to the moon and to the sun, and I think it's for a combination of good luck and also for a combination of showing the world, but it's not really the world. It's done facing out of the cave, out to the moon and up to the sun. And I don't know, and I'm not supposed to know that stuff, but I don't know exactly what or why, but it's for good. We do they do the same thing for baby boys and baby girls.

Howard: Does Ah-lah-lu go hunting with other men?

Ileka: Um-hmm. When they have enough strength and they have enough spears. They have to make more spears all the time because they lose them or they get broken. I don't even know where the wood comes from for the spears. It's some place that they find that's not in my sight area.

Howard: When they're out hunting or something?

Ileka: Um-hmm. I don't go far from the cave; it's not safe. We don't need to go too far on the plateau area away from the cave, from the women and children.

Howard: All right. You said that the soil there is not really good for growing things? So it's just the animals there that you can find and eat?

Ileka: Um-hmm. And the grasses and reeds around the water.

Howard: How do you prepare the grasses for eating?

Ileka: We just eat them. If it's a seed grass, we just strip it between our teeth. And we do kind of the same with the reed, we try to strip it with our teeth and get the tender part of it which is usually down in the water.

Howard: Good. Tell me about this water place. Is it a river or a pool?

Ileka: It's like it comes up out of the ground, and it's not a big pool, but it always has enough water for all of us.

Howard: That's good. That would be another reason for not going too far from the cave, wouldn't it?

Ileka: Um-hmm.

Howard: OK. How do you feel about this lifetime? What are you learning?

Ileka: To stay alive, to interact. That's about it.

Howard: All right. Now come forward in that lifetime and get even older, and tell me how old you are here now.

Ileka: Thirty-eight.

Howard: And what's happening?

Ileka: I'm just sitting there, feeling tired. Worn out.

Howard: Has it been a good life?

Ileka: Um-hmm.

Howard: Has it been a hard life or an easy life?

Ileka: Both – meaning the harshness was the lack of food, and the goodness was the security of us together, all of us, and my mate protecting me and my children.

Howard: Very good. OK, Mm-tata, thank you very much. I want you to reflect on that lifetime, and pick one event in your lifetime that made you feel the happiest. What was that event, what happened?

Ileka: Actually, it was when I was dying. Two things – because everyone was around me that was close to me in that life, and were caring or showing me that they loved me, and then the other side of it was because I knew I was leaving this life and moving on up into the spiritual... I knew that I was leaving this earthly life right at the peak of one existence, and going into the other.

Howard: OK. And just take your last breath, and as you let it out just rise above the body, and just feel yourself lifting, rising, free once again, moving back into the spiritual realms – one, two, three, completely back in the spiritual realms, just floating and drifting, looking down on that scene. Is there anybody you'd like to say goodbye to before you leave?

Ileka: My daughter.

Howard: Just move to your daughter now, just let her feel your energies.... Does she recognize your energies?

Ileka: Um-hmm.

Howard: Good! Send her love.... Good – any others?

Ileka: Uh-uh.

Howard: All right. Just continue to lift and rise, fully back in the spiritual realms now, home once again! And I want to thank you for this very interesting and very important information. Is there anything else that you'd like to relate before we conclude – anything at all about that lifetime?

Ileka: No, not really, just that it was OK for the first step.

Howard: OK. And Saywanda is always there with you; ask him how you did. Ask for his impression of how that lifetime went for you, and what does he say?

Ileka: He says he was glad he could be with me.

Howard: (Emerges client from hypnosis.) Welcome back!

Dee: Thank you. I think what was interesting was when I first got to Earth, I was not any shape, you know, I didn't have any shape of a human. And then to find that I was going to end up in the cave, you know, that was kind of interesting. I tried to go in the snow and ice, but I didn't... (laughs) There wasn't much up there, let me tell you! It was pretty barren.

Howard: But you survived, and that's good! That's a good lesson in itself, isn't it?

Dee: Yeah, it wasn't horrific, and nothing really extremely terrible happened in that life, so if that was my first step, then was kind of a soft break-in to the rest. I think if I came in kind of crashing and banging, it would have.... But it was soft, so I think that was the point of maybe taking that life where they didn't go out and challenge the world, so we were basically kind of protected, and that kind of makes sense, to me anyway.

Howard: Very good. Any questions?

Dee: Um-um.

* * *

Case Study 3:
SJ-08: First Earth Lifetime   April 30, 2014 – Directed by Howard Batie
Subject: "Karen"   Subject's HS: "Anaka"   Subject's Guide: "Joshua"

In this session from an earlier version of Spiritual Journeys, the Hall of Records was used as a metaphor for that place in your Spiritual Area where your own 'Book of life,' the Akashic Record of all your prior experiences, is 'located.' As you obtain your Book of Life and re-live your prior lifetimes, you are in fact accessing your own Akashic Record. Although the present version of Spiritual Journeys does not use the Hall of Records metaphor, the results are just as effective, as shown below.

Howard: Welcome Home, Anaka! Have you done the three things you must always do?

Anaka: Yes.

Howard: Wonderful! Now, Anaka, I want you to ask Joshua if it's permissible for you to access your own personal Akashic Records for the purpose of investigating your very first incarnation on Earth, and what does Joshua say?

Anaka: He says Yes.

Howard: Thank Joshua for that. Now I want you to begin by moving with me and Joshua as we move through your Spiritual Area here in the spiritual realms, and very soon you'll recognize or just become aware of your Hall of Records. Now let's enter your Hall of Records, move right in. And become aware of your Record Keeper, and just describe how he or she looks.

Anaka: It's a man, he's young, he has glasses, and he sits behind a big desk with books piled everywhere.

Howard: And you know, another thing about your Record Keeper is that he knows what your intentions are, and he knows the information that you're seeking, so ask him to fetch your Book of Records, your Book of Life, and as he brings it to you, describe it to me – how big it is, what it looks like, how heavy it is...

Anaka: Pretty good size, about three inches thick and a foot wide and a foot and a half tall.

Howard: OK. Now, as you receive your Book of Life from your Record Keeper, take it to a place there in your Hall of Records where you can examine the individual records – it could be a table or a desk somewhere, or just a comfy chair, or anywhere else that you like. But just describe where you take your Book of Life.

Anaka: It's like a big library table, dark wood and chairs – they're comfy. It's like an old library in a university.

Howard: Very good. Now I want you to open your Book of Records, your Book of Life, open it to the very first page – the very first time that you incarnated and had a physical lifetime on Mother Earth. Is your Book of Life opened?

Anaka: Yes, but I just see colors – gold and purple, and they're moving, there's anticipation, and I know I'm going somewhere.

Howard: Let those colors and that movement begin to coalesce into a wonderful feeling, a wonderful image, a wonderful knowing of who and what you truly are as you prepare for this very first incarnation. And describe to me everything that you're aware of just before you incarnate.

Anaka: I feel very fresh, very young, very new, like it's a beginning. I can tell it's starting.

Howard: All right. Just begin focusing and directing your attention on that body that you're going to inhabit for the very first time. And as you come into it, tell me what you're aware of, how it feels, about how old are you here?

Anaka: I'm still a baby. It feels limiting because it's a body, but it feels good, it feels warm, it feels safe.

Howard: Good. And what is the name that she is known by?

Anaka: Jun, like J-u-n, Jun. Yeah, just Jun. I feel warm. I feel where I live, the sun is warm. I feel it on her skin and my skin. And I see others around. We live together, but we don't stay in one place. I feel that we must move to find food. Around me everything is brownish, it's like very dry and very warm and sandy. I think I'm in Africa.

Howard: In Africa. Good. Now I want you to look at Jun, your mother, and describe to me what she looks like, what color her skin is, how tall she is...

Anaka: We're small, we're all very small, and she has brown, very brown eyes. I wouldn't say Neanderthal, but not totally human yet. We haven't grown tall yet because we need to be small where we live to survive.

Howard: OK. Now in that lifetime, I want you to come forward, come forward to the time when you're just a young being, a few years old. Are you male or female?

Anaka: Female. Five or six. I'm with my family still. We still move together. We stay near water when we can, and we gather food and we hunt.

Howard: What kind of foods is it that you gather?

Anaka: Mainly grains, some fruit, small animals. We eat small animals and eggs from birds. We have enough that we're not hungry, but there's not lots – we have to move to find it. We stay together, we move along waterways and when we stop for the night, we might stay somewhere for a little while to gather what's there, and we ... it must be warm – we don't have to build homes, we make maybe just little shelters, and I see maybe ten or twelve of us – very few.

Howard: Good. What kind of clothing do you wear, if any?

Anaka: Not much, just something wrapped around us to help us hold the things we carry, kind of like belts and clothes combined.

Howard: Very good. What are the kinds of things that you do carry with you?

Anaka: We have primitive tools, things made from sharp sticks and tied together, and sharp things, mainly hand-made, but skilled hand-made, and they work well. Like to kill the rabbits, we have a rock that has a handle that's tied together, and you hit them with the rock.

Howard: Good. And what are these beings doing now?

Anaka: They're sort of all gathered together, and we're eating and we're talking. We don't talk a lot, we don't have a lot of language; it's a simple language because we understand each other without a lot of talking.

Howard: Do you understand each other through your mind, or through your gestures and actions?

Anaka: It's kind of both because we know each other so well. We know what we need, and what the other person needs from us. We can also talk, but we don't have to talk a lot. We just describe the places and the things in our lives.

Howard: Good. Are you able to describe things you can't touch, like your feelings?

Anaka: I don't know words for that. Mainly you know if someone's angry, you know. If they're happy, you know.

Howard: Good. Now as you're moving along in this group, do you ever encounter other groups of beings?

Anaka: Yes. We share, we trade things. A lot of times, you cross paths when you're traveling, so they could be North and you could be South, and you gather things and you share. Like we have to go to the ocean for salt, and we share. That kind of thing.

Howard: Good. What kinds of things do you trade the salt for?

Anaka: Beads and things to make things with feathers and sinews, and furs. Simple things like that. And we share food with each other, and we share ceremonies.

Howard:	I'm interested in your ceremonies. What do these ceremonies celebrate, or what is their purpose?
Anaka:	I think they're seasonal, and they celebrate new people in our group, you celebrate when the rains come, and you celebrate when the animals give birth and there's new food for the year, so it seems seasonal. It's like we're very Earth-tied.
Howard:	Is there ever negativity, anger?
Anaka:	Not so much anger. Sometimes if someone has died or... that's a negative, but it's there.
Howard:	What do you believe about the person that's died?
Anaka:	We know they have a spirit; we don't know where it goes. We know that even in the creatures that they're alive and then they're gone, so something leaves, and it happens with us, too. We wrap them up in a lot of reeds, and we bend them in what we now call a fetal position – we didn't call it that then – but we rolled them up together and we tied them really tightly and then we place them in rocks – I don't think we bury them, I think we place them away somewhere and cover them, but we don't put them under ground. We cover them with rocks, like up against other rocks so the animals don't come and eat their body.
Howard:	All right. Thank you. Do any of your ceremonies focus on what happens to the spirit?
Anaka:	Only in that when they die... Ah, I just saw some we burn. I wonder if there's a difference, because in their smoke we send up their smoke. So maybe only some people get buried, and some people get burned. Different! It feels more like it has to do with when they die. I don't know if it's a seasonal thing, maybe I don't understand yet. It's a difference – where we are. Maybe sometimes you don't want the smoke; the animals see the smoke. When you don't want them to see the smoke and you don't want there to be fire, then you cover them with rocks. And I don't know why the difference is. It just has to do with the smoke. We like the smoke because that helps their spirit to go up, but it can also go up when they're in rocks. I don't know the difference.
Howard:	Good. And in this group of ten to twelve beings that you move with, how many births are there in a year, a complete set of seasons?
Anaka:	I think there's a birth every two or three years. I think there are only four children here, me and my sister and two others. Six women and four children and two men. I know who's my father. He's also our spiritual guide. He teaches us to care for each other, to pay attention to the seasons and the signs of the seasons, to pay attention to the animals and what they do – they guide us, the animals show us. When something's wrong, they know. Sometimes when the fires come, they run and we see them. Sometimes if there's an earthquake, they know; they sit down, or the wind comes up really strong they lay down before it happens, or they get really quiet, especially the birds. The birds really know, especially the sky events, like when there's an eclipse; they calm down, they know, but the birds get quiet.
Howard:	And how do the people feel when the sky gets dark?
Anaka:	Afraid! But my father says it's OK, and the sun comes back – he's seen it before. He says it's OK, and everyone believed him.
Howard:	OK. Just come forward in that lifetime to a very pleasant event, and tell me what's going on here – how old are you?
Anaka:	I think I'm thirteen. It's called a naming ceremony. I have a name, but now I'm a woman and I have a new name.
Howard:	What was your name before?

Anaka:	Un-Jun, and I think it meant daughter of Jun. Now I am... they haven't told me... wait, my father is naming me... he says my name is Sirah (Si-**RAH**), which means white bird. It's like egret – that's the image that I see.
Howard:	All right, Sirah. Come forward even more in that lifetime as you get older to another happy, very pleasant event, and what's going on right now? What's happening here?
Anaka:	My child is born! A boy.
Howard:	Good! How old are you here?
Anaka:	Eighteen. I was mated shortly after I was named, but I didn't have a child for a while.
Howard:	All right. And who was it that mated you?
Anaka:	Rana. R-a-n-a. He and I were together at our age, and no one else. He's a child of the other father, so we always knew. His hair is lighter than mine and my father's and my mother's, and it's curly, it's got blonde streaks, and his eyes are greener, but his eyes are brown. His mother is light, she must have joined us. I think sometimes when we meet other groups, we trade daughters, and so his mother was a daughter from someone else. That's what happened.
Howard:	All right. Now I want you to look at your skin, your hands, and I want you to tell me what color they are.
Anaka:	It's very dark. I'd say it's a really rich brown, it's not a dark brown, but it's definitely what you'd call a black skin in today's world, but it's really not black, just a really rich brown color. Rana is much lighter than me; so is our son, and blonder hair with curls. I don't know if our baby will have curls.
Howard:	Good. And what do you and Rana decide to call your son?
Anaka:	Ra-**ZHA**! He'll have a new name when he grows up.
Howard:	Describe this naming ceremony to me. When somebody is coming to the age of getting a new name, why do they get a new name?
Anaka:	Because you are a woman or a man. Because your child name means child-of. Like Un-Jun was Child of Jun. And RaZha is Child of Rana. I guess it's different for boys and girls. I don't understand why it's done that way, it just is what it is. For the naming ceremony, my father is sort of the naming official, and he sings to the skies and he sings to the earth, and he receives a message of what your naming should be, so he tells you. We named our child, but the leader names your adult name. Maybe he sees how you are until then, so he knows.
Howard:	Good. Now come forward in that lifetime again to another very pleasant event and be there right *now*. And describe to me how old you are first.
Anaka:	I think I'm about twenty-five.
Howard:	OK. And what's happening here where you're twenty-five?
Anaka:	There's happiness, a lot's going on. I'm not sure, I move forward without knowing what's happening, but it's a happy, happy time, people are dressed in white, there are young people there... I'm trying to see if it's another child. Everyone feels good, and there's a lot more people there than there were before. I think we're with another group, and I think it's like a marriage or a mating ceremony. We have someone new who has come, and my father and their leader are choosing... RaZha is with me, Rana is with me, and we have another child, a girl, and she's the one who is dressed white, and she has flowers in her hair.
Howard:	How old is she?
Anaka:	Two, maybe. It's about her. I think that we've gotten a boy for her. That's what's happening. The other leader, they have a boy, and they don't have enough people because

you can't marry your siblings, so he will live with us. Yes, it's a promise ceremony. But I think that... let me listen... I think that we're all to be together, so there will be twenty-five or thirty of us.

Howard: And is the other group just like your group, or are they more advanced, or is your group more advanced?

Anaka: I don't think we have a concept of advanced.

Howard: OK, do you use different kinds of tools?

Anaka: No, we all use the same kind. And we all dress similarly – we've known each other before. The other leader is my father's brother! Yeah! He was given away as a child, so that must be how we keep helping. Our children exchange, but it has to be a close group to us, so they're safe with them. So my father's brother's group stayed near us, but did not live with us until now, and now we will all live together. With us all together, we can gather more, and we will be able to work on things together, work on projects together, make gathering places and instead of move so much around, we'll have shorter distances and have like a base, a place to stay, a place to keep the children safe, and then the people who gather will gather, and the people who hunt will hunt. Before, the hunting party was only two or three people – the two men in my group, and sometimes my mother would go, and then when we grew older, Rana and I would go, but they still had to hunt small things, because the big animals can hurt you. But with more people, we can hunt bigger things and have more food.

Howard: Good! What kind of bigger animals do you hunt?

Anaka: There are like cows... I don't think they're like cows like American cattle, but they have horns like cows, maybe like water cows or big cows. If you can isolate them, they're easy to kill, but if they stay with a group, you can't, because they're like herders, and they circle and protect the little ones in the middle like we do. We have to wait until they don't know you're there, and run into the middle of them so that hopefully some get frightened and run the wrong way, then you isolate them.

Howard: Do they ever try to attack you?

Anaka: Yes. They don't want to be attacked! Yeah, they will chase you. You have to be near trees, and they are in the open where their food is, and you have to be near trees, and surprise them, and then stay near the trees because if they surround you, they kill you.

Howard: And what kind of implements or tools do you have to kill the animals?

Anaka: Spears and arrows.

Howard: Arrows? Do you have bows and arrows?

Anaka: Bows? I don't think so... I think arrows are just thrown like little spears, and we have big spears, too. Sometimes you wound them, and then they get away still.

Howard: Do any of your own kind ever get wounded in these hunts?

Anaka: Yes, men have been killed. That's why we stay near the trees, because when you get in the open, that's when you can get killed. The men are providers, especially when the women are pregnant or have new children. When the children are lots older, you can do more, but when they're little you can't. I think my father's father was killed by an animal. I think so. That's all we have to tell each other, the stories that we know. And that's a lot of what we do when we meet other groups; we share stories. And the ways we describe, we act things out a lot. It's kind of like charades where we don't use as many words, but you act it out and you tell the story. It's most fun after you've eaten, and the little ones are sleeping, and you can sit down and all share and talk, and it's quiet. In the day, we're busy, but you can still share stories because you all work together.

Howard: Do the women share stories as well as the men?

Anaka: Oh, yes. In our group, women are weaker, but we're not lesser. We all have our roles, and we all need each other – that's how we survive.

Howard: Describe a typical day in your life – in the morning when you wake up, what happens, what do you do?

Anaka: As an adult, I go outside and in the summer the grain is growing, so I gather the grain and soak it in water and cook it sort of like a mush. When the grain's not growing, then we eat what's there. I have learned to store food, although where we live, we don't have to store often because there's enough food all the time. We make baskets. We do simple, but we make baskets. It's from... we can even take skins and make them into baskets. Anything you can fold – leaves that don't dry fast, things that can wrap and can tie, you can use like that. And you can put grains and medicines, 'cause we use plants for medicines, and you just keep them. When we travelled more, we couldn't carry so much, but now we stay longer.

Howard: Is there vegetation with large leaves around that you can make into baskets, or do you have to take many leaves?

Anaka: Yeah, if they're small leaves, you use them to line something. You can weave them together, open weave and line with small leaves, just something to hold it. There's lots of grasses. I think we must live near high plains or plains, 'cause there's lots of grasses; it's very brown.

Howard: What other tools do you have that make life so much easier for you?

Anaka: We have some stones for grinding the grains and smashing medicines, but not very many stones; it's mostly sand there. They must carry the stones from places when they find them. And we have sharp-edged stones; like when a rock breaks, it has a sharp edge and you can scrape skin from dead animals, that kind of tools. And definitely things to hit with, like a hard rock, so you can tie rocks to sticks so you can bang things, and the men use spears. I'm not sure with the points... the points are bones, they file bones! Interesting! I thought it would be rocks, but it's not. They're made from very sharp bones, and they're tied on, and then – poke! Sometimes it's actually the bone itself, the whole bone like a long leg bone. So we use what we have, but we don't have flint – we don't have that kind of thing.

Howard: When you move from place to place, do you bring the fire with you, or do you make the fire where you are?

Anaka: I think we make the fire. I don't think we bring it. I think we use friction like rubbing sticks on sticks. Somehow I feel like I rub my feet and hands together to roll the stick, so I must be against something creating friction, I have that impression.

Howard: All right. Now you mentioned some time before that these pouches or bowls carry medicines. Tell me about some of the medicines that are made. Who makes the medicines? Does everybody make them, or is there...

Anaka: We all do. We all have different herbs, some leaves that you know can make you go to the bathroom if you can't, some especially for wounds. I don't think we have lots of aches and pains other than wounds. If your body gets injured, a lot of things that you chew and grind and put on the wound itself and tie to things.

Howard: And this knowledge about what substances are good for wounds, is that like from a medicine man, or one man or woman in the group, or does everybody know all these things?

Anaka: Everyone knows. My father does ceremonies, but he doesn't tell us what to do for medicines... we know that. So I think you just watch each other and see what each other uses, and you know, you know what the plants are. I remember my mother told me, "This is for a wound, and this is for infection, and this is for your tooth-hurt," different things like that.

Howard: And how old is the oldest person in your group?

Anaka: Forty. But they're very wrinkley and bent.

Howard: All right, Sirah. Now come forward in that lifetime even more, come forward to the last day of that lifetime, and I want you to BE there right NOW, and I want you to tell me what you're aware of, what's happening here? How old are you?

Anaka: I think I'm about thirty-five. I seem to be awake, sitting by a fire, it's daytime. I think I've been sick, but I don't feel really well, and there are still people moving around, but I'm not moving, I'm not helping them, just there, so... I must be ill, although I don't feel really ill. They're all just sitting with me, we're all just sitting. I feel a blackness or a darkness, I feel something there that's... dark, even though I know it's daytime, so... I don't know.... It feels heavy on my heart – I don't feel afraid of it, I just feel it's change...

Howard: Now, Sirah, before you take your last breath, I want you to just pause there for a moment and reflect on that lifetime that you've lived. Was it a happy lifetime, a productive, learning, growing lifetime?

Anaka: Yes. I got to see and feel and know the earth, to begin my Earth journey.

Howard: Why did you want to experience an Earth journey?

Anaka: Because that's how you feel, that's how you learn. You can only be you in spirit, and you can be you and more on Earth. You're still you, but you make you more. And I got to be close to the Earth. I lived right ON the Earth. I liked it! I feel I got to know my family and my people, and to understand how I would fit in, and I began to see how I would successfully interact with others that are on Earth at the same time. That we were together, we have to be together and know each other to move through....

Howard: All right. Just continue lifting, and feel yourself being pulled higher and higher like a magnet, pulling, pulling, pulling, rising, lifting, and become aware of the beautiful angels that have always been there. They've come to help you transition back into the spirit world. Continue rising and lifting... and now fully in the spirit world... allow those wonderful, beautiful Angels lift you and carry you to a beautiful garden, a wonderful garden, a Garden of the Angels! Thank them for being there with you. And ask that they give you a signal or a sign, a token of some kind that you can recognize them with. It could be something physical that you see, or it could be just a feeling, a pressure in your right shoulder or anywhere else in your body, or just a beautiful aroma, a rose perhaps, something that they bring to you now. And let them bring this gift to you, and accept this gift as your way of knowing and connecting with them again whenever you wish. (Pause) Do you have this gift that they've given you?

Anaka: Yes.

Howard: Good! Feel that gift! Look at that gift, see it! Taste it, touch it, feel it, know it! Move right into its energies, and record all the sensations, all the images, all the insights of this wonderful gift in your Garden of Angels. *(Pause)* And now, Sirah, it's time to leave this lifetime. Return to the awareness of Anaka, your own Higher Self. And Anaka, I want you to thank Joshua for coming along with us today on this Journey. So just let yourself permanently record all the insights, all the sensations, the sights, the energies, the feelings of your Journey into your very first incarnation. And I want you to begin to come back to full conscious awareness again. I'll count from Five up to One, and as I do, at the count of One and not before, you'll return to the current place, the current time, the current you. Five... Four... Three... Two... and One! Open your eyes and emerge completely from hypnosis. Welcome back!

Karen: (Giggles) That was great! It was weird because I felt Joshua wrap around me, I felt him there the whole time. And I kept waiting for the sign from the Angels. I finally just got this feeling in my heart, it started there and then just radiated up, and that was just a feeling. I kept thinking, "Oh, I'll see something!" but it was just a feeling.

Howard: Everyone is different, and their signal is unique.

Karen: Well, good! That was very, very nice. I liked it, interesting! It was weird, because to describe things, I had to use modern words sometimes, and I knew that wasn't what... but it's like there still a part, a connection, that says, "OK, you have a word for that, it's not there, but this is what the word for it is now." So that was interesting!

Howard: See, you're training yourself to live in two worlds at the same time! Any questions?

Karen: I don't think so! Well, I have no idea what time in history that was, other than it was a long time ago, a loooong time ago!

Howard: You mentioned that you were no longer Neanderthal, but not quite a human yet, so it's that transition period. So you can look it up and see how long ago the Neanderthals...

Karen: I was very aware of being smaller, and I didn't look simian, but I didn't look human, so kind of in between.

Howard: Good! Thank you!

Spiritual Journey 09 – First Soul Memories.

Your client's personal Akashic Record has within it all the memories, feelings, and experiences of its entire existence, including the moment it was liberated into the universe as an individual consciousness. This Journey is another extension of the one preceding it – instead of visiting the first incarnation on Earth, the client is guided to recall the very first memories, feelings and impressions at the moment of realization that they were an individual and independent consciousness. Some of the interesting information recalled includes: Why was I created? What did I FEEL at that moment? What was I aware of? What capabilities and characteristics did I know I had? What soul purpose did I choose – helper, explorer, healer, etc.? Who was there with me to help show the way? Where did I choose to go after being created?

This is a unique opportunity for the client to dig even deeper into her own soul purpose, and to learn how she initially navigated and operated in the dimensions of pure consciousness. Additionally, open-ended questioning such as "What did you choose to do then?" and "Where did you go next?" have led to many unexpected experiences such as visiting or incarnating on planets and worlds other than Earth (what Dr. Michael Newton calls "Hybrid Souls"), exploring non-physical worlds of sentient beings, and visiting and comparing the characteristics of other dimensions and universes. And not coincidentally, after describing their earliest soul experiences, several clients have come full circle back to the reason they chose to begin incarnating on Mother Earth.

Among the possible lines of inquiry here are:
> At the instant that you became a separate, individuated soul –
> How does it feel to be separate and unique? What were you aware of?
> What were your capabilities and characteristics?
> Did you know who or what created you?
> Did you know what your purpose for existence was? Who told you?
> Is your Guide there with you?
> Where do you choose to go first? Next? What do you choose to do? Why?
> Visit and explore each 'place'. This is where you should begin to learn about other worlds/ dimensions/universes, and investigate visitations of lifetimes in or on each as a physical being or as a non-corporeal (energetic, gaseous, etc.) consciousness or life form.

Process:
1. Client moves into their Spiritual Area and does the three things she must always do when coming up to her Spiritual Area.
2. Client's Higher Self (CHS) calls for her Guide and challenges him/her.
3. CHS asks her Guide if permission is granted to visit her personal Akashic Record for the purpose of investigating her experiences and memories at the instant she became an individuated soul essence.
4. If permission is granted, record all the details of her first soul memories.
5. CHS returns to the physical planes, reintegrates her Higher Awareness with her physical body and conscious mind.
6. Client emerges herself from self-hypnosis.

Case Study 1:
SJ-09: First Soul Memories   May 8, 2014 – Directed by Howard Batie
Subject: "Emma"   Subject's Higher Self: "Shirella"   Subject's Guide: "Samantha"

Howard: Now Shirella, I want you to move to your Akashic Record of all experiences as an individually created soul, and from the very beginning of the record of all your experiences, I'd like you to describe what you're aware of and what you were aware of at the very first moment you were aware that you were an independent and individual consciousness. What can you tell me about that instant of your awareness?

Shirella: It is a slow awakening. It is a question – what is this that I am? I am a bit confused, bewildered, unsure. Not frightened, but this is new, a new sensation, a new feeling. At this moment, I am just separate, just beginning to leave the Oneness.

Howard: And how does that feeling of separateness make you feel?

Shirella: Lonely. But I somehow know it is for a great adventure, and I am ready. That has come with my creation; my essence is to grow and explore.

Howard: All right. Are you aware of who created you?

Shirella: Oh, Yes! It is the One That Is All.

Howard: And are you aware of the process by which you were created?

Shirella: It is by thought. It is by manifesting by thought.

Howard: And why did the One That Is All create you?

Shirella: I am not aware at this point of the answer to that question. At this point, I am understanding that I will grow and that there is a purpose, but I am still becoming familiar with the separateness.

Howard: All right. Now search your awareness and describe to me any particular characteristics or qualities that you feel you have, or that you might want to attain, to acquire.

Shirella: I have a great need to grow, to learn, to experience.

Howard: Do you know what you want to experience?

Shirella: It will come as I coalesce.

Howard: And what did the One That Is All decide that you should do?

Shirella: I am to grow and to learn all that I can about the spirit.

Howard: Do you understand how you will do that?

Shirella: I am to trial-and-error. I am to go through experiences. I am to be a creator, and before I can create, I must grow to that power through learning about myself and others, so that experience can go into my creations.

Howard: Good. And once you grow into those abilities, are you aware of what you will create?

Shirella: There is a new planet that requires special growth, special life.

Howard: So at this point of your creation, the Universe is already in existence?

Shirella: Yes.

Howard: Are you aware of this special planet?

Shirella: Yes, I have heard of it. I am to help seed that planet, to grow with it, to support its growth.

Howard: Now before you move away from this point and move toward that planet from where you are, I want you to look back at Creator and just describe what you see from the outside. Does Creator have a shape, a size, a color?

Shirella: Creator is thought. Creator surrounds, even in my separateness.

Howard: Surrounds you?

Shirella:	Yes. It is always there. I am from within His thought. I am form which helps Him, not Him.... helps Creator to think.
Howard:	Helps Creator to think?
Shirella:	To manifest, to bring thought into being. We are of ... at this point... I need Samantha.
Howard:	Samantha, please help us out here.
Samantha:	At this point in a soul's growth, there is little defined consciousness. There is a sense of separateness and the innate desire to grow, and a sense of purpose. And, therefore, it feels still a part of the thought. It is very difficult, Howard, to explain. It is without shape as you know it. It is consciousness within consciousness. Even in individuation there is still connection to that consciousness. At this point in Shirella's growth, she is aware of herself, and only when she fulfills her destiny of going to Gaia and to Earth will she then understand complete separateness from that which created her.
Howard:	Now Creator has created Shirella. Is Shirella able to create other consciousnesses?
Samantha:	She will learn. But she will learn to create small. She will help create the seeds that will go eventually to Earth. That is why I am assigned to her as a Guide.
Howard:	And what is your role in Shirella's growth?
Samantha:	To protect her and to teach her the way of form-making and becoming one with that form eventually herself.
Howard:	So she will create form, and then become that form?
Samantha:	To incarnate, as you say, yes. She has elected that path.
Howard:	OK. Her path was decided by the Creator?
Samantha:	Yes. And it hard to explain, but the Creator sets a path, and then when the soul begins to individuate, it can either accept or deny that path as its own. It must accept and agree. Howard – Shirella was formed of Creator essence, similar to that of we Elohim. It was her choice, then, as she learned and grew in experience as you call a soul, to then move on into the incarnation on Earth. It is, as you might call it, an extended assignment. She has great strength, this one, and she decided that she wanted to help support Gaia and the ascension of planet Earth, and she was blessed with that decision, and, therefore, that has been her path. The Creator is well pleased, for it is a decision that only the will of the soul can make because it is a hardship for one like Shirella to take that form. A soul has a direction and a purpose from the Creator that at some point in its growth, as it becomes aware, it can choose paths and amend its initial journey plan. I am weary now. Howard, I must take a break from this communication. Shirella can perhaps go from here.
Howard:	Just rest for a moment. Thank you, Samantha. Shirella, would you like to continue to rest for a moment?
Shirella:	I am fine now, Howard. Thank you.
Howard:	Now at this moment where you're aware of what you want to do...
Shirella:	Where am I, Howard?
Howard:	You are at the beginning of your creation.
Shirella:	Thank you. I rested while Samantha was speaking. I am at the beginning of my creation.
Howard:	Yes, and you are aware of your mission that you've chosen.
Shirella:	I am aware that I'll create, and I will grow with experience, knowledge.
Howard:	And is this experience only to be gained on Earth?
Shirella:	No. In the beginning we become aware – it is a new sensation. It takes, as you say, time to become comfortable with that sensation, to understand. I am aware now, and then we grow into purpose, and then we experience within that purpose and move beyond.

Howard: Now, knowing that you are to create and help Earth, how do you feel about that assignment, that challenge that you've chosen?

Shirella: I am blessed to have the opportunity to work on this project. I am humbled and blessed. The Creator feels I can make a contribution, and that my skills, my awareness, my consciousness, my desire to help and contribute are such that I will be allowed into this project.

Howard: Good! We need strong souls to work on this project. Now review the Akashic Records of your soul and just be certain – have you ever visited another planet or world other than Earth?

Shirella: Yes, I have, to gain the experience I needed, to help to grow in my creative skills, and to grow in my strength to help Earth.

Howard: Was this other world in this collection of stars we call a galaxy? Was it within the Milky Way Galaxy?

Shirella: Yes. I am of this place. I am of this universe.

Howard: All right. You went to another planet within the Milky Way Galaxy to gain the experience that you would need for your work on Earth – is that correct?

Shirella: Yes. I went to The Pleiadies. I am with the Pleiadians to learn to coexist, to communicate, to learn the feeling of a body.

Howard: Was it a comfortable feeling?

Shirella: It is difficult, but doable.

Howard: You learned to communicate. How did you communicate?

Shirella: It is again difficult to explain. Communication between souls is instantaneous. When one begins to define the shape and form of the soul by taking body, that process of communication changes and is codified.

Howard: So as a soul, you could communicate instantly with other souls, but when you incarnated into the Pleiadian body, the form of communication had to be changed?

Shirella: Yes.

Howard: Was it verbal communication or telepathic communication?

Shirella: With the Pleiadians, it is more on a telepathic level, which made it easier to learn communication and definition.

Howard: When you communicated your thoughts, were feelings a part of that communication as well, or was it only the intellectual ideas...

Shirella: Emotions and feelings were also explored.

Howard: Are the Pleiadians a very emotional race?

Shirella: They are very kind, very positive. They are very good instructors in that way.

Howard: Good. Can you describe the level of spiritual advancement that they were at?

Shirella: Very far. They are... it is hard... they have multiple purposes, complex. One is to allow the incarnation of new souls for learning.

Howard: And do these souls come from various sources?

Shirella: Yes, depending on their purpose. Soul energy is divergent, depending on its purpose.

Howard: Divergent in what way? How does one's soul energy differ from another?

Shirella: Depends on their purpose. Again, it is nuance to you. It is characteristic difference that is extremely difficult to delineate.

Howard: I understand. I'd like to learn more about the Pleiadian social structure.

Shirella: It is group. It is equality. It is commerce without competition.

Howard: All right. Are there many races of Pleiadians?

Shirella: No.

Howard: So it's very homogeneous?

Shirella: Yes. Because they serve multiple purposes, it would be confusing to also have multiple races. They are a tool of the Creator for helping souls, planets, other civilizations to grow in positive strength.

Howard: Is the Pleiadian world similar to that of Earth in that there is polarity and duality?

Shirella: The duality is minor, and therefore experienced for teaching only.

Howard: Is there still gender differences – male and female... do they have a two-gender...?

Shirella: Yes, and that gender can change. If they elect to be, they can be androgynous. They are a tool of the Creator for spreading love and for helping. They are a step in the process of a soul's incarnation into beings like humans, into more dense life forms.

Howard: I see. And when you incarnated into a Pleiadian body, did you incarnate into a female or into a male?

Shirella: I was male. I was also female.

Howard: All right. In your learning process there in the Pleiades, what was your role or your occupation, your function there?

Shirella: I was a student of spirituality, and then a teacher. It was to be my purpose in going to Earth – to keep its spirit alive. I needed to strengthen in all ways possible my connection and understanding with that form of spirit that is the Creator of All, the essence, the power to touch that while being in a dense body of duality. And it became vastly important for my survival in my Earth experience.

Howard: You mentioned that you had incarnated into a male body and also into a female body in the Pleiadians. Did you require many incarnations to learn these lessons and to grow?

Shirella: It seems that there were several; however, it did not seem like a very long time. The Pleiades... because I was a student, a soul student, and they are also of essence, I could transfer if needed.

Howard: From male to female?

Shirella: Yes, and from body to body. If I learned an experience such as a child, and I learned it more quickly, I could transfer, move along as I needed, rather than at the pace of the body.

Howard: I see. And did this require an agreement with the body that you came into as well?

Shirella: Yes. The Pleiadians are flexible, and understand when a soul comes to them that may need rapid growth, such as I. And so the body adapts and grows at the speed of the soul. There are Pleiadians whose bodies are not as defined as some of those who visit planets like Earth. There are learning bodies on Pleiadies that are flexible, and there are bodies that are more rigid, more defined, because they have a different purpose. Their growing and learning requires a different body. The body is a tool of the soul for the Pleiadians.

Howard: So after you had several lifetimes on the Pleiadies....

Shirella: It is hard to measure because of that flexibility. I know of two, but they may have been long or short by your standards.

Howard: Good. And who decided when you were ready to leave the Pleiadies?

Shirella: It is a Council of my guardian, Samantha, a Pleiadian Council, and other high level beings close to the Creator.

Howard:	Not Pleiadian, but they're closer to The Creator?
Shirella:	Yes. Correct. Correct. Not Pleiadian, but such as other Angels, Ascended Masters. It is a Council to be sure the soul is truly well-prepared and protected, that it will not be released too soon.
Howard:	I understand. That's good. And how is the soul protected before it's released?
Shirella:	With the loving energy of its guide and other beings who oversee its journey.
Howard:	And all this time, your Guide Samantha is providing this – is that correct?
Shirella:	Correct. Samantha and the Elohim who were assigned to me from the beginning, knowing of my ultimate goal. Souls are not single – ever – as if only in a human body. We choose to forget who we are, or are unable to remember due to circumstances. Souls are in communication always with a Guide and other companions as necessary, as needed on our journeys. The concept of unit – single unit – is a concept created in a place such as Earth where the bodies are very separate, the minds are very separate from each other. Souls understand a sense of identity, but it is not a unit, a complete total individuation. We are an energy with purpose defined, but still an energy essence form.
Howard:	Good. And as you complete your learnings there on the Pleiadies and prepared to move on, tell me your next experiences as you left the Pleiadies.
Shirella:	I then went to the Sun to learn my creative skills in advanced form.
Howard:	And they were enhanced by your sojourn to the Sun?
Shirella:	They were trained. They were dedicated, amplified.
Howard:	All right. How did that amplification work? I mean, what was the function of the Sun? How did that visit amplify your abilities to create?
Shirella:	That is strong energy, nearly uncontrollable. It is powerful creative energy, and so I learned to manipulate it, and in doing so, strengthened my own, and learned to carry that energy with me, that stronger energy.
Howard:	Thank you. And did you spend a lot of time in the Sun?
Shirella:	I spent enough. I did not need a great length of time there. My skills were already strong coming from The Creator, and only needed to be enhanced and modified to help Earth, to help Gaia.
Howard:	And during this energy modification process, how were your energies modified... what were the modifications?
Shirella:	It added strength and frequency distribution for Earth.
Howard:	And as you completed your amplification activities on the Sun, what were your next experiences?
Shirella:	I was then part of the Group, the beings, the souls. I had at that point incarnated into a life form that could carry seeds, carry life, carry this energy to Earth.
Howard:	Was that life form corporeal?
Shirella:	No.
Howard:	And as this life form, this energy form carried the seeds of life to Earth, what were your next activities?
Shirella:	We released the energy onto Earth at a designated time.
Howard:	And what was the approximate time that you released these energies? Was it during the early formation of Earth as a barren rock, or were there already oceans and mountains and air?
Shirella:	Yes. It had been determined that life that would have formed cosmically would not amount to much, and it had been determined, as we have talked, that there needed to

be a planet of consciousness and conscious life in that sector. And so it was that Earth and Gaia met, and we brought transmuted life, transmutation, new life form opportunities to Earth.

Howard: Did those energetic life forms that you brought to Earth include specific DNA from specific civilizations?

Shirella: Yes, it is the project.

Howard: What civilizations or races or worlds contributed their DNA?

Shirella: Many. I am struggling with those kinds of details, Howard. I am in a consciousness now, in a place where that kind of details are not accessible easily to me.

Howard: I understand. Just relax and rest. We've come full circle with your previous discussions, and I thank you very much.

Shirella: Thank you, Howard. It has been nice to take that Journey and see it in its completion.

Howard: And I want you to be aware of that knowledge, that completion, aware of it consciously. Record this conscious experience as a part of your eternal soul record... all the good that you have done, and the good that you are doing. And Samantha, I'd like to thank you as well for being with us on this Journey and amplifying the information where appropriate. We really appreciate your guidance.

Samantha: You are most welcome, Howard, and as always, we are in service to your project.

Shirella: Howard, this is Shirella. Please be aware, as you probably are, that while Samantha and I carry the burden and the joy of the communication, there are many other beings who are involved in helping this project, and are grateful also for your help. This is a means by which we hope, we pray, that humanity will begin to understand more of its history, of its origins, but more importantly of its future. And so, accept the gratitude also of the others who, you would say, are in the background.

Howard: And there are many, I know. Thank you. And now, Shirella, do you have anything further to add at this time?

Shirella: Only that it is a bit sad to leave you.

Howard: Thank you, and I always look forward to talking with you, too. You're a dear friend.

Shirella: Yes, and it is a respite, it is fun, it is my nature.

Howard: Yes, it is! And thank you very much for this wonderful information this afternoon, and we release you now to go about your own activities with heartfelt thanks and deep gratitude. And Emma, I want you to take a deep breath and just relax.

* * *

Case Study 2:
SJ-09: First Soul Memories   May 21, 2014 – Directed by Howard Batie
Subject: "Karen"   Subject's Higher Self: "Anaka"   Subject's Guide: "Joshua"

Howard: Good. Now, Anaka, I want you to move to the Akashic Record of all your experiences as an individually created soul, and from the very beginning of this Personal Akashic Record of all your experiences, I'd like you to describe what you were aware of and how you felt at the very first moment that you were created as an independent and individual consciousness – what were you aware of?

Anaka:	Purple energy, warmth. Not like heat warmth, but like security warmth, and movement, other sparks.
Howard:	And how did that purple energy make you feel?
Anaka:	Curious, expanding, curious about where I go from here, what there is. There are other sparks of souls around me here, and we're together but individual like little balls of sparks – there's a bunch of us balls – and I'm in a ball of sparks.
Howard:	And what are you, with this particular group, to learn?
Anaka:	I don't know if we know yet. We'll all have many things to learn and we'll all sometimes be together and we'll help each other learn, but I don't know what we're learning yet.
Howard:	Are you aware of what you were created to do, to learn?
Anaka:	To learn to bring love and light, to learn how to expand it, to learn how to lead other souls to the love and light, to help them learn.
Howard:	All right. And how do you decide where you're going to go and what you're going to do? Is this something that you decide by yourself, or are you told or given a mission?
Anaka:	I think I decide what I want to learn, and the Guides and the other soul helpers help us decide how we're going to learn that.
Howard:	Wonderful! Now I want you to return to your earliest memories, and in this first instant of your awareness, is that before or after the creation of this Universe?
Anaka:	I think it's here already.
Howard:	So your creation would be after the creation of the Universe? Is that correct?
Anaka:	Of this Universe, yes.
Howard:	And are other souls being continually created, or were they all created in one big expansion?
Anaka:	No, always. Always more.
Howard:	Excellent. Now, Anaka, I'd like you to go to the next part of the Akashic Record of your soul and tell me what is recorded there. After this initial awareness of being yourself, an individual consciousness, what do you do next?
Anaka:	It's like I'm very young, and I go an area to meet with other souls and to learn what choices there will be. Joshua's there, or a teacher. And there are four of us, five of us...
Howard:	And what does Joshua do?
Anaka:	He has us all stand together in a circle, and he gives us energy. It's like telepathy. He shows us in our mind... I see stars, and Universes. He's showing us places that we will probably go... we can choose. Then he shows us ... I don't think we are all getting the same message, but in my mind I see our Universe, and I see Earth. So he's showing me Earth. I think my work is to be done on Earth. I think so, yes.
Howard:	But you were aware of other choices, other Universes, other worlds? Why did you choose Earth over these other places that you could go to?
Anaka:	I think it was so beautiful there. It appealed to me. I liked how it felt there. I liked the energy of Earth, and the potential of Earth. And I think I even knew Earth was to be very important. Earth is to show the way for all, so I got to be part of that. Earth went the farthest into duality, the farthest into separation, and even though it was still connected, it had to fight to keep that connection because there were so many energies trying to block it. But to overcome those energies and to come to almost to where we're going now... we're going there soon... Earth had evolved a lot, and I got to be part of that evolution, to learn, to show the way. I feel ancient, and I can feel modern, but when I'm incarnated, I only feel what I feel right then. When I'm out of Earth, off Earth, I don't

have a sense of time of Earth – I have a sense of... Earth's life has one energetic push... It sounds strange, but a certain path that energy took through Earth, and Earth used that energy to evolve forward.... It took a long time for Earth to go from a rock to a beautiful, living planet, and many, many millions of years it was beautiful, and then in 200 years, humans began to poison her and she had to fight, and she's still fighting, but now humans have become aware. The Earth 300 years ago was still extremely healthy. She could fight the little bits of human pollution, but it multiplied and multiplied to where it's hard for her to fight it. That's why we now have to have help from extraterrestrials now to help us.

Howard: All right. Now, from outside of incarnation, from there in the spirit world where you're outside of time, when you look at Earth, what can you tell about Earth's future? Will she return to being a rock?

Anaka: No. She'll return to being pristine, but many fewer people will live on her. I don't know if they will move on when they pass over and fewer will live there. The ones who will live there eventually will be a lot more evolved, a lot more enlightened and will work with Earth's energy, not against Earth's energy. They will understand how to help Earth become better, not to destroy her. I think there will be some die-offs, because the Earth still has a lot of changes, a lot of physical changes. Already, the Earth is working to not kill people so fast. Some of the major things that happened lately, not as many people die as could die. Where there are a thousand, there could be ten thousand. So it's slow. The younger souls coming will help. The ones coming now and the new souls, and the souls being incarnated here, they're not necessarily new souls, but they are souls that come with a new agenda. They come with a knowledge that the old ways aren't working, that we are more One. The younger people won't learn to hate as much. Some do, but that group of souls will be leaving. The souls that now hate you for your color, hate you for your status, control you for your money, control and pollute the Earth because they can't stand the oneness, those will all eventually move... Some will go to Healing Centers and learn to see the love and to learn that what they did before didn't work. We are the last of the generations that have the ties to ignoring the love and the One. So that, as our children grow to old age, and as their children grow, there will be fewer and fewer of what some like to call the Illuminati, the ones who wouldn't listen. There's fewer and fewer, and so by the time our grandchildren are grown there will be very few, and so it will be very hard for them to control, very hard to learn to make people hate.

Howard: Good! Thank you, Anaka, thank you very much. Now I want you to return completely to a soul state, and back in your record of all your experiences as a soul, in your entire Akashic Record of all your experiences, are there experiences recorded there where you've just visited any other worlds other than Earth? Just visited without actually incarnating there?

Anaka: I've been to green gas planets, planets that are mostly gaseous. They were green or orange. I think they're very, very young planets. They're still forming. I went to see what it was like to see planets before they became planets, to see part of the process and understand how the energies coalesce and work together to create. Each planet as an entity is unique because each group of energies that creates it is slightly different from other groups of energies, so each space, planet, group of planets, everything is individual. That's how the One expands exponentially through uniqueness of combination of energies. And as they combine, that uniqueness creates new. So newness expands, and that's creation expanding.

Howard: Good! Now returning to your entire Akashic Record of your soul, are there any experiences recorded there where you've fully incarnated into a physical body on a world other than Earth?

Anaka: I don't know. I feel I have, but I don't see it clearly yet. I feel a female entity as an energetic healer in a way I couldn't be on Earth. I don't feel I'm on a planet, I'm more on a vessel – I don't know if I'm born on a vessel and live on a vessel, like in a huge vessel full of entities like me, but not a vessel that's tied to a Galaxy. It's a vessel that moves, maybe a space ship that moves between Galaxies and I live there and I become a healer on that vessel, and my life has been spent as a healer on that vessel.

Howard: Good. And relative to Earth time, has that experience been experienced in your past, or in your future relative to your current Earth experience?

Anaka: It's interesting. I'm getting both. I'm getting that I've done that before, and I will do it again to heal people from incarnations – that sounds odd to me, but people will come there. I don't know if they've died or if they've been really traumatized before for some reason. They will come to where I am and I will heal their energy; they will come to me in pain, but it's not physical. They'll come to me in emotional and energetic pain, and I will help them with that. Maybe I'll help people as they pass on, I'm not sure. I almost feel that's what will happen, that there will be those who come to me, and I'll help them with their energies, and they can move on to wherever else they go.

Howard: As you worked on them, they were in human forms?

Anaka: Human or ... not necessarily human, but as an incarnated form. A physical being, yes, and I worked with their physical illnesses and physical energies, but the future one will only be energy work, not with technology.

Howard: OK. How are these beings transported? You say they're physically incarnated, but you work with them on your ship. How do they get to your ship?

Anaka: They're transported there by the people on the ship, but I'm not sure of the technology of how they get them there. It seems they're lifted with energy, that they're brought on our ship with energy, and then they're physically healed and we block their memory, so I feel we're almost like a part of what some people have reported as abductions. We bring them up and help them heal and send them back without the memory, but some have the strength to remember a little bit, and they don't understand they were healed. They only understand they were taken, but we did help them – they just don't remember that.

Howard: All right. And where did this ship originate from? What's its own home planet? Who created the ship?

Anaka: I keep hearing Pleiades. Maybe Pleiades, but they had help from someone else.

Howard: All right. Now when the ship travels from planet to planet or world to world, how does it move? What is its means of travel?

Anaka: It has a crew, but they mainly work to keep it running efficiently. It can energetically move the way we can individually move, but we all move together. So on the ship, I don't have to think where I want to go and move there, the ship does it. So we've all made a consensus where we'll go next, where we're needed next, and the crew know that. The rest of us work on our work on the ship, the crew of the ship telepathically takes us where we need to go, and the whole ship goes there. We don't have to do it; we rely on them to take us.

Howard: Now you mentioned that healing is one of the major purposes of the ship. Are there other purposes as well, other major functions served by your ship?

Anaka: Some travel with us, like a transporter; they need to move from place to place, and they don't want to use their energy. Maybe they need their energy when they get there. I think entities come on board our ship, work together on plans for places that we're going to, and then when we get there, they offload to wherever they're going. Maybe they help with the movement of the people that we're to heal. I think they do. I think they go to the surface and help the people on the surface come to us.

Howard: All right. Tell me something about the other healers. Are they also in physical form?

Anaka: Yes. Some are like me, some are very different from me. We all use the same healing energy, though, and we all amplify each other's energy.

Howard: Are you taller than human?

Anaka: Yes, maybe two feet taller. They range around... like on me they're shoulder to sternum, around that height on me. No one is taller than me that are other healers. Me and two others, a woman and a man are the same race as I am, and there are four humans as Earth humans, there are two that are not human-looking at all but they're extremely strong healers; they're reddish colored and they almost look like – they're very scaly, they have multiple arms, they move unhumanly but they're very gentle; their medicine is strong. There's only two of those because they're very, very strong healers. And there are some others that are more energetic beings; they don't have so much a physical form as an energy form, but there are a lot of us, and we work in groups of three or four. We're like a healing ship where many different groups come together. That's why we move around the Galaxies and the Universes with them. Our combination of healing from all the different human and human-like creatures come together, and because of our particular way of evolving, when we come together it creates yet a new healing energy even stronger than our individuals' (energy). Part of that evolvement is how it works.

Howard: All right. Can you describe the dimension you work in physically, emotionally, mentally and spiritually?

Anaka: OK. Physically, it's linear in a sense, in the sense that we can observe each other physically. Emotionally, in that we can tap into emotion. Emotion is pretty much, other than love emotion, is pretty hard to describe the emotional part of it. Emotion is 3D, but emotion can branch out from 3D in that love is multi-dimensional. Love is what we work with, love is what we feel, love is always there. And it's when you deny love that you move away from Source, and you move away from your ability to tap into energy. Mental is you think of that part of your brain that's telepathic – that's one side of mental. The other side of mental is the thinking, processing part, and that is partly 3D and partly not 3D. And then above emotional and etherically, you get into spiritual dimensions which ... Spiritually you can be in many dimensions at one time. And on the ship when we're healing, we're tapping into that energy of multi-dimensions because that makes our healing energy much stronger. The physical part of what we do is accepting that multi-dimensional part of the healing energy and concentrating it on the physical, that level of physical existence, but it's using many dimensions to do that. It's difficult to put into words what you can describe in 3D thinking.

Howard: You're doing very, very well! How many Earth years do you continue to live and exist?

Anaka: Many hundred. I think I live to be four hundred there, and my life is different there.

Howard: And how do you choose to end that life, or do you choose?

Anaka: I think I choose – I feel I've learned what I need to learn in that lifetime as a healer, and I'm ready to go back to my spirit space where I can choose to move into an even more evolved spirituality. I still incarnate on Earth a few more times, so that existence on that ship was a few more times of life ago, because there are things on Earth I still need to do, and I still need to help Earth evolve. So I go forward from that healer to a physical existence on Earth where I learn some lessons that will help in the incarnation when I finally am the healer in spirit, but I'm not there yet.

Howard: OK. And how about the future physical incarnations? Do you plan those, or choose them?

Anaka: I choose them after I plan them. In spirit, I see what and where my energy will be needed, and I work with other spirits to decide how we can best incarnate there to use our energy to bring knowledge, and to gain knowledge together, and then when we incarnate there when we feel like we've done what we need to do, we ... I'm getting the word dis-incarnate. So we don't die, but we dis-incarnate into another space. As I'm in physical body now, if I were to dis-incarnate with this physical body, I would retain a lot of the form without any of the physical disabilities or physical challenges of the body breaking down as it ages, and the body changing as it becomes less strong, and less usable.

Howard: So this physical body would then take on qualities of being eternal?

Anaka: Essentially, yes, of being able to rejuvenate perpetually to where you could stay at a young age because the cells wouldn't stop reproducing healthfully like they do in human bodies. We always reproduce cells, but as we age, they're not as perfect as they once were.

Howard: All right. Joshua, I want to thank you for all this assistance, help and advice that you've been able to provide Anaka today. And Anaka, I certainly thank you for this information as well. And Joshua, I would like to know if it's permissible to use portions of this information as examples in a forthcoming book, or publication, or speeches that I might give.

Anaka: Joshua says, "We are here to help you share this word. So absolutely. We are here to help you enlighten others, and it is for us, through you, so that's how we're helping you, by giving you the information so you can bring it to others."

Howard: Thank you! I do appreciate that, and I'm very grateful for that.

Anaka: We love you, Howard!

Howard: Thank you. Now Anaka, I want you to just rest for a moment here in this very spiritual space that you're in, and I want you to permanently record all the information that you've given me here today, record this permanently in your eternal spiritual memory, and also allow all this important information to be consciously recalled by Karen, even after she emerges from self-hypnosis. And let it all be remembered by your conscious mind as well to guide and instruct you as you return to your everyday life and all of its challenges, its joys. And just rest and relax now, and in a moment, I'm going to count from five up to one, and at the count of one and not before, I want you to take a deep breath and emerge yourself completely from self-hypnosis. Again, Joshua, thank you very much for your efforts, for your presence here today, and Anaka as well. All right, beginning now, Five... slowly starting to return to full conscious awareness... Four, coming up more and more, clearly remembering all the information clearly and consciously... Three, easily and gently becoming aware of your physical body resting comfortably there in the chair. Just wiggle your fingers a little bit, wiggle your toes... Two, coming up even more, just stretch your shoulders, and... One! Take a deep breath and open your eyes. *(Pause)* Welcome back!

Karen: That was great! Whoo! I feel a little dizzy!

Howard: Yes, it takes a couple of minutes to readjust. You did very, very well – a lot of excellent information!

Karen: It was – that was interesting! Amazing! I was seeing amazing things!

* * *

Case Study 3:
SJ-09: First Soul Memories   July 27, 2014 - Directed by Howard Batie
Client: "Dee"   Client's Higher Self: "Ileka"   Client's Guide: "Saywanda"

Howard: Good! Just feel the love that's there, just for being who you are. And thank Saywanda for coming and communicating with you. And now I want you to ask Saywanda if it's permissible for you to access the very beginning of your Akashic Record so you can consciously recall and understand your earliest memories and impressions immediately after you were aware that you were a unique and individual consciousness. Is that permitted today?

Ileka: Yes.

Howard: Excellent! Now, Ileka, I want you to move to the beginning of the Akashic Record that contains all of your own experiences as an individual consciousness, all the way back to the time and the place that your soul essence first became aware of itself as separate from Creator, and I'd like you to describe now what you're aware of at that instant, how you FEEL in this very first moment that you're aware of yourself as an independent and individual consciousness. How do you feel?

Ileka: I feel like I didn't want to leave the Creator, the One.

Howard: What are you aware of?

Ileka: That I'm not internally connected anymore.

Howard: All right. Are you aware of why you were created?

Ileka: I am among many others. We were created to explore all possibilities in the Universe; I don't have a direction, though.

Howard: All right. What do you choose to do? What was the very first thing that you chose to... DO?

Ileka: Meet other like minds.

Howard: Good. Does Saywanda offer any guidance or any suggestions as to what you should do?

Ileka: He's pointing to a taller being that stands out, and there's light around the being.

Howard: All right. Call this being forward and challenge him. Say, "Being, are you in service to the Light and Love of the One Infinite Creator – Yes or No?"

Ileka: Yes.

Howard: Good. Ask this being who it is, and what do they have to tell you?

Ileka: I'm not getting any answer other than I just know he's supposed to be with me. I'm just going to call him The Golden One. He's my Guide – The Golden One. He's going to help lead me because this is all new and foreign territory to me. He's my Traveling Guide, my guidance to where we go. Not like a protective Guide. I'm to follow him.

Howard: Good. Just follow him for a while, and what are you aware of as he leads you and Saywanda?

Ileka: We're heading toward a real bright star. It's too bright, but I see pinkness as I get closer. There's gold in with the pink, too.

Howard: OK. Tell me what going on here, what you're doing, and what The Golden One is doing.

Ileka: We're just BEing right now, absorbing the energies of this star. It's like, acclimating me to it, to the bright light of that star, to be able to be here.

Howard: OK, then feel the energies of this star, empowering you, strengthening you... and ask The Golden One what you're supposed to do next.

Ileka: He's going to take me out away, and there is like a planet that kinda would be if I could... it's kinda like the moon is to Earth, kinda like that.

Howard: All right, let The Golden One lead you out toward this planet, and what does this planet look like as you become closer and closer to it?

Ileka: It's all white, and maybe it's all this cloudy, foggy white swirling around it.

Howard: And why are you visiting this planet? If you're not sure, ask The Golden One what the purpose of your visit to this planet is.

Ileka: He said just to learn more, to acclimate myself to the atmosphere and the planet.

Howard: Good. Just move across the planet, still staying above it, not touching the ground, but just moving through the atmosphere, noticing any terrain or mountains or hills or clouds. What is it that you notice as you move across this planet?

Ileka: It's more like it's not really solid. When I saw it from afar, it was almost like a flat screen, but when I'm closer it's just this atmosphere, air, fog. There's no mountains and trees, it's all gas.

Howard: Now as you move through this atmosphere safely and very easily, are you aware of any other beings or consciousnesses?

Ileka: Actually, I see other new beginners like me doing the same thing I am, coming here for the same purpose, to be able to get used to that experience, to experience it and feel it.

Howard: This gaseous planet, do you know what it's called? ... Ask Saywanda or The Golden One. Do scientists have a name for it?

Ileka: They said Wy-aynee.

Howard: Good. Here on this gaseous Wy-aynee planet, do any beings live here?

Ileka: No.

Howard: All right, just become familiar with the energies and the feelings here in the atmosphere. Are you able to share the information you have about this planet with the other new consciousnesses?

Ileka: They are aware of us, but they are in contact with their Guides and their protectors.

Howard: Can you share any information with the other beings directly?

Ileka: If I directly try to make contact, yes.

Howard: It's OK to do that, so just send out a thought to the other new consciousnesses here and say, "Hey! I'm here, too! Are you aware of me?"

Ileka: They are now! What we can share is the feelings where we see them at this point, how it makes us feel, and that could be cold and cool, or emotionally and all that, a sense that we are awakening. It's all new to us! All new!

Howard: It's always nice to have somebody to share with when everything is new, isn't it?

Ileka:	Um-hmm. There's seven of us. It feels like we've been together before, and I'd like to join with them. I think it's OK to go together now.
Howard:	Good. Just join with their group now, and does each consciousness in this group have their own Golden One?
Ileka:	Right now we're actually even touching, and that's part of the sharing.
Howard:	Is it like a physical touch, or is it like an energetic touch?
Ileka:	Kind of like both. Something we can sense and feel, plus our minds.
Howard:	Wonderful! You're all at about the same stage, just starting out; you're all at your own beginnings. You mentioned before that one of the things that you were supposed to do is explore. What about the others? Do they have the same path or a different path?
Ileka:	I feel like now we're supposed to allow the paths to be together. Not all of them, but a lot of them will be together to help each other learn, and we will be together in lifetimes and in experiences, but not always.
Howard:	Wonderful. And what do you as a group decide to do?
Ileka:	We want to take off! I know where my soul wants to go; I don't know where their souls want to go. Mine wants to go to the Pleiades. It will be another experience.
Howard:	Right! That's what you're doing – you're collecting experiences. As you approach the Pleiades, tell me what you're aware of. Is there a special star that you pick?
Ileka:	This one right here (points to her right).
Howard:	Good. Let's head toward that. And tell me what you're aware of so I can stay with you.
Ileka:	It's getting closer and closer. It still looks like a star – very bright. ... I feel warmth and light like golden... more golden and white light, kind of a fuzzy star.
Howard:	All right – let's go exploring! Just get closer and closer to your destination. Your Golden One will guide you to the place that you need to be at, so just float there, just allow yourself to drift there, and what are you aware of here?
Ileka:	It's still just this really bright light, and all this light is just energy and a high intelligence also. So it's more like a... star! But it's still all this high intelligence and high energy and high everything!
Howard:	Is that intelligence from the star or is it from beings around the star?
Ileka:	It's a combination. The totality makes the star. It not a cold planet that's on fire, it is... oh, gosh! It's like the body of the Universe kind of thing, it's the creation of all that is! It's not the place, it's just part of a.... It's just all this energy, all this intelligence and knowledge and everything is right at this point – not the only place, but this place. It almost felt like they just gave me a brain! Here's all this information, and now it's gotta go somewhere, it's almost like it got received into a brain almost. A place for it to go.
Howard:	Just ask to receive all that you can understand, and integrate that into your own being. All that you can understand – let it become a part of you. And as we continue, you'll be able to integrate more and more, with each experience you'll gain more knowledge, wisdom. Good. Let's just stay here and absorb all this information, this wisdom and knowledge, and describe to me how it feels and what you're becoming aware of.
Ileka:	I feel a lot of tingling, a lot of energy, a lot of knowledge is going in without it being individualized, it's going into my receptive area, into me, but it's not that I can break it down into small components. It's just knowing that it's flowing in and being stored there. The Golden One says, "As you experience your different lives, you will understand as you go." I could stay here forever, and it would be fine!
Howard:	Ask Golden One if it's possible for you to come back here from time to time.

Ileka:	He said at first, yes.
Howard:	Good. That's comforting to know, isn't it?
Ileka:	Um-hmm. ... I don't want to leave!
Howard:	Is it time to leave?
Ileka:	I DON'T WANT TO!
Howard:	What does Golden One say? You know you can come back here again, so it's alright. There might be other exciting adventures somewhere else in the Universe to explore.
Ileka:	(Pouting) Won't feel the same!
Howard:	No, everything will feel NEW!
Ileka:	It'll be a trial. There will be hardships along with all the gradual knowledge and experiences.
Howard:	Yes, and what will the hardships teach you?
Ileka:	Growth.
Howard:	Sure! And you can make it an interesting challenge or you can make it a real hard-ship. It's more fun to have it be an interesting challenge, though.
Ileka:	Um-hmm.
Howard:	Good! Alright, Golden One, is it time to move to another place now?
Ileka:	Um-hmm.
Howard:	Alright. Ileka, hold onto Golden One's hand as he leads you to another place, and describe to me what you're aware of as we go to another place, another dimension perhaps, another world, tell me what you're aware of.
Ileka:	He's showing me the Earth.
Howard:	And as you look down on the atmosphere and the Earth below, what do you feel about this place?
Ileka:	It's going to be my home for a long time! And I'm going to miss where I came from!
Howard:	Well, you can go back any time you want to in the dreamtime. Remember that! Golden One said you could! So, knowing that, are you ready to taste a bit of that Earth energy? (no response) Just begin to drop a little lower, coming closer and closer, and tell me how it feels as you move into the atmosphere.
Ileka:	I put my brakes on – I don't want to go! (pulled feet up and put hands out like pushing) I think it's just like the pre-knowledge of knowing how hard it's going to be, how this is so different – SOOOO DIFFERENT! It's so heavy! And so dark, so dense. This is going to be sooooo hard and take so much energy. That's what I know now before I get there.
Howard:	Remember you got so much energy when you visited that first Sun; that energy will help keep your batteries charged. And also, when you're on Earth in a lifetime, in those lifetimes you have to go to sleep at night, and in the dreamtime you can go back to the Pleiades, you can go back to wherever you want to.
Ileka:	I just realized something, that those other six souls – I'll be meeting them, so it won't be so bad.
Howard:	No! You can help each other, give each other strength and support, and they can give strength and support to you, too. So that was very good to get your soul group formed before you had these challenges, wasn't it?
Ileka:	Um-hmm! I feel them, there's about three others going with me.

Howard: Alright, just move closer and closer now, become aware of any changes like in temperature, able to feel hot and cold.

Ileka: I'm just back in that first jungle again. The others aren't there. They are in another part of the world. They went elsewhere.

Howard: But you know that you'll meet them again someday because you all planned to do that. Now, thank The Golden One for leading you to the Sun and then to the Pleiades and finally here to Earth. That was the proper way to get prepared for Earth, knowing that you'd have the strength from the Sun and the peace and the tranquility from the Pleiades, you can bring those with you, and they can be your tools for meeting the challenges, the opportunities that present here on Earth. (Pause) Now are you still in the jungle are there?

Ileka: Um-hmm.

Howard: OK. Where else would you like to move to now?

Ileka: I don't have a choice.

Howard: Where are you drawn to?

Ileka: (Frowning) They're going to take me back to that cave.

Howard: Alright, go back to that cave now, right back to Mm-tata and join with that baby, and KNOW that you're beginning your adventures here on Earth, feeling very strong and confident, knowing that you have all these powerful friends that you're with, and this loving mother who is caring for you, cradling you in her arms, protecting you. Now, Ileka, we've come full circle. Are there any questions you want to ask Saywanda about your progress here, your journey to Earth.

Ileka: He just put his hand on my shoulder and said to know that he's with me, and I wouldn't be alone, even though many times I feel that I am.

Howard: Now, Ileka, is The Golden One still there?

Ileka: If I call him in.

Howard: Well, he's probably helping others now, too. You have Saywanda here to help you through your journey here on Earth, and The Golden One did a good job guiding you here, didn't he, here where you needed to be? Just thank him for that; say, "Thanks, Golden One! I let you go about your own activities now, you're released." ... Good. And take Saywanda's hand and ask him to always let you FEEL his hand in yours. Know that he's there for you. Now, Ileka, is there anything else that you'd like me to know before we conclude this session?

Ileka: No.

Howard: You know that you're at the very beginning of a very successful adventure. You know it's successful because you've experienced Mm-tata and many other lifetimes. Good. Now, Ileka, I want you to permanently record everything that you've experienced today, record all the information that you've given here today, record it all in your permanent subconscious memory as well as your conscious memory. And allow all this important information to be easily and consciously recalled even after you've returned from this very high spiritual state that you're in just now. Just let it all be remembered by your conscious mind to guide you and instruct you and help you, assist you as you return to your daily life and full conscious awareness. And when you're ready, I want you to take a nice, big deep breath, and count yourself back up from five up to one and return to full conscious awareness just like you've been taught. (Pause) Good! And emerge completely from hypnosis! Welcome back! That was a wonderful Journey!

Dee: It was. I think that what's hard right now is that I was there feeling OK, now this is the beginning of all I went through, but I don't even know half of it, but that was the harder part of it. Being in the moment was knowing and feeling like all these trials were still going to happen, yes, even though they've already done their thing. That was hard, especially where I came from.

Howard: So you were IN that moment!

Dee: Oh, yeah! I was there!

Spiritual Journey 10 – Memories of Oneness.

As you become more familiar with recovering information from the Akashic Record pertinent to your individual clients, they may also wish to investigate their earliest memories as a unique individual consciousness while still within the energy of Oneness within The Creator. These initial memories of Oneness with The Creator, as well as other consciousnesses like themselves, are also recorded in the greater Akashic Record and are available for recall as long as the three caveats previously mentioned have been met.

As an investigator into our personal and collective memories, there are many lines of inquiry that can be followed. Among these are:

Looking at the Akashic Record before Creation of this Universe occurred, what is there?
Move back in the Akashic Record to a time when you were in the energy of the Creator – what are you aware of? What do you feel? What do you see?
What is Creator aware of? Does Creator have any thoughts? What does Creator feel?
Are you aware of any others like you?
If so, are they the same size as you? Do you sense they are any particular gender?
Did you exist before creation of the Universe?
Why did Creator decide to create the Universe?
At the point of Creation of this Universe, were other universes created at the same instant as well?
What were the very first things or beings that Creator created? The next things?
What memories, knowledge and abilities did you have before Creation? After Creation?
What did you feel before creation of the Universe? After creation?
Why were you created? Why were the others like you created?
Are there beings greater than you are? Smaller than you are?
Are you aware of the thoughts of others?
How do you communicate with the others?
Does Creator continue to create additional individual consciousnesses?
What was the very last thought you had before you left the energy of Creator?
How different did you feel at the moment you left the energy of Creator?
At the moment you left the energy of Creator, did you know what you were supposed to do?
Did you know that before you left Creator's energy?
Who told you to do that?
Etc.

Following these lines of inquiry and others that will come up during your investigations can bring to light much knowledge about our true spiritual nature, our spiritual characteristics and abilities, and about the spiritual realms our Higher Selves live and play in. The information is there for those who are ready to know it: "Let those who have eyes to see, see. Let those who have ears to hear, hear." The veils of forgetting that prevent us from consciously remembering who we are and where we come from are beginning to dissolve like the morning mist that evaporates in the sun, and our awareness naturally expands to the limits of our ability to absorb and integrate this information into our knowingness and experience.

I've also found that during the recollection of personal experiences in this Chapter and especially in the Memories of Oneness Journey, it is usually better to have the information obtained from the Akashic Record by the client's Guide rather than by the Higher Self. There have been several times when the understanding of the client's Higher Self was not sufficient to relay detailed impressions or knowledge that are recorded, and the client's Guide needed to step in to provide additional clarity. On the other hand, there may be times when the Guide has difficulty expressing emotions or feelings of individual souls while incarnated, and the Higher Self can then be asked to step in and provide the requested information from its physical experiential perspective.

Process:
1. Client moves into her Spiritual Area and does the three things she must always do when coming up to her Spiritual Area.
2. Client's Higher Self (CHS) calls for her Guide and challenges him/her.
3. CHS asks her Guide if permission is granted to visit her personal Akashic Record for the purpose of investigating her experiences and memories before she separated from the energy of Creator as an individuated soul essence.
4. If permission is granted, record all the details of her Memories of Oneness within Creator's energies.
5. CHS returns to the physical planes, reintegrates her Higher Awareness with her physical body and conscious mind.
6. Client emerges herself from self-hypnosis.

Case Study 1:
SJ-10: Memories Of Oneness   June 4, 2014 – Directed by Howard Batie
Subject: "Emma"   Subject's Higher Self: "Shirella"   Subject's Guide: "Samantha"

Howard:	Samantha, we would like to ask you now if it is permissible to visit the Akashic Record so that we can become consciously aware of and understand the earliest impressions of your own existence.
Samantha:	It is.
Howard:	Good. Samantha, I want you to look at the Akashic Record before creation of this Universe occurred. And what is there?
Samantha:	It is energy. It is thought, although not that limiting. It is a knowing, it is ethereal, it is uplifting.
Howard:	Good. And now, move back into the Akashic Record to a time when you were in the energy of Creator, and what are you aware of there? What do you feel?
Samantha:	At one with the energy, the thought, the love. There is a knowing, and simultaneously there is a question. It is a question of exploration, a desire to grow the knowing. It is a curiosity, it is a simultaneous knowing and a question, a curiosity, a strong desire to know more.
Howard:	What is Creator aware of?
Samantha:	Itself, its knowing. It is expansive, expansion. It is directional without limits.
Howard:	Thank you. Are you aware of yourself as a part of Creator?
Samantha:	Not at this point. I am with the amalgam, with the beginning energy.
Howard:	All right. Are there others like you?
Samantha:	We are all One. We are not defined. I AM the Creator, I AM the One That Is All. I AM that energy, I AM that knowing, I AM that curiosity. I want to learn, to grow, to expand. I want to share my joy, my love. The knowing is that having love and not sharing it is a limitation with which I cannot live.

Howard: How would you go about overcoming that limitation?

Samantha: We must create something, an entity that can receive and return love. We must step away from ourselves to have this sharing. We are One, but to share, to grow, to expand, we must subdivide, find a way to subdivide without losing connection, self-defining in smaller units perhaps. It is a simultaneous oneness and a dividing into smaller units. Without doing so, this love that is the nature of the Oneness cannot be expressed, and that is its essence. The love must be given to be fulfilled.

Howard: Thank you. After you had decided to create, what was it that you created first?

Samantha: We began with form, we began with a shaping and a process of individuating.

Howard: And what did that process individuate your energies into? What became?

Samantha: Creative energies like myself, only condensed. To begin this process first was the individuation which came through condensation of the energies, and it would therefore follow that it would have the same purpose of love and creation, curiosity.

Howard: After the first creation of this condensed energy, in our limited way of thinking, is there a name or a classification or a category of being that this is called?

Samantha: Not at this point. It needed to succeed at this level. We needed to know we had achieved a level of individuation. How do you know you are separate from another Hu-Mon? It is a knowing. I know myself in all forms. I could feel something different. At this point, the next step would be form with more definition and purpose, and the logical act of purpose would be creativity – creation with a purpose, and so I condensed further and created what you know as The Elohim. These are extensions of creativity with the purpose of giving creativity form, and of taking form themselves when necessary.

Howard: Wonderful! How did you feel about these creations that came into being?

Samantha: Excited, joyous, loved, and purposeful. It is hard to explain how the act of creation is a purpose unto itself.

Howard: You stated before that the Elohim created the Archangels. Was that the next creation?

Samantha: Yes, therefore my reason for moving in that direction. The Elohim are less condensed than the Archangels. The Archangels are more individuated with a more refined purpose.

Howard: Are there other types of beings that are further individuated and have difference purposes?

Samantha: What you know as Angels.

Howard: There's another classification or class of being that I'm curious about that have been talked about, by humans anyway, and that's the Seraphim. Are you familiar with that classification of beings?

Samantha: They are a form of Angels. Their function is to sing on high, to spread joy. It is a human definition. We have a group who are charged with the purpose of focusing the energy of love.

Howard: And that's the purpose of the Seraphim – focusing love?

Samantha: Yes. That is the best that I can explain. The Seraphim have a specialized ability to concentrate what you call love, what we experience as unconditional acceptance, et cetera. They are like a laser. They can send a highly concentrated focus to life forms to be used as seed. They break apart blocks of the negative. Is this helpful?

Howard: Yes it is. But I'm curious about the statement that there is negativity at this point.

Samantha: We are in two places at one time, Howard. The Seraphim, in the beginning, were the Keepers, the joy, the protection. They were formed as a guardian. As creation continues and grows, we know that it will not always be close... Let me step out, Howard. ... In the beginning, the One That Is All only divided, individuated, condensed to certain degrees, and then formed the creative Elohim, and then the Archangels with purpose, and began in its knowing to understanding that if it created beyond its control with free will.... It understood that it would be creating free will and would therefore need to have a means of influencing with the positive, the love. You are asking me in the beginning, but there is knowing at all times, and as creation expands and free will is given, there is a knowing that the opposite of the love could be selected.

Howard: I'd like to return to that earlier time when you were still in the mind of God before creation had occurred. As I understand it, individual soul energy had not yet individuated – is that correct?

Samantha: Correct.

Howard: At that point, the Elohim have been created, and the Seraphim are in existence. Has the physical Universe been created at that time?

Samantha: No.

Howard: Before you individuated, were you aware of an individual purpose or mission that you would be performing?

Samantha: No.

Howard: So it was only after you individuated that you were given or chose a mission or purpose – is that correct?

Samantha: Yes.

Howard: So at that point just before you individuated, what were you aware of?

Samantha: Being in the One.

Howard: And when you individuated just after that instant, what were you then aware of?

Samantha: The understanding that I was now unique. Your language words carry more than one meaning, so to say I was aware I was separate is too distinct. I was unique, but not yet separate. It is a new experience to feel I believe what you call limits. On one hand I have all of the creative energy of the One, but now I am aware and know it is more defined and directional. There are boundaries in the strength and the power, but not in the essence in the love or the creativity. The creativity and the love, I am understanding, is part of all who will come forth in this process.

Howard: At that point where you became aware of your uniqueness and individuated, did the Universe exist? Had that been created yet?

Samantha: It was in the Beginning. It was... It appears to be a simultaneous rather than linear creative act. The intention to create created both the Universe and the beings that would explore the Universe.

Howard: At that point of creation, were other Universes also created, or is this a continuing process?

Samantha: Yes to both parts of the question. Once the forces were set loose, so to speak, the One That Is All decided to create companionship, create life. It is a process, not an event.

Howard: At the moment that you became aware of your uniqueness, did you understand and know what you were supposed to do, to create?

Samantha: Not in its entirety. It was evolutionary.

Howard: How did you learn what your mission was?

Samantha: Let me try. The soul energy, as I understand.... Perhaps we should see if Shirella might do better with first-hand knowledge, as she is soul energy.

Howard: Shirella, at the moment you became aware of your own individuality after being let loose from the body of God, did you know what you were supposed to do? Did you have a good feeling about what your mission and purpose was?

Shirella: We knew from the beginning we would be the experiment in extended growth and learning. We would take on a more defined form by inhabiting experiences in the newly created universes.

Howard: Samantha, were the individuated souls that were created – were they able to express or experience in other universes as well, or only in the universe that they were assigned to?

Samantha: Some chose a multi-universe experience, and others selected to stay within one particular universal experience. It is part of the growth creative pattern that continues through life forms and life at this conscious level – the ability and necessity to make certain choices part of the growth experience. It is more arduous because a soul energy begins to define itself, to align itself with the energy patterns of its universes, so if it chooses multi-universe experiences, it must be able to realign as needed, and it is sometimes difficult – takes a longer time to complete the soul journey. However, it is not better than, it is different than a more interesting experience.

Howard: Thank you very much, Samantha. Do you have any further questions or information that you'd like to provide along this line of initial creations?

Samantha: It is that the concept of free will and choice began early in the expansion of this process because choice is part of the ability to give back. The One That Is All, in a desire to share love and to have it returned, did not want it as an automatic process. The process of sharing love must be a free choice in order to feel, understand the full nature of that experience. But in creating the opportunity to experience the full sharing of love, it also opened for the alternative choice, and so souls were created with the initial practice of making choices, of understanding the consequences of making choices. And for souls, the process is always positive in choosing to incarnate into such as Hu-Mons with duality. They then had the opportunity to learn the opposite and to grow in that experience without necessarily doing damage to their soul, their Selves. There are rules and guidelines when one incarnates, and if those are broken, the soul energy can be damaged; however, it may be part of that soul's experience – it may be the soul's choice to experience that extreme.

Howard: Can you give me an example of how the soul might be damaged?

Samantha: It steps outside of the love, the oneness that is with us at all times. It becomes totally individuated, not to the point of being lost, but to the point of needing focused help to come back.

Howard: Thank you. Now, Samantha, you said before that the Elohim are the creators of the souls or consciousness. Is that an event, or is that an on-going process? Are new souls being created continuously? Or am I thinking very linearly with the time concept?

Samantha: In essence, you are. It is both – souls can complete a cycle when they have served their purpose, and their energy is, in your terms, recycled and it goes back to The One. However, it is a difficult concept for me to explain because I am without limitations. My limitations are expansive – I have creative energy, but I have boundaries within which I can use it. So in that sense, I understand the limitations, but I find it difficult to convey this process in your limited conceptual abilities.

Howard: Yes, I understand the difficult position I'm placing you in. Do souls continually be born, be created?

Samantha:	Yes.
Howard:	It's not just a one-time event when all the souls were created, it's an on-going process....
Samantha:	It is, and if I can convey to you the sense that the Creator that is One is an on-going process....
Howard:	I understand. You've been very patient with me today, and I appreciate that.
Samantha:	It is not a problem, Howard, you have been patient also, and it is always great fun and challenge in growth to attempt these kinds of dialogues, and we are all working toward a greater awareness of this information. We live without definition, we live with knowing, and we live without time, so it is interesting to attempt to move into something more restrictive, and it is one reason I chose this path to become for a short time what you call a Guardian Angel or Higher Self. It helps me understand the full growth experience.
Howard:	You used the term Guardian Angel. Is that synonymous with the concept of Guide?
Samantha:	No. In this place, in your definition, I am doing both jobs. This incarnation of this soul needs protection, as well as guidance. The protection comes from the Guardian Angel function; the guidance comes from what you call the Spirit Guide, and I am both in this particular case because I carry the powers and the ability to do both.
Howard:	And we also give thanks to Emma for allowing this conversation to happen.
Samantha:	This one, Howard, was difficult for her. As her Guardian, please do not limit what you feel you can ask, but know some are more difficult than others, and we will always be here to assist, and to put boundaries if necessary. It is hard to explain why it is difficult. She wants to please and do well, and at some times is uncertain.
Howard:	And I'm sure that you'll always let me know if it's time to conclude; if I'm pressing ahead, you'll tell me.
Samantha:	I will because she is not able to set those limits for herself. And she insists I say she is fine.
Howard:	Good. But it's time now to conclude this session. Thank you very much again. It's been a wonderful and informative discussion. My deepest gratitude to you, and to Shirella, and of course to you, Emma. And Shirella, Samantha, thank you for your presence today, and you're now released to go about your own activities with deep thanks and gratitude. Thanks for being here today. And Emma, just relax now, and come back in an awareness of where you are today, here in the room, resting peacefully in the chair. And when you're ready, return to full conscious awareness in a way that's most appropriate for you.

* * *

Case Study 2:
SJ-10: Memories Of Oneness   June 17, 2014 – Directed by Howard Batie
Subject: "Karen"   Subject's Higher Self: "Anaka"   Subject's Guide: "Joshua"

Howard:	Good. Now Joshua, I'd like to know if it's permissible to visit the Akashic Record so that we can become aware of and understand the earliest expressions of Anaka's own existence – is that permissible?

Joshua:	Yes.
Howard:	Now, to begin with, Joshua, I want you to look at the Akashic Record before creation of this Universe occurred, and what is there there? What are you aware of?
Joshua:	Swirling energy, and I'm being directed at it, light from many places being directed toward where the Universe will be.
Howard:	All right. Good. And I want you to move into the energy of Creator now, to a time when you were in the energy of Creator. What are you aware of there, what do you feel?
Joshua:	I feel green light, a strength, a calmness, an intention to grow by creating all that is and will be, by diversifying into many Universes and many beings of energy. Everything is energy, so everything will expand and expand and become more and more layered and complicated. Depending on which way the energy is directed and used, the outcome will be different than if you were to use it in a different way.
Howard:	So is it your intention to create multiple outcomes?

(Note: Here where Joshua's awareness is the same as Creator's awareness, I'm beginning to shift my questions to Creator of this Universe as well.)

Joshua:	Yes, to know all, to know the possibilities of what could be, of what will be.
Howard:	All right. It sounds like you're curious.
Joshua:	Yes, curious but calmly confident about it, curious but I know that I can do whatever I... that I can make the energy go wherever I want it to go, and it can be what I wish.
Howard:	Wonderful! What are you aware of as Creator?

(Note: I'm now addressing Creator)

Creator:	That my energy is infinite, that as long as I call upon it, it's there and can be sent out. It creates upon itself. It's hard to describe. It's as if I'm energy, but that energy expands exponentially and I'm aware of it as it happens. It's like my mind can be in a million places at once. I'm expanding energy in different ways. Every time you expand energy, it creates something new, and you build on that newness.
Howard:	Good. And in one of those places that you are thinking about, you're planning on creating a Universe, is that correct?
Creator:	Yes.
Howard:	All right. And what is the purpose of this Universe that you're going to create?
Creator:	It will be unique in that there's where the Earth Experiment will be eventually.
Howard:	Tell me about the Earth Experiment.
Creator:	The Earth Experiment is the duality where those that live there will forget, and because they forget, they will evolve in different ways than those who always remember. They will think they have fallen, but they never really fell, they just went sideways.
Howard:	OK. As we come up to the point of creating that Universe, are there any other things that are created before the Universe is created?
Creator:	Other Universes, and beings within those Universes... beings that don't exist within the Universes that are energetic still. They don't move down to the Universe – they stay closer to the center.
Howard:	Are they like you, other beings like you?
Creator:	Some are, some are older and are closer to the Source.
Howard:	What do you know of the Source?
Creator:	The Source is The One That Is, The One That's Always Been, the One that we are all part of. Some of us are a part from early on, and some are new. I don't understand about always being, but there being a beginning. That part even I don't understand.

Howard: So there is a Beginning in the Akashic Record?

Creator: There seems to be, but it stretches backward on along long energetic lines that I don't know how to go backwards on it. But it's as if it was always there, and then blossomed. And as it blossomed, the Oneness just began to spread all throughout.

Howard: Investigate the entirety of the Akashic Record and let me know if there's anything at all in the Akashic Record that lets you know how you were created.

Joshua: I was created from light energy like we all are, but with a purpose to help souls develop. There are many, many beings like me that help souls develop and watch that process, and then help guide the souls. We are a certain type of energy.

(Note: It now seems that the answers come from Joshua instead of from Creator of this Universe.)

Howard: And what other types are there that might have different purposes?

Joshua: There are other energies that create the Universes in which the souls live and be... they're a different kind of souls – there's Universe souls, and planet souls, and the kind of souls that aren't stuck in one place like a Universe or a planet is, like humans have the kind of souls that really can move from place to place – they're a different sort of soul or light energy. Each Universe has a consciousness of its own. But like us, its consciousness is just a part of the whole.

Howard: All right. Now we have various terms for spiritual beings, or energetic beings, like Angels and Archangels and Elohim. Are you one of those classifications, or are you more a Source of Creation?

Joshua: Less a Source of Creation, and more a separate type of being. I help with creation, and I contribute energy, that's the best way to say it. You create energy – creation comes from contributing energy, and that can come from many places, mainly from The Source, but they can be influenced by all those things you mentioned – Angels, Archangels, Elohim – all can contribute. As a part of Oneness, I'm a part of creating All That Is. As Joshua, my role is not the creation of, but the guidance of, souls after they are created.

Howard: Now at the point that the Universe was created, what were you aware of during its creation?

Joshua: Huge amounts of energy changing and moving and forming and swirling, always moving, always moving. The moving helps the Universe to settle into the energetic patterns so that the parts of the Universe can work together better, and the energies take form to hold it in place. And I observe and watch as it happens, and as the souls that I guide become ready, I help them to move into the Universe.

Howard: Good. And what did you observe when the consciousness of Anaka was created?

Joshua: I observed a ball of golden light, and it was purple and gold and green and bright, and it swirled, so I knew that Anaka would lean toward working with other people and wanting to be with other people, helping to heal eventually, but that she would have many incarnations in that Universe, and in other Universes, too. I could see that it was a bright soul, and I could feel that. She called to me to Guide her as I went to her, too. Apparently, Anaka's aware from the beginning that I was to be her Guide.

Howard: All right. Now Joshua, at the point when Anaka was first created, the Universe is already in existence – is that correct?

Joshua: Yes.

Howard: All right. Good. And what is Anaka at the instant she is created?

Joshua: She's aware of the light, she's aware that there are other beginning souls around her, but she's not in contact with them. They're all there together and growing together, but they don't really interact until they develop more. As soon as you are created, you are, you exist. So your soul or soul spark is, as soon as God creates you, you exist and you are there. You don't exist in a separate place – there's not a God's mind – God's mind is everything.

Howard: Yes. I would now like to talk with Anaka. Anaka, at the point where you were first created, what did you feel? What were you aware of?

Anaka: Warmth, a feeling of security, that I'm taken care of. I'm aware of Joshua, and I'm aware of others as well. Joshua is there with me and other souls, but there are others like Joshua all around us, and I'm aware of all of them, and they all send me warm, comfortable kind of energy – a safe feeling. There's a place where we're all together there, and once we're finally actually created, then we go with our Guides and learn. I decided to begin the adventure! To me, to incarnate felt like an adventure, that every time I would incarnate, I would learn and I would find things happen that I would find interesting, and exciting. And each time I incarnated, I would understand more and more about how all of our energies work together, and how each of us is individual but each of us needs each other's energy to help us grow. So it all seemed very exciting and wonderful to me – I was excited to incarnate and to begin.

Howard: All right! Good. Were you aware of any individual mission or purpose you had or that you chose? Other than just choosing to incarnate and experience, what did you choose to experience?

Anaka: With each incarnation, I sort of chose a theme, a thing I wanted to learn, like when I first incarnated, I was pre-human, but I was in a small group and I learned independence and dependence. I learned how we needed each other in a very basic world. And even though many, many incarnations passed, I still kept that lesson and learned more. I learned different lessons of how each thing that we do affects the other entities around us in different ways, how my use of energy affects other people's reception of energy, as a way to put it. I'm learning to use energy.

Howard: Tell me some different ways you used energy.

Anaka: I used energy as power, I was a soldier and I learned that energy can be used to subject other people, and to overpower other people, and that did not feel good to me. It felt good in the incarnation because I was a winner, but after, when I looked back at that life, I thought that was not good for the other souls that I affected. So I learned that lesson from it. And I learned healing, and I learned how to help others to work with their own energies, helping people to be in touch with their spirituality, and in some lives I was a spiritual consultant, not so much like a leader, but like a consultant. And I learned to help people in their own beliefs and their own thoughts, and to look inside themselves.

Howard: Good. Now Anaka, I'd like you to return to the Akashic Record and examine that part of it that may contain any experiences that you may have had in other Universes.

Anaka: They're not open to me now. They're there, but I have visions of green places that have lots of plants, but no other people, there are not a lot of people there – there might have been, but I can't see them right now. I just have visions of places that were very green, and places where I could fly.

Howard: All right. Joshua, is it possible to assist Anaka with additional clarity? Are those places in the Akashic Record available? Is it permissible to visit those places for additional clarity and understanding?

Joshua:	Yes.
Howard:	Good. Now help her to do that now so that she can recall those experiences.
Joshua:	OK.
Howard:	Good. Anaka, tell me what you're aware of here in other Universes.
Anaka:	I'm aware of being on a planet that was very young and very green, and not a lot of people around. I'm a flying creature! I'm not like a human, but I have intelligence like a human, so I'm aware of myself, I'm aware of all the things around me. I can reason and discern, it's not just instinct. And there are human-like beings here, and I'm not like them but I interact with them. We can actually speak – it's telepathic, but we speak. We accept each other as fellow creatures of the planet, although we're very different, and we don't live together. They live in cities and I live in the forest, but we interact.
Howard:	OK. And in relation to a human's size, are you shorter, taller, bigger, smaller?
Anaka:	Slightly smaller in my body, but I do have wings, and they're very large, kind of like a bat's wings, but not exactly. I can lift upward as well as float. The air is very light here, very thin compared to Earth air. We all are light – there's air, atmosphere, but it's easy to rise up from the surface.
Howard:	Good. And the humans, or human-like creatures that are on this planet – what do they do? You say they live in cities?
Anaka:	They work, they create, they interact with each other. There's not a huge population of humans here, but they all get along well. They don't have a veil like on Earth, so they're all aware of who they are in their own spirituality, and because of that, they accept everything well. I communicate with them, and we solve problems together, so if something needs to be built or needs to be done, they and we are enlightened enough that we work together. They understand they can do things we can't, and vice versa, so we work together to solve problems like creating spaces for the new souls that come to the planet to live, and making sure that the planet stays healthy.
Howard:	Good. And what are some of the characteristics of this Universe that are different from or the same as the Universe that we live in?
Anaka:	We have a Central Sun in our Universe, we have more than one world that is occupied by creatures, and we're in communication with those worlds. It can be telepathic, but you can go there. I don't think we use ships – we must teleport. We must just want to be there, and then be there.
Howard:	So you have a physical body, and you're able to teleport the physical body?
Anaka:	Yes. Not all of us on this planet can. There are different levels of evolved creatures, but the humans and others like me, we can all teleport.
Howard:	Good. Do you ever visit other worlds in this Universe?
Anaka:	Yes, I often do. I explore... it's like a vacation sometimes. There's a lot of water on some of them, and I love the water so I spend a lot of time near the water. I have others like me – maybe families – I think I have family on many of the other planets there, so I visit them.
Howard:	And there's others like you on these other planets?
Anaka:	Yes, we're all through the Universe there. We evolved the ability to fly as an experiment in the Universe. And it was a successful experiment, so there are many, many of us here, more than the human types.

Howard: Good. Now what kind of communities do you live in?

Anaka: We live in the forest in the trees. We don't build things like the humans do; we live in nature, and we're happy with that. Our interests don't go to building and creating structures and that kind of thing, we create new plants and we nurture the plants we have. It's like the world is like a giant greenhouse, and the humans are a part of it. They built a community within this, but sustain the planet by helping the plants diversify and stay healthy and keep the atmosphere healthy. So we're sort of like planet guardians in a way. We cross-breed plants, and if it makes a particular kind of fruit or vegetable, we might even create new ones from what we have already. We can take a plant and focus energy into that plant and you can change the way that the plant grows and becomes... what it becomes.

Howard: Hmm. Very interesting. What other abilities do you have?

Anaka: I can heal the water with energy if the water has become polluted. If the humans are building, sometimes the by-products are not as healthy, and we can disperse them or get rid of them with energy. We know how to go into the cells and change the way the atoms react. It's like the atoms can absorb the things that are not healthy for them, and change them. And we do that with our intent.

Howard: And what did you learn from those lifetimes in that universe?

Anaka: The possibilities of energetic infusion, and... it's not something I can use on Earth because Earth's not ready for it, but eventually I'll be able to use those energies that I learned then... the abilities to influence the energies. I can do that in little ways on Earth, but as Earth rises, I'll have a lot more influence. I can affect the energies that are coming through the Earth, helping clarify them, helping focus them, and in some ways, I can use energies from myself to affect the things around me, but a lot of humans there are still very resistant. When that resistance begins to fade and people start to evolve, by then I can help people heal themselves, help them to use the energies too, and help things that aren't as conscious like smaller animals and plants in energetic ways. Now as Karen, I send energy when I can and I give energy as much as I can, but it's nowhere as strong as it will be, or else I can do it in spirit form.

Howard: OK. Now I'd like you to return to the point in the Akashic Record where the Universe was just created. And at that point when the Universe is being created, are all the other Universes created at the same instant, or is this a continuing...

Anaka: No. There are a lot, and a lot are created all at once, but they're always being created. Our Universe will be a new Universe when Earth has ascended all the way, and the people on her have ascended. It will be our Universe, but it will be a different Universe. The energies will flow more freely throughout all because the Earth is free from the resistant energies that it had. Resistance is negative, but it's also a part of what is, so it's hard for me to think of it as negative-positive, it's just resistance, and as long as there's resistance, energy can't flow. Some have to have the resistance because they're not ready to receive, so it doesn't make them bad, it just makes them not ready. If they're not ready in our Universe, they can move to a Universe where they can still get ready, still can evolve. Our Universe will change to a different Universe that's more open and free with energy that freely flows. But those who can't accept that energy yet, can't stay with it. They have to go where they can feel the way they need to still. Many will do it through death, and then start again.

Howard: Thank you. Joshua and Anaka, thank you very much for coming and sharing your wisdom with us today, and you're now released to go about your own activities. *(Pause)* Good. Now just rest and relax there in the chair, become aware again of where you are, and when you're ready I want you to return to full conscious awareness in the most beneficial way that's appropriate for you. Go ahead and do that when you're ready. *(Pause)* Welcome back!

Karen: Thanks! Interesting Universe where I was flying!

four

Spiritual Exploration

Over a hundred years ago, Carl Jung identified a state of consciousness that he called the Collective Unconscious where all information and experiences by all people who have lived and are now alive on the earth are stored. The psychic Edgar Cayce and others like him have popularized the term Akashic Record or the Akashic Plane for this Library of all knowledge, but by whatever name it is called, it appears that while in deep hypnosis, we are able to move our awareness into a state where all information is available under certain conditions.

In Journey 7 of Chapter 3 we began our introduction to the information recorded in the client's personal past lifetime experiences, all of which are recorded in their Personal Akashic Record. Journey 8 extended this investigation back to the record of their first incarnation on Earth; in Journey 9 the hypnotized client recalled their first impressions and feelings after they were created as an individual spirit essence separate from or 'outside' the energy of The Creator, and in Journey 10 they extended their recollection back to their earliest memories of oneness while still within the energy of Creator.

Since these earliest personal memories were recalled by virtually all of my hypnotized clients who had successfully progressed through Journey 3, I decided to investigate the structure and composition of the Akashic Records themselves. My lines of questioning were initially directed toward understanding if there is a separate Akashic Record for each person on Earth? For each planet in our solar system? For each galaxy? For each universe? And what about all the events that did not involve sentient beings such as creation of a galaxy or an individual world – are these all recorded as well? How are they recorded? Where are they recorded? (Yes, it's probably obvious: My name is Howard, and I'm a recovering Engineer!)

Fortunately, the spiritual beings with whom my hypnotized clients were communicating (usually their own Higher Self and primary Spiritual Guide) were very patient with me, and my knuckles did not get rapped too often. They explained that, yes the one Akashic Record did have a structure to it that my human linear mind could understand – that of a single book that could be opened to a separate Chapter for each Universe, a sub-chapter for each Galaxy, a sub-heading for each Solar System, a paragraph for each world, and a sentence for each sentient being who had lived on that world either in physical or non-corporeal form. Further, when permission to access the Akashic Record was specifically requested by myself or my Guide, or of my hypnotized clients' Guide, the spoken words "Akashic Record" acted as the password that allowed access to the specific information requested, again with the three caveats discussed before, and the locating of that information was done automatically.

It was patiently explained to me that the Akashic Record can be considered to be the complete awareness of the One Infinite Creator, Who is constantly receiving and recording all the information and experiences within Creation, and aware of everything and everyone that has been created, as well as the motives, principles and actions involved in their creation. This is a concept that was initially difficult for me to get my linear mind around, so one day I asked Emma's Higher Self the following questions and received the information indicated.

Howard: Does the Akashic Record contain any information about an individual soul from the times before that soul was created?

Shirella: That is separate. That is in the Beginning. (*Note: She didn't provide an answer because the question was outside the scope of the information I had initially requested*)

Howard: All right. Now talking about the separate individual Akashic Records, is there another greater Akashic Record for Mother Earth, or Planet Earth?

Shirella: It is not greater, it is different.

Howard: Now the beginning of Earth – how was it originally created?

Shirella: It was determined that this galaxy and this part of the galaxy required a conscious planet to assist the development of the galaxy, the universe, and so it was created.

Howard: And what was it that was determined to be needed?

Shirella: At one point in this part of the galaxy, civilizations were very separate and unwilling in their consciousness, their limited corporeal beings, to come together. And it was determined that it was time for them to learn to associate, and so a planet was needed that would help them over generations to learn to come together to work on a project and create life that blends, that becomes an amalgam.

Howard: Now, back to the Akashic Records, are there any limitations to the amount of information or the type of information that can be stored and recalled from a being's own personal Akashic Record?

Shirella: There are no limitations because all is open; there are, however, limitations to access.

Howard: And what would cause those limitations?

Shirella: Unpure motivation, not able to comprehend the information being requested, interference with a growth, a current lifetime growth, it is not time for them to know that.

Howard: Does each planet (in our Solar System) have a separate Akashic Record?

Shirella: If it has consciousness. (*Note: some planets are reported to have consciousness, others do not.*) The Galaxy is a consciousness, and so it has its own record.

Howard: Our Galaxy covers a large area. Does the Galactic Consciousness create other forms of consciousness such as planetary systems?

Shirella: Yes. It is a guiding consciousness, it is a creative force that helped with the creation of Gaia.

Howard: So we have a separate level of Akashic Records for Solar Systems, for Galaxies...

Shirella: Yes. As you would call them "categorized," but it is like searching – you go to the Akashic Record and you search for what you need. Then the sorting is done automatically.

Howard: So it's one large Akashic Record...

Shirella: It is consciousness. ... The One That Is All _is_ the Akashic Record in a more defined form in the sense that the One That Is All knows all that has happened, and therefore, when it is appropriate, the Akashic Record is a term that is used here for asking for that kind of information from the One That Is All. ... And then you say, "Akashic Record, I need..." So it is hard to define for you an organizational structure. ... It is only the consciousness of all places, all universes. Access to information from the One That Is All is always done in a form suitable to those who are asking. ... It is the One That Is All who knows all that has been. In this Gaia and in the human experience, the term "Akashic Record" is used as a password to that information.

So with an understanding of the infinite scope and contents of the Akashic Record, all we need to do to receive the answer to any question on any subject at all is to meet those three criteria for access to its already-recorded wisdom and knowledge. Again, this is the central purpose of the Spiritual Journeys program – to assist in the development and expansion of the awareness of those who are ready to receive the Truth.

Spiritual Journey 11 – The Akashic Record.

The following topics of investigation are among the infinite number of subjects recorded in the Akashic Record, yet the investigation process is remarkably similar: once permission is granted for access to the Akashic Record, simply ask for the information to be provided, and it will. "Ask and ye shall receive." Yet sometimes, a further expansion of our awareness may be required to fully understand and integrate the information.

Possible Topics of Investigation:

SJ-11a. Atlantis

SJ-11b. Lemuria/Mu

SJ-11c. Energy Lines/Ley Lines on the Earth

SJ-11d. How the Giza Pyramid Was Really Built

SJ-11e. The History of Mars

SJ-11f. Interactions with The Galactic Federation

SJ-11g. Where would you like to go?

SJ-11h. What would you like to investigate and learn about?

Etc., etc., etc.

If several visits to the Akashic Records are made for different topics, you may want to label each as Spiritual Journey 11a, Spiritual Journey 11b, and so on to conform with your system of notation for the different topics investigated.

Process:
1. Client decides on the topic for which she wants additional information, and structures the questions to be answered.
2. Client's Higher self (CHS) moves into her Spiritual Area and does the three things she must always do each time she rises up into her Spiritual Area.
3. CHS asks her Guide, "Is it permissible to access the Akashic Record for the purpose of understanding _____ (e.g., How The Giza Pyramid Was Built)?"
4. If not, the client is emerged from self-hypnosis.
5. CHS asks for and records the specific information or answers to their questions.
6. Client returns to her cocoon and returns to full conscious awareness.

Case Study 1:

SJ-11: Akashic Record (Giza)   June 28, 2014 – Directed by Howard: Batie

Subject: "Karen"   Subject's Higher Self: "Anaka"   Subject's Guide: "Joshua:"

Howard: Now, today I'd like to investigate the origins of and the reasons for building of the Giza complex in Egypt, the three pyramids there. And Anaka, ask Joshua if it's permissible for us to visit the entire Akashic Record today to gain a greater understanding about this topic.

Joshua: Yes.

Howard: Thank you. And now, Joshua, I want you to move to a time before the pyramids were built, before the Sphinx was built there in the Delta area of Egypt. And first I would like to know who is considering building the complex of pyramids.

Joshua: The King of the people in Egypt. I hear Ra. Maybe Ra.

Howard:	All right. And what dynasty or what year is this in the way we reckon years now?
Joshua:	I can't get it – I don't know.
Howard:	Is it older than eight thousand years ago?
Joshua:	That seems closer.
Howard:	Is that time more than ten thousand years ago from the present date?
Joshua:	No.
Howard:	Thank you. And who are involved in this concept of building this complex of pyramids?
Joshua:	The King has advisors like scientists – they study the stars and the people; I suppose they're religious leaders, too. The guys are responsible for teaching people their view of everything. The King has a woman there too. I see a Queen, but she's also a priestess.
Howard:	All right. And how many are there who are considering designing and building this complex?
Joshua:	Seven or eight. They are advising the King. The King wants to be more aligned to the Deities or be more god-like to the people.
Howard:	And how will this complex of pyramids help in that desire?
Joshua:	It will awe the people. They will be amazed at the grandeur of it, and therefore give the credit to the King.
Howard:	And in the people's eyes, how do they regard their King?
Joshua:	They worship him, and love him, and fear him. It depends. There are a lot of separations in society – there are slaves, and there are people who own the slaves. And the slaves are afraid all the time of everyone, especially the King.
Howard:	I see. And as these seven people huddle together and come up with their designs, what are their considerations for completing this design? What are they trying to show with the design of this complex?
Joshua:	It has to do with the skies, with pointing to the skies or reaching toward the skies. Apparently astronomy is important to the priests. The sun and the moon are important, the constellations are, too. I see Orion, and I see... I think I see the Big Dipper, but it doesn't look like it looks here – it must be a lot farther north. It's very dim. And I see Orion, and I see others I don't know the names of.
Howard:	All right. Now as these plans for this complex of pyramids begin to take form, what do they want to show in the shape and the orientation of the pyramids? Is there a reason for, say, three pyramids in this complex, one bigger than the other two?
Joshua:	Yes, there is a reason. The two serve the bigger one somehow, energetically. It's like the smaller ones give energy to the bigger one. It's like it's channeled through the pyramids. Maybe that's why they're oriented the way they are – to receive specific energy, and then send it on. It goes inside the pyramid, and it seems to be concentrated there. I guess you could say it's modified. It comes in from more than one direction, and it's concentrated, and then it goes out again. There are different shafts built in that help transport the energy. I think the Sun goes into certain shafts and moves and bounces. The rocks are light colored, and so they help the sunlight move.
Howard:	All right. Let's move to the point in the Akashic Record where they're just beginning to do the actual work, the construction on the Great Pyramid. We want to select some stones for this. Why did they select stone for the pyramid?
Joshua:	The kind of stone that they select for the pyramid assists with the energetic movement, and with the building of the energy inside the pyramids.

Howard: All right. Let's move to the quarry where the stone is cut from the earth, and how is it cut from the earth? What kind of tools or implements are used?

Joshua: I see people chiseling, but I also see an entity there – I don't know if it's human or not, but they're able to direct energy toward where the rocks are cut from, and they're assisting somehow... I don't know that part. It's human size, it's a man, a male. If it's a human, it's a very powerful human, but I can't get a clear picture, but I see that entity using energy from themselves, like directing energy, like they're pointing in their mind. It helps the blocks get cut out faster. I see them sort of in a cliff of rock, or in a small hill that's being taken down and cut into the blocks, and a lot activity, a lot of people moving all around, a lot of pulling and a lot of moving. There's not just one, there's more than one of these beings. I don't know if they're priests. Helping energetically, all around where the rocks are being harvested and helping those harvesting. I see three or four all around. They have very dark robes and I can't see what they look like.... Now that I'm closer, he's smaller than most of the humans a little bit, and I guess they're sensitive to the Sun. There's so much sun here – that's why they have so many dark robes on covering their face. Just the ends of their hands stick out when they're directing energy. And you get the feeling of their mind energy is working through that. I see them with very pale skin, light-skinned, very thin, no hair, human-like features, but not exactly human. Hands, and eyes and nose, but not much of a nose.

Howard: Is the mouth about the same size as ours?

Joshua: Kind of, a little bigger maybe in proportion to the size of the face, tiny little ears, almost like bird-hole ears, a little ear. I still don't know if they're a type of human, or something not from here.

Howard: All right. Now I want you to view all elements of the Akashic Record and understand, or just know, where these beings have come from.

Joshua: (Pause) I hear Atlantis, but not originally. They were just there for a while. But they were scientists there, and so they came to help the priests. The have knowledge of the energy that the people in the pyramid didn't have. They still know how to use it and direct it in ways that the humans have forgotten. I'm seeing that these are beings that came to Atlantis and lived there and were scientific and interacted with people, but were different from people. And they were different from the Atlanteans, too. I don't know who they are – they're from another world in another Galaxy.

Howard: And what do we call that Galaxy? Not the name that they use, but the name that we know it by.

Joshua: I see numbers and letters. Like AR-782 ....

Howard: All right. Now let's return to the quarry where the beings are assisting the humans in quarrying the rock. Do they do any of the actual work themselves?

Joshua: The energetic work.

Howard: And how do they focus their energy? Do they use their hands to point....

Joshua: To direct it, yes. They bring in the energy with their mind, and focus the energy, and use their hands to direct that energy. The energy works between the cells of the rock, and helps to separate the cells so that the rock comes clear. It's almost that smooth when they cut it. They don't have to do very much to it.

Howard: And how do the beings know where to direct the energy so that it will fit correctly when it's put into the building?

Joshua:	They understand math very well, and in the planning they know how big each side of each block needs to be so they fit together, so it's pre-designed. That's why they need energy workers to help with the cutting – the humans can't do that math.
Howard:	Were the other beings part of the designing process?
Joshua:	A little bit, but I'm getting that they built them in other places and then eventually Egypt, they helped to build them in our Earth and in other parts of other planets. They have the technology that Earth people are using to make the pyramids. They couldn't do it without the help of these people, entities. And they designed it. Humans say, "We want it to look like whatever," and then these beings say, "We know how to make it do that." That's how they help them do it.
Howard:	All right. There's many, many stones. This must have taken a long time.
Joshua:	Yes it did! More than that King's lifetime. I'm getting eight hundred – that's a long time.
Howard:	Yeah, many generations. Now these energetic beings that are assisting with the cutting of the rock, did they stay throughout the entire period to assist.
Joshua:	No, they come and go. They also have more than one generation involved.
Howard:	Good. Now once the stone is cut from the hillside, how is it transported to the construction site?
Joshua:	It's moved on logs. They must have had pillars or trees somehow, long tubes that look like logs and they're rolled and pulled with ropes and moved. Four or five miles, I think. They had animals to help pull, oxen-type animals.
Howard:	So once the stone is cut from the hillside, how is it lifted onto the logs?
Joshua:	The energetic people help get it started. It's a matter of everyone working together for each block, and they all help it move. There's an energetic person whose job is just to move back and forth. The energetic movers help with all of the construction – the cutting, the moving, and the ... piling the rocks up – I still haven't seen that part yet.
Howard:	And how are the blocks lifted from the ground onto the logs? How do the energetic beings accomplish that?
Joshua:	I see two or three of them working together, moving the energy together to help it move, to make it lighter. Somehow they make it lighter. I don't know – they kind of affect the density, and when the blocks get to the pyramid, it's like they're pre-energized because of all the energetic work just to get them there. Somehow, that makes them a lot easier to work with once they get there.
Howard:	Good. Well, let's move to the construction site. As the logs are rolled onto the construction site, how are they moved from the logs to where they rest on the ground?
Joshua:	They're just pushed off, and there are ramps. I see ramps, so somehow they're pushed up ramps level by level. There are a lot of blocks that go inside, too, so it's done layer by layer, but pre-planned shafts for light and for energy are worked around, pathways to get in. It's all planned ahead, and then it's just built up layer by layer as they go. The block gets to the edge, and then it has an energetic push to get up, so the energetic workers do a lot of the heavy part.
Howard:	Do the humans have to do any additional lifting, or is just energetic pushing...
Joshua:	Yes, they help to guide... It's like all the energy is concentrated and that's so much work for the energy beings, the humans then put it in the precise place with guidance, there's still guidance there. But because the energy workers are concentrating all their energy,

they're not working on placement, they're working on making it light. So then there's like a guiding architect or one of the designers that helps them put it in the right place.

Howard: And as the pyramid is half-way completed, and there are tunnels that are situated in the rock, the rocks are shaped so they create the tunnels as the pyramid is being built, another block comes in to be raised and lifted to that level. Do these energetic beings lift it all the way to the level where it's required to go, and then the humans just guide it to the exact spot – is that correct?

Joshua: Yes. That happens all the way up.

Howard: OK. And during the construction of the pyramid, are there only seven energy beings, or are there more?

Joshua: There are more. They come and go, depending on where they are in the construction, and I see the big one nearing completion and the little ones near it like, I see the square of it on the ground, and off to the side of it, I see the little ones being started.

Howard: All right. And were the designs for the little pyramids completed before the construction of the big pyramid started? Were the designs completed...

Joshua: Yes. I think they were all designed to work together.

Howard: Very good. Now, as the pyramid is being completed, and these rough stones are quarried from the hillside and put up there, how is the pyramid finished? Are the faces covered with any smoother type of rock? We have a lot of blocks stacked up. The blocks... they don't create smooth sides.

Joshua: I see that later. That happens later. It gets smoothed later. For a long time when it was first built, I don't think it had a really smooth edge. That must be added later, and all the time it's being built, there are people inside putting messages and designs in these various chambers, they're carving inscriptions and things, messages and information that will help those who go there to use the energy.

Howard: Good. What do these inscriptions say?

Joshua: A lot of them just talk about the religious philosophy, a lot of them describe the Kings and the designers who started it, some tell the story of the pyramids being built – I don't know if they've found that one yet. I don't know.

Howard: Do any of these inscriptions give a clue as to the purpose of the pyramids?

Joshua: Only if you understand their religious philosophy. It has to do with how they believed the King and the priests were representations of the god energy of the Sun. So the energy of the Sun is part of what is utilized in the pyramids, and it fits in with their religious philosophy to support the King and his ... deification? To prove to the people that he's a god. I'm not sure about that. Inside, the writing talks about the Kings, about the skies...

Howard: Is this about the King that designed the pyramid?

Joshua: Yeah, and the kings before. It goes back to Kings before that as well, it's like a Creation Story.

Howard: All right. I want you to read that story from the Akashic Record, and tell me the Creation Story that's recorded in the pyramids.

Joshua: I see a King and a Queen on a ship with a lot of people, with oars, and they're coming down a river to begin the civilization. And when they land there, the people recognized them as gods. There was a family that was in the boat, and whoever this family was, when they came to the people, the people were still very primitive, and they were able to show the people how to grow some things, grow food in better ways, how to use the delta so that they didn't flood and have either flood or drought, how to direct the waters, and how to raise more food so they would have food year-round. So they sort of somehow had the knowledge to bring these people forward in a civilized way so that their society could evolve better.

Howard: Where did the boat come from?

Joshua: I'm getting that they came from the ocean. I don't know if they also came from Atlantis. It had to be they came from somewhere that knew more than most other people on Earth at the time, but it's still from Earth... I'm not sure, but they came there by boat, and that's how they knew of the mathematicians and the scientists, and that's how they knew to call on them for help. They had been with them before. I'm getting that Atlantis had beings from many other places altogether, it wasn't just humans there. There were a lot more advanced scientific races of peoples, and a little bit of information went out in this boat into the world.

Howard: Why did they leave Atlantis?

Joshua: They didn't like it there any more, they felt they were losing their connection to feeling a part of God or to the One, so they wanted to go where they would still be a part of God and be as God, kind of a control thing a little bit, a power thing. But they would also bring knowledge that people would use, that would be good for people.

Howard: And when the boat landed in what is now Egypt, did they immediately start planning the pyramids, or was there a lot of time before they started?

Joshua: Time went by. I'm getting a couple, a few thousand years went by of them establishing their hierarchy. Because along with bringing the people advanced civilization, they enslaved part of them, so that their lives could still be easy and comfortable. They would teach, but they didn't want to work. And to do that, they had to have people who they could make do the work. And the people were willing to do the work because they had been starving, and so they gave up their freedom for survival.

Howard: Good. And later, when the pyramids were nearing completion, were there any ceremonies that were conducted at or in the pyramid?

Joshua: Many. The King wanted everyone to give him credit for it, so there were huge ceremonies and huge celebrations for the completion of it.

Howard: And you say that it took eight hundred years for the Great Pyramid to be completed. Search the Akashic Record and tell me the name of the King when the pyramid was completed.

Joshua: I'm getting Ra-Men. Almost like the noodles – Ra-Men. He was not as strong as the original designer king. He was a descendant, but it seems his power was not as strong in that in his mind the pyramid reaffirmed his divinity to the people, apparently they were starting to lose faith in him, but it deified the King and the King's family to the people.

Howard: That was important for the king. Was it important for the people?

Joshua: Not in their minds – in the King's mind. He thought they needed to know that he was a god and couldn't be questioned. But they were like all people, and they were willing to listen, and willing to be a part of the religion, but it didn't serve them, so it didn't feel as good to them, so they doubted it.

Howard: And did the priest caste also begin to doubt it?

Joshua: No. The priest class were a part of the ruling class, so they encouraged the thought that the Kings were gods, because they were the advisors to the gods.

Howard: Did they actually believe that the kings were gods?

Joshua: In that they knew all were God, but they didn't want the regular people to know that. You can't control people when they're equal to you, and they knew that.

Howard: And you said they were aligned with Orion?

Joshua: Some with Orion, yes. Orion was an important.... Orion's more with the apex, the top of the pyramid has more to do with Orion ...

Howard: Is the apex of the pyramid used for transmitting energy or receiving energy?

Joshua: Both.

Howard: And when it receives energy, where does that energy concentrate?

Joshua: Inside the pyramid, and then it's sent out from the pyramid. I keep getting that energy comes in in beams, but that it radiates out in waves, so that all those who are around the pyramid are affected by the pyramid because they're in the air space of the pyramids.

Howard: OK. Is there a special reason or a purpose for the King's Chamber?

Joshua: It receives a particular energy. They believed it received the most god-like energy into that chamber, and that the King would eventually rise to Heaven from there. To the skies, yes. It's not like they believed of Heaven like we do now, but they believed there was an afterlife, and they would be much as they were on Earth, that they would still be Kings and Queens and gods, and they would be even more powerful than they were on Earth.

Howard: Did they believe that the slaves would also go to Heaven?

Joshua: They believed you'd stay the same, they wouldn't go back to Source or Spirit, you stayed what you were on Earth.

Howard: And what was the original purpose that the designers conceived of for the Queen's Chamber?

Joshua: It's a different kind of god-energy, and it's more of a compassionate or healing kind of god- energy. I guess they saw a difference between the male and female energies, the male being strength and leadership and guiding the people, and the female being compassion and love and healing energy, although there were men and women healers both. And the Queen must have been the leader of the healing priests, and the King was the leader of the ruling priests.

Howard: All right. Did the Queen have any healing ceremonies, or did any of the priestesses participate in any healing ceremonies or practices?

Joshua: Um-hmm, they all did. She was healed always by the priestesses, they always anointed her and sent her energies, and then she believed that she received the healing and then transferred it out to all the people; the people had to come through her for healing.

Howard: So that established her divinity as well, in a sense for healing, for health.

Joshua: Yes. She wasn't weaker than the King status-wise; her energy was just different. She was still revered as much by everyone. I think the people liked her better than the King; they saw her as understanding them better.

Howard: Good. Now when the Great Pyramid was completed, the other two lesser pyramids were still being constructed. And how long did it take for the completion of those lesser pyramids?

Joshua: I think a total of a hundred and fifty years – they were faster, and they were started before the big one was finished.

Howard: Good. And when the smaller pyramids were completed, what did the energetic beings do – did they stay, or did they go somewhere else, or return to where they came from? What happened to them?

Joshua: They moved on to go build other places. They are advisors and scientists and builders, so when the job's done, they just go to the next job, so to speak.

Howard: And after the pyramids in Egypt were completed, did they go to other sites where pyramids were being built here on Earth?

Joshua: Yes. I'm getting some were built before the big pyramid, and then some after – I'm seeing the ones in the Americas, I think those are younger, but some are older ones, but they're not found.

Howard: And you mentioned that these energetic beings also assisted in the construction of stone monuments or temples or buildings on other worlds. What other worlds in our Solar System might they have worked on?

Joshua: I don't have names for the worlds, but four or five other Galaxies – they've been to numerous worlds on those.

Howard: All right. Are there any other worlds in our own Galaxy that they worked on?

Joshua: I'm getting Venus. I'm not sure where on Venus, or when it was... a very long time ago. And I think they went to Mars, but they didn't build there.

Howard: They did *not* build there?

Joshua: I think it was too late when they went to Mars. They knew it wouldn't last. Somehow they knew, they could feel Mars was dying. They knew.

Howard: And when they went there, how many years ago was that from the present time?

Joshua: A billion, a long, long time.

Howard: So this is a very ancient race of energetic beings.

Joshua: Yes. That's why they can use the energy so well, they've evolved for a long time.

Howard: And they go to many Galaxies and help with the construction. Do they do anything else, or is construction their purpose?

Joshua: I think it's their main purpose. They do small projects for fun in other places, like spires, and artwork and buildings that have the design to use the energy to fuel the building, so to speak. They know how to build buildings that use the energy in the air and the energy coming in from the sun there to be used by the occupants of the building, and it's in the design of the building, so they understand how to do that.

Howard: All right. Do they always work with stone, or are there other forms that they use as well?

Joshua: They use what's available on any given world, it's different in different places.

Howard: So it's not the material that's important – it's the shape?

Joshua: Yes, and the density. It's the shape and the density, because they specialize changing the density to create form and use the energy. Like when they cut the blocks for the pyramids, as they cut the blocks, the blocks become energized, and if they move the blocks, the blocks become even more energized. And as they set the blocks, the blocks become even more energized. So once the pyramid is built, all that energy in all those blocks, because of the way that they're made, combine and works together. And it makes it that the pyramids are extremely efficient at sending and receiving energy because of that design. It happened when the density was changed – there was a release of energy when that density changed, and that's what they do when.... I see a building that's almost like a spiral building, and it has like a smooth spiral that goes around it, very tall, and then all the residences are in between the spiral, and the spiral collects and distributes the energy, and the spiral was designed by these beings to do just that. It's from material of that planet, and they energized and they changed it when they built it. Because they did that, it now absorbs and sends out energy in forms that can be used by the beings. So these energetic beings have really strong abilities to control even the atoms inside each cell to release and to collect energy.

Howard: Good. Now in the pyramids in Egypt, when the rock was quarried from the hill, its density was changed as it was energized, and then when it was set in the pyramid itself, it was energized even more. I'm wondering when the density was changed back to its original form so it became very heavy again.

Joshua: I would say that it never came back to exactly what it was before, but our perception of it is that it's like it originally was because the energetic beings are no longer there influencing it. So when they left, it became to us what we knew it to be before, very solid and very heavy and very dense. But it's still really.... If you were to look at it at a microscopic level, it looks different than where it came from. If you were to go to where the rock was quarried, at the atomic level, that rock is yet different because the rock in the pyramid was changed. We don't have the ability to perceive the change, but it is changed. And if one of those energetic beings were to come now, it could easily influence it again because it has already been influenced by them. The energy is still there; we just can't still perceive it, but it is doing its work.

Howard: Does that have any relation to our perception to this level of consciousness? In higher levels of consciousness, would we perceive the pyramids to be lighter structurally?

Joshua: Yes. I see us almost able to see into them. If we look at them from a spirit perspective, we don't see them as solid. From a spirit perspective, you see them as energetic, you see the energetic movement in and out of them through that rock. You have to be the kind of rock for the energy to work the way it does. I see the energetic beings working with the rock, but they choose the material and the place that they're working that's going to use their energy the best.

Howard: All right. I'm still a little confused as to when the beings left, the density of the stones returned to its original density – is that correct?

Joshua: Yes – they always were the rock, they always were the same block. It's like if you look at a human, there's the physicality of that human, and the human can be very dense and the energy can be tight and closed in, or that same physicality can be very light-infused and very pliable. From the outside it looks the same, to touch it, it looks the same, but energetically it's very different. So the rocks in the pyramid are very different than what they used to be, even though they look the same. And they still appear to us as very dense and very heavy because we don't understand the energy, we don't know how to tap into it yet.

Howard: When we understand the energy, would we perceive them differently?

Joshua: Yes. They would be also semi-transparent. I mean they're there and they're solid, but they're energetically solid instead of physically solid. It's hard to put into words that make it easy to understand; it's all about their energy, but they're holding a LOT of energy. A density of, say, granite, it has energy, but the energy is locked into solidity, and it moves very slowly, and it moves sluggishly. And the energy of a cotton ball is open and light, and moves easily in and out and through. So if you take a block in the pyramid, it appears to be that dense, solid, hard, non-moving energy, but because it was made the way it was and because it constantly receives and gives off energy, it really is more like the cotton ball energetically. It's open, it's more alive, more fluid – we just don't perceive it because we live in the physical world from our human perspective.

Howard: And that characteristic is still part of the pyramids, even though the beings have left?

Joshua:	Yes. You can feel it if you sensitize yourself, you could go there and feel it.
Howard:	Thank you. Joshua, it's been a real treat, a real pleasure to have you with us this afternoon, and to share this very important information with us. Thank you!
Joshua:	Thank you!
Howard:	And Anaka, do you have anything else you'd like to add before we close?
Anaka:	No, I'm excited to see this unfold!
Howard:	Thanks again for coming, Joshua and Anaka. And you're released now to go about your own activities with much love and gratitude. And Karen, just let yourself rest even deeper... and place your attention on your body resting below in your cocoon of light. And when you're ready, come back to your cocoon of light, merging completely and totally with your physical body and conscious mind... and then when you're ready, return to full conscious awareness using the most beneficial method that's appropriate for you. Go ahead and do that when you're ready. *(Pause)* Welcome back!
Karen:	Thanks! Wow!
Howard:	Wow is right! A lot of good information there – actually more than I expected. Thanks!
Karen:	Yeah – interesting! I wasn't even sure I was going to be able to get there, and Joshua kind of stepped in and took over, so that was good.
Howard:	I've found it better to work with the Guide, rather than the Higher Self, when you're looking at the Akashic Record – it's from a higher spiritual perspective.
Karen:	And I find a lot of times when Anaka's looking, she can't see it, she's like I don't know, and then Joshua will come in and say This is what it is.

* * *

Case Study 2:
SJ-11: Akashic Record (Crop Circles)   July 8, 2014 - Directed by Howard Batie
Client: "Emma"   Client's Higher Self: "Shirella"   Client's Guide: "Samantha"
Howard's Higher Self: "Artoomid"   Howard's Guide: "Michael"

In this session, Emma rose into her Spiritual Area and, as Shirella, called for her Guide Samantha to come forward. After greeting us, Samantha provided a message for Shirella and Emma. Then at that point, I was guided to also call for my Higher Self Artoomid and my Guide Michael to come forward, join the conversation and provide the information regarding Crop Circles; Michael spoke through Emma.

Howard:	Michael, come forward now and join our group this afternoon.
Michael:	Hello, Howard.
Howard:	Hello. And, Being, are you in service to the service of the One Infinite Creator – Yes or No?
Michael:	I am.
Howard:	And are you in fact Michael, my Guide?
Michael:	I am.
Howard:	Thank you very much for coming, for being with us and joining our group here this afternoon. This afternoon, I would like to address what the Akashic Records have

recorded about the Crop Circles that appear in various countries around the world. Michael, is it permissible for us to gain access to the Akashic Record for investigating the origin, the nature, the purpose and the messages of the Crop Circles?

Michael: It is.

Howard: Thank you. Now, let's begin with the crop circle that was sighted recently in the United Kingdom, in England, not too far from Stonehenge. Michael, what does the Akashic Record have to say about the origin of that crop circle?

Michael: That came as a message from another world and planet that they are present and observing what is happening on Earth, and wish to be known to Hu-Mons as soon as appropriate. They are from this galaxy. The crop circles are one way that life from other parts of the galaxy indicates that they are interested in communicating with Hu-Mons, and that it is safe to do so, at the time that it is appropriate. Hu-Mons must lose their fear of communication with beings off-world to the point that the exposure of these other beings will not cause panic on a wide-scale basis.

Howard: What are the purposes that these craft are here for? How do these purposes change – from what to what?

Michael: Some who have been here for a long duration are willing to step back somewhat, to allow newer visitors the opportunity to participate in standing watch over Earth and its process. It must be monitored carefully, for as we have spoken earlier, too many in too close proximity could cause an untimely exposure and jeopardize an appropriate time for meeting. We are waiting patiently, all of us, monitoring who is coming and going, so that there is not again an untimely viewing or landing that could jeopardize an appropriate disclosure. It is somewhat complicated for you to understand the numbers of beings who are visiting Earth and the logistics in managing these numbers and being sure that all are agreeing to and honoring the limitations for their presence. This is a very exciting new venture, and as it becomes more known throughout the Galaxy, as we come closer and closer to a stronger Ascension path by Hu-Mons and Earth and Gaia, there are more requests for the opportunity to participate or observe in the ascension monitoring and assistance with energies, as well as observing the process and being a part of those groups who will eventually make first contact.

Howard: The beings that are observing us from, let's call them UFO's or ships, how do they create crop circles?

Michael: They are a dispensation, a release of a pattern of energy that has been formulated into a specific design which impacts the material on the ground level on Earth.

Howard: And these material designs contain information, a message?

Michael: Yes. In general, the message is all the same, which is "We are here, we are interested, we are safe." Specifically, in some cases the designs are artwork which helps to identify the beings and the ships which are creating the design. It is true some of your investigators talk about mathematical symbols and designs, and these are correct. However, they are being used in a more artistic individualistic pattern. In some cases, it is almost a creative play for the beings who are creating the crop circle images. They are identification symbols, and there are embedded messages; however, they will only be discovered once Disclosure has happened and translation has been provided.

Howard: So there is nothing embedded in the messages that would correspond to an alphabet, or a sense of translation itself?

Michael: To some degree, some are attempting that.

Howard: Is that with letters or with mathematics?

Michael: Mathematics is the easiest language to translate and use across multiple beings. Mathematics is a more universal language. It carries less emotional nuance, confusing contradictions in definition – is that more clear?

Howard: Yes. But there is little in the design themselves that carry a message other than "We are here and we are safe" – is that correct?

Michael: No, there are some with messages, yes, but the ability to fully discern that message will not be possible until Disclosure and translation information begins to be shared. Is that better?

Howard: Yes, yes. Now, there was one very unique crop circle – I don't know who it was made by –but it had on it a pictograph of the image that was on one of our spacecraft, and the crop circle image carried that same information back with a few minor changes that led us to believe that the changed information indicated the planet or planetary system that the originator came from.

Michael: Yes. You must understand, Howard, that in some cases, these crop circles are a way to entice humans to look further into the Universe. The replication of that information, with the changes that you mentioned, was an enticement to get humans going to looking beyond the obvious, to look for meaning in the crop circles.

Howard: To my knowledge, though, the only thing it has created is a lot of head-scratching. But we don't have that translation yet.

Michael: No, but humans have taken an important step and are asking and head-scratching, rather than total denial, rather than fearful ignorance. And that is what keeps the seeking, for curiosity is one of the inherent beginning qualities of the human that was encouraged to be developed. It is not possible for a human to exist and think without curiosity. The difference is the way in which each chooses to use that part of their being, and the extent that they allow it to guide them to higher, more open ways of viewing their Universe. It is one of the greatest gifts given to them when it was determined that this particular animal would be chosen to advance in its evolutionary path. To understand that the crop circles are identifications is a good thing, of different planets, beings, that they are asking for welcome, and that they are indicating friendship is important.

Howard: Well, perhaps it's time we give Emma a rest. Thank you very much for your insights, and the attendance also by Shirella and Samantha, Artoomid. Thank you all for coming. I do appreciate this! And I release you all to go about your own activities now with much love and very deep gratitude. It's a wonderful team I have here, and I do appreciate the value of it.

Michael: We acknowledge that love from you, Howard, and thank you.

Howard: Thank you. Good. Now Emma, just relax even deeper. Good. That it, just relax. And when you feel it is right, when you're ready, just return yourself to full conscious awareness using the techniques that are most effective and beneficial for you at this time. *(Pause)* Welcome back!

Spiritual Journey 12 – The Angelic Kingdom.

Several additional topics of investigation are also possible within this Journey. For example, Spiritual Journey 12a may investigate the nature and capabilities of The Elohim (the creative aspect of Creator); Spiritual Journey 12b may investigate the various Archangels and their characteristics; Spiritual Journey 12c may investigate the role and mission of Angels and/or Guides, etc. However, the process associated with each separate Journey would be very similar:

Process:
1. Client moves into her Spiritual Area and does the three things she must always do each time she rises up into her Spiritual Area.
2. Client's Higher Self (CHS) asks her Guide, "Is it permissible to access the Akashic Record for the purpose of understanding the nature and characteristics of the Angelic Kingdom?
3. If not, the client is emerged from self-hypnosis.
4. CHS asks for the specific information or answers to her questions.
5. Client returns to her cocoon and returns to full conscious awareness.

Case Study 1:
SJ-12: The Angelic Kingdom   May 12, 2014 – Directed by Howard Batie
Subject: "Emma"   Subject's Higher Self: "Shirella"   Subject's Guide: "Samantha"

Howard: Now Shirella and Samantha, in our previous Journeys, we've discussed many topics.

Samantha: There is great joy here today that you are interested and want to talk about the Angelic Kingdom, that you wish to know more, and there are great hosts here today, and great, great joy!

Howard: I'm honored to be in your presence. Samantha, I would like to know first, before we begin, is it permitted to access the Akashic Record for additional information and understanding on the nature of the Angelic Kingdom?

Samantha: It is.

Howard: Thank you very much. And Shirella, please tell me what you can about the Angelic Kingdom. And Samantha, if you would like to elaborate at any time, please jump in, but identify yourself as Samantha speaking first.

Shirella: It is unbridled joy and love. It is the epiphany of experience. It is nearly uncontainable. It is as we have spoken before in layers, in divisions as you call them for the purpose of their assignment, for their purpose, for their assignment. But all are deeply and immediately connected to the One That Is All and feel the strength of the unlimited joy, and to allow Emma to experience, communicate... please forgive if this is not appropriate, but the only term we find is we have to "dummy down" our energy, reduce without ruining the integrity. It is overwhelming as a human to feel that joy and excitement, and makes it difficult to function intellectually.

Howard: I understand. Shirella, is it safe and allowed for Emma to feel just what she is able to feel of the energy of the Angels?

Shirella: Yes. We have protected her and she has felt the touch of that.

Howard: Now, Shirella, now that you have access to that Akashic Record, tell me what you can about why the Angelic Kingdom was created.

Shirella: It is to have an organization for the creative energy of the One That Is All. It is to help as a communication dispensation to have a way for other beings to touch the creative energy of The Creator. It is not possible for life of any kind outside of the Angelic Kingdom to survive, to feel the full impact of the creative energy, and the Angelic Kingdom is a go-between, it is a dissemination body of creative energy. It allows the Creator to interact also with other life forms directly and indirectly through the Angels. The Angelic Kingdom stands between The Creator and other life forms, such as human, such as the gaseous, and even essence life forms which are neither corporeal nor gaseous. They come closest to the Angelic Kingdom, and yet are not able to feel the direct unbridled energy of The Creator.

Howard: In our limited way of classifying, we tend to believe that there are different classes of beings such as Angels, Archangels, Elohim and soul energies of incarnated beings. What can you tell us about the nature of these different elements, as we describe them?

Shirella: I have been using the word Angels to encompass all of those in the Angelic Kingdom, and we do have and understand your terms Archangels, Elohim, and angels with a small "a" as opposed to big "A" general category. Each has a separate function and connection to The Creator, to the One That Is All.

Howard: Then do I understand that the Angelic Kingdom is that part of spiritual beings that never incarnate, but souls do incarnate?

Shirella: Correct.

Howard: Yes. OK. Can you describe the difference in the functions between the Angelic Kingdom and those who incarnate?

Shirella: Those who incarnate are energies with a purpose to grow and expand, through which the Creator expands its experience of living, of creating. The souls help the development of The Creator by adding concrete experience, knowledge, information of the ramifications of the creative energy. It is as if the purpose, and I understand that this is not so, but I understand that it is as if a human child were to expand the information for the adult to help the adult to grow, to create a better or different experience next time. Is that confusing?

Howard: Well, let's look at the different parts of the Angelic Kingdom. First let's look at the Elohim and their functions. What can you tell me about the Elohim, their purpose, functions and methods?

Shirella: The Elohim are responsible for the direct creation of the souls and life forms, following the directive of The Creator, as well as gathering information to help make it so. We have discussed the new seeding of Earth, and through Emissaries to Earth to discover what was necessary to create positive life for Earth in that environment. The Elohim oversee such a project, and when all is good, they are allowed by Creator to manifest.

Howard: So the Elohim are the creators of the soul?

Shirella: The form, yes. That is your word. The energy with which The Elohim work is still nebulous, it is less concrete than you might perceive, and yet it is distinct from that direct creative energy. It is starting to take shape and purpose under the guidance of the Elohim.

Howard: As I understand it, The Elohim are the creators of form, the energetic template that will form the structure of the incarnated physical being. The Elohim are also the creators of the soul essence that incarnates?

Shirella:	Yes – it is one package.
Howard:	OK. Is there anything else, concerning the role and function of The Elohim, that you can share?
Shirella:	As with all of the Angelic Kingdom, their work is deeply sacred. And to serve in the Angelic Kingdom as an Elohim depicts great honor, trust. Each of the Angelic functions is sacred. It is difficult to explain. It cannot go wrong, and it cannot be misused, but Elohim and all Angelic Kingdom beings have awareness of a special trust and a deep gift from the Creator. It feels that with each project, with each assignment, with each purpose that sacredness is imbued in each of their creations.
Howard:	Is there one Elohim, or are there many?
Shirella:	Many. Many Elohim. A legion. There are many.
Howard:	And does each Elohim have a particular area of expertise such as a specific planet?
Shirella:	The groups do. They tend to function in groups and as a group consciousness. Depending on the theme, the project, it can be as few as ten or twelve, and as many as several hundred.
Howard:	Thank you. How does an Elohim come to be elevated to that position?
Shirella:	They are not elevated. Again, the Elohim, the Angelic Kingdom is the first creation of The Creator as a method by which the One That Is All could disseminate Creation in a variety of pathways and at a variety of levels. The Elohim were born directly of The Creator and given consciousness to allow them their function, but they are without ego, without division. They are aware they are a part of a group, as speaking between Elohim and Archangel and Angel and lesser angelic beings.
Howard:	The Elohim were created first?
Shirella:	Yes, but not superior to. The Archangel energy was undefined for individuation. Individual Archangels were not defined at the beginning. As the Elohim created the life of other beings, then Archangels formed in concert with that world or being. There is an Archangel for each world, for each life form. It is hard to explain because the term Archangel is Hu-Mon. Other beings understand, at some point in time, a higher source of energy which helps guide them, but which may not call them Archangels. The Archangel group is an energy of guidance and communication and serves as is needed, and for the life form or world as needed.
Howard:	So, in general, there is an Archangelic form of energy to guide the specific life forms that incarnate on each planet – is that correct?
Shirella:	Yes.
Howard:	A different Archangel for each different planet?
Shirella:	Sometimes multitudes, as in the case of Gaia. There are multitudes of Archangels assigned here because of the complexity of the life form and the ascension process. Multitudes, thousands, unnamed, some named. The unnamed work beyond the consciousness of the human. The unnamed support and guide Gaia specifically as opposed to the humans. The unnamed channel energy as needed to assist Gaia and those who are working on ascension, but they are not in the foreground, but no less important. They are the worker-bees of the Angelic Kingdom, of the Archangelic form.
Howard:	You said that there are several named Archangels that are assigned to Gaia. Name the Archangels that are assigned to Gaia.
Shirella:	The Archangels assigned to Gaia are unnamed. She does not need a name. There are many. Of course, you know Michael intimately, Uriel, Metatron, Mezekiel,... I am not

to go further. It would take too long to list, and some are for you to discover – we cannot give you all the answers, Howard. Samantha has said that it is an inappropriate use of this time and energy for a list of names. And perhaps Michael can help you with that list at another time.

Howard: Thank you. What can you tell me about Archangel Metatron, his functions?

Shirella: He is as-needed, he functions as to what is needed at the time to problem-solve. It may be communication, it may be decision-making help, it may be teaching, but he is one who deals more directly with issues.

Howard: Thank you. Now you mentioned before that Elohim are creators of souls. Are Archangels also creators of souls?

Shirella: No.

Howard: All right. Thank you. Back to the Elohim for a moment. In addition to being creators of souls, are they also creators of planets, of galaxies?

Shirella: Yes, and they oversee that process for universes. We mentioned earlier another group of angels. The Elohim will at times delegate the creative process to a group of angels, and that is often the creation of a physical world, a galaxy, a universe. They are of the One Who Is All, so they will work in other universes as needed. Again, it is highly complicated – your word – it is not a simple structure, a simple program.

Howard: I guess I need to understand the difference between universes.

Shirella: You have mega-companies, corporations, and there are different businesses with different purposes within each of those corporations, and they may not have a relationship in their product. They may not seem, on the surface, to have a connection; they have just been accumulated or bought out by the corporation. That is similar to, but grossly limited in definition, how the Creator, the One That Is All... A universe is a company within a corporation, so there are other universes within the corporation, and the Elohim are the Board of Directors – that is the closest I can come to ...

Howard: The Board of Directors which is the parent company...

Shirella: Yes, which is The Creator. Despite the human definition of the universe as being all-encompassing, it is only a name for a large collection of something. So you have in your science world coined the term "multi-verse." Human mind is now beginning to understand that the term universe as a definition is now archaic. It is not the be-all and end-all. Thank you. But there is ... I hesitate because your human brain will immediately ask the next question. If I say to you there is creative energy, the human brain will want to know what created that. It is not possible for you to understand that at this point. It is simply an existence – it is what it is.

Howard: At this point, I understand that the human mind is only able to get its imagination or its understanding around the idea of The Creator as the CEO of the many corporations which we call different universes...

Shirella: Yes, and the essence and the form of The Creator is unknowable when living in a limited life form such as the Hu-Mon.

Howard: Is the creative energy limited only to Creator and Elohim?

Shirella: No. The angels have creative powers, and they have also designated certain life forms and certain levels within all life forms as creative. Please define and explain how you mean 'creative.' Are you talking about the ability to create life?

Howard: Yes.

Shirella: Howard, you ask such complicated questions.

Howard: I'm only trying to understand how it works.

Shirella: I understand. Give us a minute. (*Pause*) Creative energy is the essence imbued to all beings at all levels. Certain life forms have ... we are now talking about incarnated beings such as humans... have awareness and understand they can be creative in a variety of ways. In moving to the spiritual, as you call it the un-incarnated, realms there are beings who can assist the Elohim in creating life forms, or who take the Elohim seed and refine it. They are acting out, they are functioning according to their own creativeness. All beings at all levels have the directive to create, including humans, including ants, including all life forms. They are to create. What is created is driven by the level of consciousness. Some is by instinct for those forms of life whose consciousness level is not as developed as the human, for example. And a human consciousness at this point is not as developed as other being such as the Pleiadians or the essence beings we have discussed in relation to Emma's soul, and pardon me, but I also believe that your soul is of an essence being. And those of higher consciousness create differently. So the manifestation of creativity is a matter of consciousness and directive within their own creative spirit. As anything that is discussed with The Creator and creative energy, you are asking to take the air around you and put it in a box so that we can see what it is like. It is almost impossible, so we work at doing our best to help you understand the magnitude of what you are asking to know.

Howard: Yes, it's a challenge trying to fit things into our limited consciousness.

Shirella: And yet, we are overjoyed, it is so gratifying to see those of you who are willing to make the struggle, to attempt to expand your understanding and therefore your knowledge and your consciousness.

Howard: One other question I want to clarify a bit – you said that the Elohim were kind of like the Board of Directors in other universes as well as this universe. Do the Archangels also work in other universes?

Shirella: Yes. They function in other universes. It is a way of the Creator beginning to give its creative energy form and function. And I believe Samantha needs to say...

Howard: Samantha, what is it you'd like to add?

Samantha: Only that we are deeply honored to serve you, Howard, and we ask that you be patient. You will receive all that you need, for you are a light among us, with whom we are honored to associate and serve. And while you may feel that somehow we are above you, we are with you, next to you in service, and wish to see the human race and the human life form, as individuals, complete their journey of ascension and growth and expanded consciousness.

Howard: Thank you. I would like to come again and ask your counsel and wisdom on that subject, the ascension of Gaia if that is permitted – we'll do that another time. Thank you very much. And now, Emma, I want you to permanently record all this information that we have received here today, record it in your conscious memory as well as in your eternal spiritual memory. Just let it be remembered by your conscious mind very clearly to guide and instruct you as well as we return to our daily life with full conscious awareness. And again, Shirella, Samantha, and all those who have attended today – Thank you! I send you my deep gratitude for your wisdom...

Shirella: You cannot see it, Howard, but they are bowing to your recognition and honor, and acceptance of your gratitude.

Howard:	I acknowledge that, thank you. Now Emma, just place your awareness back on your physical body resting in the chair, and when you're ready, just take a deep breath and return to conscious awareness *(Pause)* Welcome back!
Emma:	Thank you.
Howard:	That was wonderful.

* * *

Case Study 2:
SJ-12: The Angelic Kingdom   July 12, 2014 – Directed by Howard Batie
Subject: "Karen"   Subject's Higher Self: "Anaka"   Subject's Guide: "Joshua"

Howard:	Hello, Anaka. It's good to be with you again. Have you asked that the white light of Creator surround you and protect you always, that a clear channel of communication now be established between yourself and the highest levels of love and wisdom, and that all information you receive be only for the Greater Good of all concerned?
Anaka:	Yes.
Howard:	Wonderful! Thank you. Now just take a moment and feel how good it is to be here again, and when you're ready, ask Joshua to come forward so we can meet with him and discuss things with him today.
Anaka:	He is here.
Howard:	Challenge him: Are you in service to the light and love of the One Infinite Creator – Yes or No?
Anaka:	Yes.
Howard:	Are you in fact Anaka's Guide, Joshua?
Anaka:	Yes.
Howard:	Good. Welcome, Joshua! And Anaka, just go over to him and give him a big hug. Let him know how glad you are to see him as well. Just be in his energies, feel his presence here.
Anaka:	He's here!
Howard:	Good. Now, Anaka, Joshua, today we'd like to explore the Akashic Record for any information we are able to learn about the Angelic Kingdom. And Joshua, is it permissible for us to visit the Akashic Record to learn about the Angelic Kingdom today?
Joshua:	Yes.
Howard:	Anaka, I'd like you to read the entire Akashic Record as it pertains to the Angelic Kingdom. And what can you tell me about the Angelic Kingdom today?
Anaka:	Angels are co-creators with The Creator; they are His way of contacting and manifesting. Creator is always with us, but sometimes He needs to contact us in the way that we can hear Him better, and He uses Angels for that.
Howard:	There's another class of Angels that some call the Archangels; I'd like to know what the difference between an Angel and an Archangel is, differences in their energy strengths or missions, purposes, functions, and how those two classes interact with each other.

Anaka: They do interact. They're aware of each other. They can work together, but don't always. They have different purposes or duties.

Howard: What are those differences? First the functions, duties of Archangels.

Anaka: They're closer to Creator. Their duties are more in the higher realms. They do most of their work in the spiritual world, whereas Angels do most of their work with incarnated beings.

Howard: Do Archangels ever work with incarnated beings?

Anaka: Sometimes. I see it kind of filtered or cloudy a little bit, so maybe not as directly as Angels do.

Howard: All right. Go on with the mission and functions of Archangels.

Anaka: They move about in the spirit world. They help with souls who are in between lessons, in between incarnations where they've had to learn lessons and they're in the spirit world when they're processing what they've learned or need to learn. They also work with the Guides a lot. The Angels don't work as much with the Guides, the Archangels work with the Guides. The Angels are busy elsewhere, I'm hearing. As we're incarnated, we're more likely to be in contact with Angels, or to be guided by Angels, or assisted by Angels.

Howard: I see – while we're incarnated.

Anaka: Yes.

Howard: But then after we die and return to the spirit world, then do the Angels continue to work with us, or is that Archangelic work?

Anaka: The Angels can, but mainly our Guides and the Archangels, and there are other Angelic types of spirits that aren't called Angels and Archangels that also work with the Guides. They work more in the Creator levels, of creating souls and deciding which souls go where.

Howard: And what is that class of Angelic beings or spiritual beings called?

Anaka: Some are Elohim, some don't have names, but they're there. They're on the level with the Elohim.

Howard: I know that numbers are difficult, but are there great numbers or just a few numbers of, say, Elohim?

Anaka: A few compared to all others. It's hard to say few, because that could be a million compared to twenty million. Many fewer.

Howard: Are they, in numbers, greater than or fewer than Archangels?

Anaka: Fewer than.

Howard: There are more Archangels than Elohim?

Anaka: Um-hmm. And more Angels than Archangels.

Howard: I see. Is there a ratio or multiplication factor... I mean, are there ten times as many Angels as Archangels?

Anaka: I don't know that.

Howard: All right. Numbers are difficult when you're working with infinite concepts. Back to the Archangels first. What is a more detailed description of their functions, their missions, how they go about their work?

Anaka: I see them moving a lot, moving throughout the spirit world, moving as if they're supervising and checking and monitoring and helping to keep things all connected and running smoothly, kind of. I see lots of different colors of energy in them.

Howard: Are the colors indicative of any particular function?

Anaka:	I think so. I think that different energies are different colors, and different energies are for different functions, like healing or enlightening or uplifting. Purple and gold are for enlightening, green is for healing, and orange and pink and peach, kind of mixed together are for raising, rising.
Howard:	And these Archangels have these colors associated with hem?
Anaka:	They all have intense white light, but from their source, their energy within each, also come the colors mixed in with the bright white. It comes from their core, like from their heart center.
Howard:	All right. Are there any other missions or functions or purposes? You say overseeing, checking...
Anaka:	And guiding. They consult the Guides, they advise the Guides. The Guides are very wise, but sometimes they need advice.
Howard:	I'd like to know more about the Guides. When we say a Guide such as Joshua, has Joshua ever incarnated for example? Do Guides incarnate?
Anaka:	Joshua says he never has. He can be with incarnated beings, like with me, all the time, but he's not a physical being.
Howard:	So when working with Anaka, if Anaka has questions, then Joshua can answer them, or if she needs guidance, then Joshua can provide that guidance – is that how Joshua would work with the Higher Self of the incarnated person?
Anaka:	Yes, like he does with me. Joshua and I have such a long history that he doesn't need a lot of guidance when it comes to me, he knows our plan, he knows how we're going to get to where we're going. But with the new souls, sometimes he consults with other Guides and Archangels and other Angels. Joshua can be considered an Angel. An Angel is not one kind of entity. An Angel can be a Guide, can be an Earth Spirit, can be many forms. And because of that, depending on how it's perceived, it functions differently. But Joshua, he's like an Angel to me, but he's not Angelic all the time, he's fatherly, and wise and guiding.
Howard:	Does Joshua work with other individuals, other incarnated beings?
Anaka:	Yes. They have groups. When my soul seed was created, I was with other soul seeds, and Joshua stayed with all of us. I think there's seven others and me.
Howard:	All right. Is that about the average number of souls that a Guide guides?
Anaka:	No, there can be any number, but usually not twenty or thirty, but there can be fifteen or there can be three.
Howard:	And is the Guide usually in charge of all the souls in the individual soul group that were created together?
Anaka:	Yes, but other Guides sometimes helped, too. When I was created, I was aware of other Guides coming and going, and Joshua was always there as our Guide, and we knew he was our Guide, and I don't believe I've been contacted by other Guides, and Joshua, he's the one that talks to me.
Howard:	Thank you. OK. That clarifies a lot about Guides. Guides work with Archangels, the Archangels sort of guide the Guides – is that correct?
Anaka:	Yes, advise them and help them to think of new ways if something needs to be solved. If an entity is trying to understand and the Guide needs, maybe, ideas of new ways to help, that's what an Archangel can help with because they know all. Guides know all as well, but they're kind of busy working with who they're working with.

Howard: Thank you. Now you said that Archangels kind of oversee or direct Angels. Do Angels and Guides interact?

Anaka: They are aware of each other, and sometimes they work together, as in a healing. In a healing, there can be Guides and Healers and Angels all sending energy to the entity being healed, depending on the need of that particular being. But Angels can send energy, but they don't send energy the same as the Healers do. The Healers have a different way of controlling and directing the energy, and the Angels help to amplify that with their energy. Think of a healing as a ball of energy, and that ball of energy is created by the Healer, and then other Healers and Angels add to that energy. It's the Healer's energy expanded exponentially.

Howard: Wonderful. Thank you. And you say the Guides are involved in this healing process as well?

Anaka: Um-hmm, but not as much to send energy, as to help ground the person as they receive it, ground them within their own soul.

Howard: So in a healing situation, it's primarily the Healing Angels, we'll call them, and the other amplifying Angels?

Anaka: They are not different, Angels can amplify and Angels can contribute, and Angels can observe.

Howard: You said that some Angels are Healers.

Anaka: Well, not exactly. Healers can be Angelic, but it's not exactly the same. Angels are more ethereal, they are more... not exactly gaseous, but not... They're not as dense. I see Angels as sort of ... not a feeling, but a type of warm, comforting, assisting energy, assisting wherever they can.

Howard: And what is this class of beings that are called Healers in the spiritual world. They're not Angels, are they beings that have incarnated and are experienced in healing, or what?

Anaka: A Healer can be an incarnated being, a Healer can be a spiritual being, and a combination of them. A Guide is usually not a Healer, but a Guide will assist a Healer with their energy and their direction. Angels aren't typically just Healers themselves, but Angels coalesce around a Healer. I see Angels.... Remember the Orbs of energy that are attracted to energetic happenings? Angels are like that. Angels go where they are needed by an energy attraction, and if that energy that's happening is a healing energy, they contribute to that healing energy.

Howard: All right. Now what is the nature of the Healer?

Anaka: A Healer can be ... A Healer is a choice. Like you're a Healer, Howard. Archangel Raphael is a Healer. But he's an Angel that guides and oversees and directs healing energy. He's one of the strongest Healers ever. His energy is energy that all tap into and he enhances everyone else's energy. It's kind of hard to explain. Archangels are extremely, extremely energetically powerful. Raphael heals, and Michael enlightens. It's their choice to do that. They've chosen to heal, it's not that they're a Healer and that's what they have to do. So you can choose to be a Healer, an Angel can choose to be a Healer by assisting and helping, an Archangel can concentrate their energy on healing.

Howard: I see. And these other Healer entities, are they created by Raphael, are they aspects of Raphael?

Anaka: No, no, no. Remember when I lived on the ship and I was an energetic Healer? I was incarnated, and I was using the same kind of energy Raphael used, but it was Creator energy – it didn't come from Raphael. Raphael could come there and be with us and add his super-strong energy to what we do, but my energy didn't come through him. My energy came from Creator.

Howard: So the Angels are focusers of energy, different types of energy.

Anaka: Focusers, deliverers, channelers. Creator is so vast and so huge an energy source that it's just pure white light phenomenal energy, and because it's so strong, it's sort of filtered down as it goes toward those who are incarnated like we are. So as it comes through the Archangels, they are so evolved spiritually, they can handle any energy Creator passes through them, and they can pass that on down through to incarnated beings, to Angels, to Guides, to whomever it goes to. And the energy is what you can accept when you get it. So they help to form it in a way that it's used to the best for whoever or whatever receives it.

Howard: Good. Thank you. Are there other classes of spiritual beings besides Angels and Elohim and Archangels that we haven't discussed today?

Anaka: Guides are spiritual beings, and they're separate from the others. And your Council of Elders as they call it – they're another type of spiritual being, those you go to to analyze and resolve and think about and incorporate what you've done in past lives, and those you go to who are yet different to plan what you will do next, those are spiritual...

Howard: What are those called?

Anaka: Those can be on the Council of Elders, but they're more like sort of a Planning Committee. Some people see them as the same, and there can be ... Let's see if I can see my Council... there are four, and I go to the four when I come back.

Howard: And each time you come back, do you go to the same four?

Anaka: Yes. And when I'm ready to leave (the Spirit World), I go to another Council first to make a decision. And then I go to those four (in the Council of Elders).

Howard: And what does this other Council....

Anaka: They're like a Planning Committee, kind of. They're like a.... They show you there are lessons you can choose to undertake at this time, and this is how you can do it. And in each of those lessons you can choose a way to find that lesson. And you decide – you can see options. You know yourself that if you take Option A, it will affect your soul and your spiritual growth in a particular way. And if you take Option B, it could be completely different, and a different lesson could come from that. And then after you've chosen, then you see your Council of Elders, and they advise you, they.... I don't know if they sort of ... It's like they give you a blessing. And then you incarnate, and you see how you do with that lesson. And they're not Angels, and they're not Archangels. They are their own kind of spiritual being.

Howard: It's another class of spiritual being... does that have a name?

Anaka: No, but Joshua calls them The Planners.

Howard: And how does one get on the Planning Committee?

Anaka: When you evolve to a point, you can choose to do that. Once your spirit evolves to a point you can incarnate or not... You incarnate enough times to where you and your Council and your Guide feel you've learned the lessons that incarnation can teach you, and you may have other things you want to learn or do, and you can stay in the spirit world and work as a Planner, work as a Teacher, or a Schoolroom for those souls who have made really poor choices in their incarnations and have harmed other souls, or harmed things. There are spirits that counsel and work with them and help them back to balance, and you can choose to do that.

Howard: So the people on the Planning Committee have evolved to the point where they can choose to be a Planner?

Anaka: Yes. They have seen so many incarnations between them, they can give you some great choices of how to learn lessons.

Howard: OK. So the Planning Committee is (made up of) those souls who have incarnated physically into lifetimes, and they understand incarnation and physical life?

Anaka: Yes.

Howard: Good. Are there other classes of spiritual beings or groups of spiritual beings that have previously incarnated and now perform other functions other than planning?

Anaka: Yes, there are many. When you get back to Spirit World, when you've reached a point where you don't have to incarnate if you don't want to incarnate, there are many kinds of lesson rooms and school rooms, it's unlimited choices. You can choose to remain as spirit and still move between planets as a spiritual being and not incarnate.

Howard: Why would you do that?

Anaka: To just ... I see it kind of like a vacation, sort of, someplace you'd really like to be, but you don't want to stay there a whole lifetime and incarnate as a born being and go through all the physicality. There are places you can go and live in spirit and return to spirit world whenever you choose without having to die.

Howard: Those type of spiritual beings, is there a continual evolution of them?

Anaka: There's a continual evolution of all of us, even Angels and Archangels and Guides, we all always evolve. They just become stronger and wiser and bigger energy balls. Bigger representations of Creator.

Howard: Do they become Creators themselves as they continue to evolve?

Anaka: We are all co-Creators. We all can create. They are close enough to Original Creator that they have huge creation powers.

Howard: And what type of things do they create? For instance, do they create Universes or worlds...

Anaka: They can. They can create space in the Spirit World. They can help with the expansion of each Universe, and interconnection of dimensions.

Howard: Can they create physical things such as constellations or galaxies?

Anaka: Yes. They can create it all. It all comes from Creator, and it's guided outward, and they're near the source of guidance. So if you think of Creator as this huge ball of energy, the next layer out would be Elohim and Archangels, and that energy just vibrates out from there. It all creates, and all creation makes more creation.

Howard: Yes, but the farther out you go, the farther you get away from Source, and the more diminished your creative abilities become – is that correct or not?

Anaka: You can bring with you strong creation energy, if you're evolved to that point, into lower levels of Creation. Say in an incarnation like (on) Earth, the incarnated beings on Earth have many different levels of creativity inside them. There can be those who have a stronger connection with Source, and therefore have stronger energetic abilities themselves for creation, and those who have blocked themselves from Source at all and don't know that they are creators anyway. They have it in them, but they don't ever use it and it's very weak. But all can create. Creation is change. Creation comes from change, and the result of change is whatever new creation there is, so every energy and every blend of energy creates yet a new energy.

Howard: Interesting! And what's the difference in the creative ability between an Archangel and an Elohim?

Anaka: Elohim are stronger and more... not in control of, but in connection with using the energetic power – a little bit, not a lot. Elohim are the biggest creators and their creation energy is fine-tuned as it passes through down into the hardest of entities in incarnation. Even the hardest of energies, say, in rocks on Earth, inside still is moving energy, and that energy traces all the way back to Creator, just growing as it grows, from the tiniest parts of the tiniest atom, all the way up to Creator – it's all moving, changing, creating energy.

Howard: Is it accurate to imagine that the frequencies of this energy increase, the closer you get to Creator, Source?

Anaka: Increase in strength and in vibration.

Howard: We humans tend to think in terms of numbers and octaves. A convenient way for us to visualize how things happen is that one level of reality exists in a certain octave, say the physical octave. Then the next level up is the spiritual octave that we go to when we die. Then the next level up is an octave of Angels or whatever....

Anaka: It's not really octaves, it's the spiritual world. You pass through the layers of vibration and get to the level of vibration that your spirit can hold in comfort. So when you return to Spirit World, you return to that part of Spirit World that matches the vibration that you've come to at that point. And you're there with many, many other souls that are vibrating at your same intensity. And as you move closer to Source, the vibrations get stronger and stronger, but you have to learn your lesson to change your vibration. Being incarnated, you have to.... A lesson is a coming to an understanding or a settling in with the resonance of the vibration of the understanding of that energy. And as you absorb and accept, and can understand that energy better, your soul is evolving, so each time you incarnate, your soul can learn to vibrate even more strongly and as you return to Spirit World, you're more enlightened as a spirit. You still are in contact with all that's in Spirit World, but more 'into it' when you get there, you're more calm and warm and in the space that is absolutely right for you. When you're a very young soul, you go back and you're antsy to keep evolving and you're antsy to reincarnate, and you're antsy to keep learning, and you want to learn fast. But as your soul grows, when you get back to Spirit World, you're calmer there, and you're more peaceful there, and you're more in tune with everything else that's there, besides just the learning and the.... I'm getting learning pods, learning places where your soul returns to learn more lessons. And the more that you learn, the less time you have to spend learning – you know.

Howard: All right. Is there less motivation to continue evolving the higher up you get?

Anaka: It's not as motivation, it's knowing. You know when your soul begins to fill with the knowledge that you need to become who you become. And so it's almost more like relaxing as it gets more filled with the knowledge that you have. It's kind of hard to explain the feeling of it – it's not exactly motivation. Motivation is like a push, and it's not as much a push as a settling into.

Howard: But the younger souls are motivated, you said – they're antsy.

Anaka: Yes – they want to learn, they see each lifetime as exciting and filling. You're like an empty ball with a little bit of energy, and every lifetime fills more energy into that ball, and more energy, and more energy. And as the energy fills you, you learn to deal with all the things that happen in each incarnation. It's not a driving force any more. You're motivated, but you just move forward. You know you're moving forward, and you're comfortable with whatever pace you move forward at. So you don't feel like you need to push, you need to learn, you don't need to run at it – you float forward, you let it happen to you, because it does! Once you reach that point of evolvement in your soul, things you need become presented to you, they're there to help you choose your path forward.

Howard: All right, thank you. Anaka, Joshua, this is a treasure trove of information, it really is. Is there anything else that you'd like to add regarding the Angelic Kingdom?

Anaka: It's vast – it's very vast, and there is still lot ...

Howard: Does the Angelic Kingdom exist everywhere in the Universe?

Anaka: Well, it's a different dimension. The Universe is physical and spiritual, but the Spirit World is overlaid throughout our Universe and other Universes. The Spirit World is multi-dimensional and it's a separate dimension from the Universe, but they co-exist together.

Howard: So do the Archangels also work in other Universes, in other dimensions?

Anaka: Oh, yes. They work with all everywhere.

Howard: Good. Do they perform the same functions in other Universes?

Anaka: Um-hmm.

Howard: All right. Thank you very much. Anaka, Joshua, do you have anything further to add today to our discussion today?

Anaka: No.

Howard: Thank you for coming today, and Joshua, again with much love and gratitude, you are also released to go about your own activities. And now Anaka, just rest, relax, and remember all the conversations here today so that Karen can bring them back to her conscious mind. And when you're ready, just return to your cocoon below, fully integrating your superconscious, your soul awareness, with your physical body and your conscious mind. And when that's complete, and when you're ready, return to full conscious awareness in the most beneficial method for you. Go ahead and do that now. (Pause) Hello! Welcome back!

Spiritual Journey 13 – The Plant and Mineral Kingdoms.

Investigations into the Akashic Record can shed much light on topics such as, What is the role and function of the Plant Kingdom? Why is there such diversity in the Plant Kingdom? Did this diversity arise solely through genetic evolution on Earth? Are all crystals conscious? These and many other topics can be researched separately in the various sessions of Spiritual Journey 13, again using the same general process of other Journeys into the Akashic Record.

Process:
1. Client moves into her Spiritual Area and does the three things she must always do each time she rises up into her Spiritual Area.
2. Client's Higher Self (CHS) asks her Guide, "Is it permissible to access the Akashic Record for the purpose of understanding the nature and characteristics of the Plant and Mineral Kingdoms?
3. If not, the client is emerged from self-hypnosis.
4. CHS asks for the specific information or answers to her questions.
5. Client returns to her cocoon and returns to full conscious awareness.

Case Study 1:
SJ-13: The Plant & Mineral Kingdoms May 21, 2014 – Directed by Howard Batie
Subject: "Emma"   Subject's Higher Self: "Shirella"   Subject's Guide: "Samantha"

Howard: Shirella and Samantha, today we'd like to explore the Plant Kingdom. And Samantha, I'd like to know if it's permissible to visit the very earliest Akashic Records so that we can consciously become aware of and understand the roles and missions of the various elements of the Plant Kingdom.

Samantha: It is.

Howard: Thank you. Shirella, what can you tell me about the Plant Kingdom, in general terms to begin with?

Shirella: It is lively, it is renewing, it is fresh, it is depth of life. Plant life precedes the human, so its knowledge runs deep. It understands the way of life, the development, the creation. It is that life without complication of reasoning. It is life.

Howard: How was the Plant Kingdom created?

Samantha: Howard, this is Samantha. You must understand some of this is not translatable into language. We will do our best. The plant life has a knowing of life that is too deep for the Hu-Mon to understand in its complicated brain; it is simple, straight-forward life energy that has developed into some more complicated species, and yet it retains a knowing that is different from the animal, and especially the Hu-Mon. So please be patient as we search for ways to help you understand

Howard: Thank you, Samantha. Shirella, can you begin the exploration by understanding why was the Plant Kingdom created in the first place?

Shirella: The Plant Kingdom was created to support, to bring life, to have life on Gaia, on Earth, and to support more complicated life forms such as animals of all kinds. It gives nuturance of itself as no other life form does for the planet. Its sole purpose is to sustain other life forms. To give back to the air, to provide food and nuturance, to hold the life energy. It is more than biological sustenance. It holds life force energy that can be transmitted to other life forms by what it creates, how it interacts, how it feeds, by its making of oxygen. So it came to Earth as a primary form of sustenance. It introduced life and life essence.

Howard: Good. In our earlier discussions, you mentioned that the Elohim were the creators of consciousness. Are they also the creators of the plant life forms?

Shirella: Yes. There is consciousness in plant life forms; it is different. This is difficult. It is aware without being aware. It is aware to some degree, however, because its purpose is sustenance and support, to be fully conscious would be painful and difficult. It does its job with pure love and joy, as children of Gaia, and so its self-consciousness has been limited to protect it, to keep it from the duality on Earth and the pain, both physical and emotional, of providing sustenance. It is a sacrificial life form of sorts. It asks nothing in return, only to grow and provide, which is its purpose.

Howard: There's many, many different forms of life in the Plant Kingdom – the diversity of plants is amazing. Can you speak to the reasons for this diversity?

Shirella: As the planet began to develop and Gaia began to develop and grow, it was determined that there would be animal life on this planet. The Plant Kingdom agreed to provide a variety of life forms to meet the needs of the growing non-plant life and the energetic needs of Gaia in the early days. And so it began its own diversification project. It grew as needed and continued to meet the needs of the ever-changing, ever-changing life forms of Gaia and Planet Earth.

Howard: Some of the life forms in the Plant Kingdom seem not to have served as sustenance for the growing animal life forms, such as large trees.

Shirella: Trees provide shelter and homes, and they carry within them a type of advanced consciousness, and their roots run deep to help connect with Gaia. We would like to call upon what may appear to be a strange reference, but is the closest we can come to explaining. Your story of the Ents (in "Lord of the Rings") is not too far from the consciousness of trees; for example, if necessary, at one time, trees could awaken if it was necessary to help project energy, to protect, or to assist in the growth of Gaia. They could spread, transmit to the Earth or to Gaia and return energy to the planet and the species. And today, they still function in that way; however, they do not awaken. Once a level of consciousness was reached in the Animal Kingdom on the planet and some animals became destructive to the plants in a non-sustenance way, trees no longer awakened – it was too dangerous, and their energy and protection in some cases has been diminished, although they still try and work with Gaia to keep the energy flow productive, positive, balanced, but it is now a struggle because so many are gone.

Howard: Thank you. Before that time, when the trees' consciousness could awaken, could you describe the nature of the activities that the trees undertook?

Shirella: There was great joy when trees in a group would awaken, would talk with each other, would communicate with each other and to know they awaken to add powerful energies to help Gaia grow and help sustain the Earth.

Howard: Do trees communicate with a consciousness or with chemicals?

Shirella: A consciousness if it is energy, with the planet Earth if physical, they were able to disseminate certain chemicals to nurture the ground, to allow life to spread and continue.

Howard: And to me there seems to be another class that doesn't seem to be in the food support role, and that's the beautiful flowers that appear everywhere. What is the purpose of the flower element of the Plant Kingdom?

Shirella: The flower is a go-between from the Plant Kingdom to the Animal Kingdom. It allows certain species sustenance and nurturing, and it also provides energy of a high level, something you would use as a term as beauty, as raising consciousness levels, they have become symbolic of that. So they do provide sometimes sustenance for some beings, but they also in their beauty create such a wonderful energy of love. It is a constant smile of joy, of fragrance.

Howard: Can one element of the Plant Kingdom, such as trees, detect the presence of another element such as flowers?

Shirella: At a certain level. They have a plant consciousness that runs through all, and it is very deep, very old. It is a basic life force. There is again a knowing and acceptance of life and of being part of the One That Is All, that is their connection, their touching point, their conversation with each other. They do not have the need for a consciousness as you are intending, I believe.

Howard: You mentioned before that the Plant Kingdom was provided on the Earth prior to the development of the Animal Kingdom. Was there another Kingdom present on Earth to pave the way, to prepare the way, so to speak, for the Plant Kingdom -- I'm thinking of the Mineral Kingdom. What can you tell me of the Mineral Kingdom and its relationship to the Plant Kingdom?

Shirella: The Mineral Kingdom began prior to that time to provide sustenance for the plants. So it is a layering of the earliest life form, not knowable by the human at this point, and growing in complexity. Minerals do not need sustenance, but provide that for the beginning of conscious life forms, the plants.

Howard: Thank you. What are the characteristics, the basic properties inherent in the Mineral Kingdom?

Shirella: They are static, they are knowing without knowing without knowing. Their life awareness is nearly.... They are deep, deep, old, very ancient. It is hard to talk about minerals and life forms as you use it. They are an ancient entity unto themselves.

Howard: All right, Shirella, do you have anything to add or to amplify regarding our original focus of interest today – the Plant Kingdom?

Shirella: Only that we feel sad for humans who do not understand the love that surrounds them in plants. Even those propagated by humans carry the original seed, and are about love and light. And Emma now understands why at least in part why people come into her garden and talk about how peaceful they are, because she allows, to the extent possible, the natural energy of the plant to come forth and exist. And the human destruction of the Plant Kingdom not only threatens its physical life, but also its spiritual.

Howard: This is beginning to change, is it not, as people are beginning to become aware of their environment?

Shirella: It is and it is hopeful, still much damage has been done, and with the ascension of Gaia, there are plans in place for a resurgence of the plant life. As awakenings happen, people will be drawn to plant life.

Howard: Good. Thank you Shirella, Samantha.

Shirella: My pleasure, and thank you, Howard.

Howard: You are welcome, with my gratitude and thanks. Shirella and Samantha, I will talk with you again.

Shirella: And the multitude who gather again salute you. They thank you. That is not sufficient, but the only word we know.

Howard: My thanks to you – I love you all. ... And now, Emma, it's time now to release Shirella and Samantha to go about their own activities, always guiding you, watching over you with love. It's time now to return to full conscious awareness, so allow yourself to come back now, becoming more and more aware all the time, and when you're ready, just take a deep breath and open your eyes. *(Pause)* Welcome back!

* * *

Case Study 2:

SJ-13: Plant & Mineral Kingdoms   June 29, 2014 – Directed by Howard Batie

Subject: "Sandy"   Subject's Higher Self: "Carlosha"   ubject's Guide: "Kwana"

Carlosha: Kwana, may I search the Akashic Records to understand all about the plants and minerals?

Kwana: Yes!

Howard: Now Kwana, I want you to move to the universal Akashic Record of all beings and all events in Creation, and from the very beginning of this Akashic Record, I'd like you to scan it and know and understand more about the nature and the characteristics and the purposes of the plant and mineral kingdoms on Earth, and how they support and interact with each other and with other life forms, including us humans. Kwana, what can you tell me about these wonderful kingdoms? First, how was the Plant Kingdom created?

Kwana: Cell by cell it evolved and changed so that each group of people could discover how they could benefit from them.

Howard: Good. Who created the Plant Kingdom, or was it strictly an evolutionary process?

Kwana: The seeds came from the stars, and evolved. Peoples from other planets had them first, and on trips here to Earth, they left them in the soils. And as they grew and flourished, the Plant Kingdom just evolved from the seeds, and changed, according to temperatures and geological locations and different peoples bringing them to other parts of the Earth. Early peoples needed food and medicines, and tried many different things, tried growing different things using what they found in their areas, traded with different peoples from their areas, mixed different things together. They had a knowing of what would work, and this knowing was handed down through generations, always searching for new and different things.

Howard: The humans, or humanoid beings, have a level of consciousness as well; they are self-aware. Is the Plant Kingdom also self-aware?

Kwana: Yes. Yes, to be sure, there is cellular memory, a knowing, a genetic consciousness in each cell of every plant that has ever been on Earth. And there is a communication form between different plants and trees and life. It can be monitored by people with technological devices, but it is an energy that moves between the cells and between the species, and they are aware of each other, mostly for the benefit of each other as in symbiosis. The plants and grasses support trees by sheltering the roots, bringing moisture down to the roots. There's some chemical interaction that I don't know. I'm seeing different diseases that sometimes can be healed or prevented by living near another species of plants – they protect each other from certain things, perhaps insects.

Howard: Tell me what you can find in the Akashic Record about the interaction between the Plant Kingdom and the consciousness of the Earth.

Kwana: Everything is welcome. Everything is meant to grow, to be. The strongest survive. Earth provides what people need, what animals need intentionally. It's all meant to be, together. Of course they need light and water and sunshine, and their genetic codes make them be what they are and they can be changed, their forms can be changed by the elements and by what is done to them by water and storms. And wind can change their forms, which can then change the next generation of them as they mutate.

Howard: OK, I understand that. How does Gaia interact with the Plant Kingdom?

Kwana: It's like love! It's wonderful! She's their mother, she's the womb for all of them. I don't know why it's making me teary, but it is! There's the giant, giant leaves of certain plants down to the tiniest microscopic life form in the Plant Kingdom. And they're all here for our benefit, for us to learn from, to make medicines from, to enjoy, to help us, to make things from, to make our lives better. They share their lives with us, and they have a knowing of what their purpose is, which is to live, to record in their memories what they've seen, but to also sacrifice so that their purpose is to be useful. There's no sadness in the plant world; they live a joyful life, understanding that their cycles are just that – they're cycles.

Howard: Wonderful! There's another element of the Plant Kingdom that we haven't mentioned, and that's the flowers. What can you tell me about the Flower Component of the Plant Kingdom, and why there is such a diversity.

Kwana: The flowers are formed to form the seeds for the next generation, of course. But it's like the ultimate combination of joy when a flower blooms. They exist and finally feel that joy of becoming what they were meant to be, and then producing seeds for the next generations. They spread the joy of their beauty to anyone who is open to appreciating it, to serve as food for some, to make Mother Earth the beautiful place that she's meant to be.

Howard: As a tree grows and comes to maturity, what is it aware of?

Kwana: The elements, the rain, the wind, the cold, the air around it, the lives that it shelters and the things that grow on it, like the birds and the lichens and the gauls, and I feel like it senses time passing. There's something majestic about a big old tree. The trees that are cut down for timber, for boards and wood, they know that this is their fate, but they don't mourn it. The trees gives us energy and clean air, and are happy to do so.

Howard: Now, we've talked briefly about flowers and trees and grasses. What other forms of plants need to be recognized and discussed?

Kwana: Mosses. There are so many different kinds of mosses. They have their own little world. They shelter the soil, and take nutrients from the soil and the bark of the trees, and they're just their own little microcosm of tiny life. Sometimes they blend with fungi and become lichens, and they spread their unique beauty on the trunks of the trees. They're just a separate thing, and they don't hurt the trees, it's just symbiosis where they can live together. They gather the moisture from the bark, but they don't really hurt anything.

Howard: What does Gaia think about the trees all over her surface?

Kwana: They're wonderful! They clean the air and they hold the soil. She wishes that they would not cut down so many in places where they are endangered. Too many trees get taken. But they can be renewed, they can grow new trees. And the balance is disturbed by man, but it will all be well.

Howard: What needs to happen to restore that balance?

Kwana: Collective energy, people caring, people doing distant healing, people putting their feet down to make it stop, doing renewable energy things.

Howard: What does Gaia think or feel about the grasses and the reeds?

Kwana: They're happy, they're natural, they're the covering of her skin to protect her. She's happy that they provide nutrients to the soil.

Howard: Good. Now we haven't talked about plants that live and have their entire life cycle in the oceans, all these plants that live in the waters.

Kwana: Wonderful kelp beds, beautiful, waving, in the water for all the animals to find shelter and protection and food, and soooo many life forms in the ocean. The corals, it's all beautiful! It's like coming home! The oceans and the fresh waters, too. They give oxygen to the water, and they're beautiful each in their own special way, every little pond, every little puddle, every bit of water has some plant form in it that renews itself and makes it pure.

Howard: And what does Gaia feel about the flowers that grow on the surface of all the lands?

Kwana: It's her crowning glory, it's her gift to the world to bring joy, they bring jobs and money and commerce. People like to share them. There's just not a lot about flowers that's not about happiness. And the fruits and the crops, all of the things we can grow. It's amazing!

Howard: Now Carlosha, I want you to look again at the Akashic Record and tell me anything else interesting about the Plant Kingdom.

Carlosha: The mushrooms!

Howard: Tell me more about them.

Carlosha: There's so much more to learn about them! We have barely scratched the surface of what they can do! We know they taste good, we know they can be psychedelic, but there are many medicinal properties to be learned about. Fungi are just interesting! It will be years before we know what they can do.

Howard: What kinds of things will they be able to do, will they be able to help us to do?

Carlosha: Cure diseases, and anti-aging properties.

Howard: Interesting! Tell me more about the aging process and how mushrooms, funguses, and molds if they're included, how they can address or slow down the aging process.

Carlosha: Spores – something to do with the spores of the mushrooms. I'm seeing – and I don't know their names – these little thin-stemmed mushrooms, little white thin stems, and their tops are reddish and rather conical with little white spots on these in groups.

Howard: Do the grow in caves or on the forest grounds?

Carlosha: Forest, more foresty, damp, dark, mossy. I see them sprouting up from within the mosses, the spongy mosses.

Howard: Good. Now, Kwana, is there anything else that you'd like to tell me about the Plant Kingdom? And how it interacts with Gaia, or with other elements of itself like trees with flowers, or grasses with flowers, any interactions?

Kwana: It's all interconnected. If you could just see it like an infra-red picture where it showed the energetic connections, it would look like a worn roadmap with all the roads and veins connecting in a good way.

Howard: Wonderful! Now I want you to also look at the Akashic Record, and tell me what you can about the Mineral Kingdom. Just examine the Akashic Record of Earth and tell me what you can about the nature and purposes of the Mineral Kingdom on Earth.

Kwana: It's incredible! Absolutely incredible how all these different elements can be blended like fire and create the most beautiful crystals and caves, form metals, how sand can spill and... Oh, the explosive, explosive things that happen to make all the wonderful things we have. Volcanic explosions from the center of the Earth, billowing up and melting all these separate things together. Oh! Wow! The formations! Oh, it's just absolutely beautiful and incredible that all these things were formed for us to see and find and use and share. Oh, it's just.... There's so <u>much</u> there that can be explained or comprehended. There's more to find, there are things that are hidden deep within the center of the Earth. Treasures! Treasures of wonderful rock specimens who we can use. We have not found it all. Must dig deeper!

Howard: Just move right into the Earth and FEEL the structures, the compositions, the forces, the energies. How can they be used, directed, or channeled toward productive applications?

Kwana: Some kind of technology that lets us see into the Earth, and when it's developed, it will be as plain as day. I'm seeing the fiery core of our planet. I guess that would be thermal energy.

Howard: Let's come back up to the surface now, and throughout all the eons of Earth's existence, all these forces have deposited such a wide variety of metals and ores, and crystals and other things from within the Earth. How can we best use them?

Kwana: Being conservative, not depleting. Still exploring, still testing and finding different compounds that can be put together to make different things. It's protecting the land, not scouring it, protecting the Earth to keep it safe. Most lf all, just appreciating what we have instead of just taking.

Howard: Good. Now I want to talk with Carlosha. Carlosha, have you ever had any interactions in any of your physical lifetimes with the Plant Kingdom on Earth? Look through the Akashic Record of your lifetimes and let me know – have there been one or more physical lifetime interactions with the Plant Kingdom? (Note: We shift to Carlosha because prior to the sessions, Sandy wanted to know why she had such an affinity for plants and minerals.) And when you were interacting with the Plant Kingdom, how were you interacting? What functions did you perform in those lifetimes?

Carlosha: I see field of flowers. Field and fields of different flowers, different colors, walking among them, gathering them, loving being there. I feel like it's in another country.

Howard: Did you have this feeling of walking among the flowers in one lifetime or in several lifetimes?

Carlosha: Mmmm, other lifetimes, too.

Howard: And how about your interactions with the Mineral Kingdom, with the rocks and stones and crystals, with any component of the Mineral Kingdom?

Carlosha: I'm finding them in every lifetime, and using them for things, but mostly just loving them, their textures and their colors.

Howard: Wonderful! And what's your feeling for these rocks and stones, minerals? When you hold them in your hand, what do you feel?

Carlosha: Close to the Earth, holding a piece of Gaia, of the Earth, grounded, being part of the Earth, almost wanting to BE a rock; they're so perfect and solid.

Howard: And if you could BE a rock for just a moment or instant, what form of rock would you choose to be?

Carlosha: A rock that has many components of different types of minerals and crystals and quartz, feldspar, metals, all of them together. Enormous energy!

Howard: Just feel that! And remember the feeling! Yes, and for just an instant, move right into those rocks and stones you're holding in your hands and FEEL what it is like to BE the stones, the rocks, the minerals. And what is the feeling? Can you describe that? Tell me about what you're feeling.

Carlosha: Complete, solid, beautiful, necessary for me, to be.

Howard: Remember that feeling. Record it, and then move back into your own being, aware that you're holding that rock, stone gently in your hands, and then set it down and thank it for that experience. Good. Now, Kwana, I'd like to ask you if there's anything else you'd like to recall or remember or relate to me about all this information that you've provided to me today... very interesting and important information.

Kwana: There's so much more. There's so much more to know and feel, to grow!

Howard: Good. Now, Kwana, I want you to permanently record all the information that you've given me here today, record it not only in your subconscious memory, but in your conscious memory as well. Just allow all this important information to be clearly recalled, even after you've emerged from this very high spiritual state that you're in just now. Just let it all be remembered very easily and clearly by your conscious mind to guide you, instruct you, and help you as you return to your daily life and full conscious life. And Kwana, you're released to go about your own activities. Thank you for coming and sharing this information. And Carlosha, it's time now to come back to the Spiritual Area and bring with you all the memories, all the images, the imprints and the feelings of your experience here today. Allow it all to come back into your conscious memory with clarity and grace. And I want you now to place your attention on your physical body in the planes below, resting comfortably, very safely. Just return to the physical planes when you're ready, and fully integrate all these spiritual memories with your physical body and your conscious mind once again, fully integrated and complete, using the technique that you've been practicing. And then, when that integration is complete, just emerge yourself from hypnosis and return to full conscious awareness, and easily and gently emerge from self-hypnosis, remembering all the details of this wonderful Journey. Welcome back!

Sandy: I don't want to come back! Oh, that was powerful for me! I'm glad I can keep it with me consciously! I'm going home and hug my rocks, Howard! I didn't know it would be possible to be more connected, but I can feel it now! Wow! I could see it happening, I could see! These explosions, and these minerals forming, and in these caves all these beautiful, beautiful stuff, indescribable! Mmmmm! That was great! It was awesome! Oh, it's going to take me a long time to absorb all this!

Howard: Well, you'll have a copy of the recording, and you can play it as often as you want.

Spiritual Journey 14 – The Elemental Kingdom.

Our myths and folklore are filled with stories and tales of little nature creatures that live in the woods, hide under bridges or deep in the forest, and tiny beings, usually female, who cheerfully flit through the woodlands and meadows and land on the flowers and mushrooms. But very little is known or written about what their purposes or functions are, beyond simple emotional qualities that some have, such as the happy-go-lucky leprechaun, the grumpy trolls, the busy little fairies zooming here and there, and the sometimes mischievous elves. Why these little creatures even exist has been as mysterious as they are themselves. So it was time to turn to the Akashic Record and investigate this curiously interesting Kingdom of 'beings' that represent the four nature elements: Earth (Gnomes), Air (Sylphs), Fire (Salamanders) and Water (Undines).

Process:
1. Client moves into her Spiritual Area and does the three things she must always do each time she rises up into her Spiritual Area.
2. Client's Higher Self (CHS) asks her Guide, "Is it permissible to access the Akashic Record for the purpose of understanding the nature and characteristics of the Elemental Kingdom, the domain of the Sylphs, Undines, Salamanders and Gnomes?
3. If not, the client is emerged from self-hypnosis.
4. CHS asks for the specific information or answers to her questions.
5. Client returns to her cocoon and returns to full conscious awareness.

Case Study 1:

SJ-14: The Elemental Kingdom July 9, 2014 – Directed by Howard Batie
Subject: "Emma"   Subject's Higher Self: "Shirella"   Subject's Guide: "Samantha"

Howard:	Welcome, Shirella! Have you surrounded yourself with the love and the light of the One Infinite Creator, established your clear channel of communication to the highest levels of love and wisdom, and asked that all information you receive be only for the highest and best good of all concerned?
Shirella:	Yes.
Howard:	Shirella, I'd like you to call on Samantha to be here as well. Just do that now.
Shirella:	Samantha is here.
Howard:	Now Shirella, describe to me what you're aware of as you gaze at Samantha, how she appears to you.
Shirella:	There is essence, not a lot of form. I am aware of her presence.
Howard:	All right. Thank you. Let's go through it just to be sure: Essence, are you in service to the light and love of the One Infinite Creator – Yes or No?
Samantha:	Yes.
Howard:	And essence, are you in fact Samantha?
Samantha:	Yes.
Howard:	Thank you.
Samantha:	Howard, this is Samantha. In these sessions, the visible is no longer necessary for Emma or Shirella. The focus and energy is on information. Thank you for validating my presence.
Howard:	Certainly. Let me be clear on that message. Are you saying that the challenge and verification is no longer required?

Samantha: No, I am explaining why, perhaps in the past, Emma has seen a form identified with my presence. In these sessions, the energy that it takes to create that form is instead used for transmitting information.

Howard: I do understand that. Thank you for that explanation.

Samantha: And I see that it is always better to do the challenge than not.

Howard: Good. Now, Samantha, today we would like to look at the Akashic Record, and investigate what we can learn, what you can tell us about the nature, the characteristics, the inhabitants of the Elemental Kingdom. Is that permissible for us to investigate?

Samantha: It is.

Howard: Excellent. Thank you. Now what can you tell us about the nature of the Elemental Kingdom?

Samantha: The Elemental Kingdom, as you refer, comes from the very beginning of the development of Gaia and the advancement of life and energy on the planet Earth.

Howard: All right. Was the consciousness level of the Elemental Kingdom at the time of Terra, was that equivalent to the consciousness level of Terra, the third dimension?

Samantha: Yes.

Howard: All right. And can you describe the functions, the purposes of the various inhabitants of the Elemental Kingdom?

Samantha: They were the beginnings and have developed into the keepers of what is necessary to provide life on planet Earth in a biological sense, to monitor those energies. It was concomitant with the development of life, for as life developed, the surrounding elements also needed to develop, especially in consciousness level. It is, please remember, always an energy exchange, so if we may speak of the elemental of water or air, those are life-giving forces that need to be monitored, and they carry their own consciousness level in order to interact energetically with the life which they support. They do not directly intersect or interact with the development of the life form, but rather monitor the growth and energy development, and then be sure that the elements supporting that life are in tune, up to date, supportive, strong enough to support, developed enough. It is a support system which has connections, but not hands-on development.

Howard: So the Elemental Kingdom observes and monitors the development of life; with whom or what do they interact to make adjustments when adjustments are necessary?

Samantha: Within their own knowledge, as well as that that comes to them from Creator, and the process that was established in the very, very beginning of this project. It is as with all life and energy, an exchange. Energy is sent, energy is received. It is the basis of all life from Creator. The Elemental Kingdom was given in the very beginning the necessary understanding, tools and information to grow, and that was provided in the beginning by Creator. If we look at Gaia as a unit, a function within which there are several contributing pieces that must coordinate and communicate, then the Elemental Kingdom is part of that mechanism, that unit. Their function is to support and enhance biological life on Earth, the planet. They are a life of themselves to some degree, because they have a limited consciousness. All of Gaia is alive if one is speaking of energy as life, and therefore all of her components are also alive if one is speaking of life as energy. The Elemental Kingdom and its components have life and consciousness to the degree that is necessary for them to perform their purpose, which is to create a viable environment for sustaining a biologically-based life such as Hu-Mons, animals, plants. It is to create the environment as well as support. For example, biological life must breathe air, so the Elemental Kingdom provides that air as well as monitors its appropriateness for the level of life and necessity on Earth.

Howard: Yes, go on.

Samantha: So if one leaves the definition of form behind, Gaia and all connected with her are within these energetic layers that interact and support the being known as Gaia. Within these energies and frequencies, form then becomes known or apparent. As frequency is slowed, we know that form is created. But at the essence level, all is interchangeable energies. The Elemental Kingdom, as you name it, is a group of specific energies which are used to support a different level of energies. So when you are asking about if it is supporting this or that, please understand that your Hu-Mon culture, history, as it attempted to deal with its environment as a basic life form, began to tell stories, to give names, to create a limited understanding within what they were capable. Some of these early human understandings, of course, have been passed down, and that is the way memory is created, that is the way that learning is allowed. One grasps a concept and then, hopefully, begins to elevate that concept as growth is continuing. Part of the issue with discussing a concept such as the Elemental Kingdom is describing it and expecting answers or discussion within the framework of these stories and myths. These formed understandings, the Elemental Kingdom as an example, is simply an energetic process which each one forms, but its interaction is primarily at an energetic level. Is this beginning to make sense?

Howard: Very much so. I'd like to look, if we can, at each one of these individually to understand them better, and also to understand how they interact with each other, and with Gaia. Can we begin with Air? What can you tell me about the Air Element?

Samantha: Air is a primary sustenance for biological life. It carries nutrients, allows life systems to function, and when withheld, what you know as life systems will perish. The Air energies are given through what you know as the chemical makeup of air: the oxygen, hydrogen, primarily of course of oxygen, and the exchange carbon dioxide. The energies have taken the form of the chemicals that create Air. All life and all support systems on Gaia at this point have some level of consciousness in order to perform, to make decisions, to take direction, as opposed to purely mechanical. Your scientists' and human understanding at this point to some degree have a very limited view of the element, for example, of oxygen. However, as your sciences and your consciousness expand, you will discover that it is a consciousness and energy, a chemical of great variance and possibilities, but in very narrow, shaded nuance form, these differences.

Howard: Yes, it's difficult for me to understand how a chemical element can have different nuances.

Samantha: A chemical element is also energy. Therefore, its frequencies can be modulated. Those modulations are done, completed at a very minute level, undiscernible to the Hu-Mon instruments and understanding at this point. Is this more clear?

Howard: Yes, but these nuances that are not detectable to science – these are energetic nuances, or are they atomic structure nuances, or what?

Samantha: Energetic would be the best way to describe. This issue I believe here, Howard, is that in an attempt to honor your question and explain, we are in an area that requires you to look beyond form, concreteness, definition. All of Creation is energy which is the best word you have to explain the essence. And therefore, it is continually malleable, controlled by appropriate devices, ... no, instructions, ... cannot find a word except owners, but that is not appropriate. So as you begin to develop intellectually and ascend the energies, vibration levels, some of these things will be known to you. However, now they cause conflict with your ability to comprehend because it is beyond your current belief system. Please just continue to understand that all is life, all is energy.

Howard: I do understand that. Thank you. The Fire Element – what can you tell me about the Fire Element? Is that similar in nature to the energies of Air and Earth?

Samantha: It is, yes. It is slightly different because it is not absolutely required for existence. In the early form heat was necessary to keep life alive for humans, and fire was an answer to that issue. And as Earth developed, Fire was also able to play a role working with the Plant Kingdom, for example, where some species require a burning, a death of sorts, in order to live again. And some of the chemicals from that process also interact with the Earth Element. So Fire is somewhat specialized. Air is not able in and of itself to be destructive, and Earth, the dirt, in and of itself is not necessarily destructive. Water, while it can destroy civilizations, it is not intentionally destructive. However, Fire can be used deliberately and with intention for destruction. Therefore, it is monitored very closely. It is a complex element, in that Fire was seen as a solution to several small problems, such as heat for Hu-Mons, and growth control for some plants as they evolved.

Howard: Was the development of human civilization in jeopardy without the introduction of Fire?

Samantha: Yes, because there were places on Earth where the cold during part of the cycle you call a year would have killed these people, would have resulted in their destruction. Remember that Hu-Mon life began in several places on the planet, and even in warmer climates at night, it can become cold. Therefore, warmth is needed to maintain and balance the body temperature required for life.

Howard: Thank you. These four elements – Air, Earth, Fire and Water – they mutually support each other through their interactions...

Samantha: Yes, as necessary and as required.

Howard: How do these elements interact with each other and with Gaia, the consciousness of Earth?

Samantha: Gaia's consciousness is like the Control Center. She provides the major energy directive, support, translated in some ways,.... Excuse me, let me explain. Gaia's energy can be directly transmitted to life such as Hu-Mons; it can also be filtered through the Elements we have been discussing.

Howard: Gaia's consciousness provides directions to the Elemental Kingdom for support of plant life, animal life, human life. Can humans interact in the same way or in the reverse way?

Samantha: Yes. We need to go back. All is energy. Energy operates at nuance of levels. At some level which is not apparent to human understanding, all systems interact. Human systems interact with Air systems. We breathe the air, and in that transaction, there is an intelligence explain (sic), conversation, discussion of how that is to happen. That is the best way I can explain what happens, but it is not knowable to Hu-Mon consciousness at this point.

Howard: Now, there's another aspect of our discussion of the Elementals that I'd like to discuss, and that's names. We humans need names for everything, and we have come up with, or created, the names of the Air energies, if you will, as Sylphs. Are there any other forms that Sylphs are intuited as or noticed, or experienced as? Is there a form to the Sylph, or is it just an energy of ....

Samantha: It is an energy, it is an imaginatary (sic) product from the Hu-Mon's attempt to explain what they do not understand at that time and space level.

Howard: But they accurately came up with the four different Elemental energies....

Samantha: Yes, by observing what maintained life and what did not, what encouraged growth and what did not.

Howard: Human imagination is just wonderful! They come up with all different kinds of images of beings that represent these energies, for instance, the Earth Elemental Gnomes and Elves and Fairies. Is there any true basis for these individual differences between these energies are manifested as? Did these Gnomes actually exist, or are they just individual frequencies of the Earth energy according to somebody's imagination?

Samantha: There were for a while, as life developed, these mutated life forms in the sense that the pathway to the human, to the advanced form of life known as human, took several different directions, and as Gaia and Terra and Earth experimented with ways of creating life, some of these, for short times, existed and therefore entered human mythology. However, they are not directly associated with the Elemental Kingdom as such in talking about earth, dirt, as a sustaining element. Does this help?

Howard: I think so. Fairies, for example. Why were they created, or the idea of fairies? What benefit did the idea of Fairies serve?

Samantha: Fairies were an interpretation of light transmissions coming to Earth to assist and increase the speed at which life was developing. They are purely mythological, but have their foundation in energy transmissions that became visible by the early Hu-Mon.

Howard: Early humans, early beings actually saw these light transmissions?

Samantha: Yes.

Howard: What about the opposite – the Gnomes.

Samantha: Again, they came out of a more grounded experiment of life form, more solid than a light transmission. It was part of the overall plan to experiment on Earth with viable ways of creating an evolutionary life form, but the chemical makeup was not sufficient, nor the ability to move beyond lower level frequencies, consciousness.

Howard: Yes. What about Elves? Are they in the same category?

Samantha: More in the Fairy category. Again, mythological, more sophisticated in the interpretation of what was seen and stories transmitted. Elves are like Fairies in that they are mythological beings, imaginary...

Howard: Gnomes, however, did physically exist?

Samantha: For a very short period, yes, until it was deemed they would not be suitable for further evolution.

Howard: OK. And what about the Fire Element, those beings that are normally called Salamanders. Why was the representative form for that element called a Salamander?

Samantha: That was a human interpretation that is not knowable.

Howard: So the Akashic Record has no reason for it – it's just a human invention?

Samantha: Yes. The Salamander is an animal that can grow, change itself a bit. Fire can come from a small spark and regrow. It may have been that pathway that led humans to identify the Salamander. The Salamander has regenerative properties. However, the energy that the Salamander expends in regenerating body parts reduces its ability to grow intellectually, to grow in other areas and complexity. Regeneration is a highly complex process.

Howard: Thank you! Now the fourth element, Water. Does the Akashic Record have any information about what an Undine is?

Samantha: Only that water takes the form of its container, and therefore, identifying a specific form to its representative would be difficult. The Undine is the mythological representation of this element which is difficult to put into a single form without major process such as ice or steam. It can take a form, but it does not hold a form. So it is difficult to assign it a representation. There again, this is coming from deep human history, perhaps at another time we could delve, but it is deep in the history of human development, and to be honest, Howard, what purpose would it serve you to go further into those areas? It is not our intention to diminish the importance of the mythology surrounding the Elemental Kingdom. It is of vital importance in the early development of humans and culture. However, humans tend to cling to outmoded ideas at inappropriate times, and do not always understand the need to move forward without hanging on to outmoded ideas. This does not mean there is not value in some of these ideas, only that they need to be readdressed, updated to some degree, with current understanding. So we do not mean to diminish the importance or relevance, only to say that the purpose at this point is to enhance ascension, moving to a time when we hope humanity will be generally happier and a citizen of the Galaxy. We are eager for this to happen, we are excited, to use a human emotion, and do not want to trample or step on pieces of human, for it all has played a part in moving the human concept forward, the human imagination, development, intellectual growth forward. Does this make sense?

Howard: Yes, I understand. I do appreciate the conversation that we've had today, Samantha, significant help. It's always a joy to talk with you. We will be with you again, but for now, adieu. And Samantha, Shirella, thank you for your presence as well, and you're released to go about your own activities. Pleasant day to you both. *(Pause)* Emma, just relax deeper and deeper. Wonderful. And Emma, when you're ready, return to full conscious awareness in the best and most appropriate way for you. *(Pause)* Hi again!

Emma: *(Laughing)* Oh, the places we go!

* * *

Case Study 2:

SJ-14: The Elemental Kingdom August 1, 2014 – Directed by Howard Batie

Subject: "Karen" Subject's Higher Self: "Anaka" Subject's Guide: "Joshua"

Howard: Good. Joshua, I would like you to access the Akashic Record and tell me what you can about the Elemental Kingdom on Earth, of what is it composed, and what are its interactions and functions with not only humans, but also with Gaia, the consciousness of Mother Earth. Let's begin with the structure of the Elemental Kingdom. As I understand it, the elements within the Elemental Kingdom are Earth, Air, Fire and Water. Are there any additional elements that need to be considered?

Joshua:	No, they are all representations of the energy of Gaia, the different forms of the base energy of Gaia, or representation or outflow.
Howard:	Maybe it would be helpful to have you describe the characteristics of that energy of Gaia.
Joshua:	OK. One by one. The energies are of different density and need different representatives because of that density, the air energy being the lightest and all-encompassing, the earth energy is the densest but the most alive as far as intensity of energy. Air Element is a light energy and flows through more easily than earth energy. Each works with each other. Earth energy is from the center of Gaia and comes through the more physical and dense trees and plants and dirt and hard rocks.
Howard:	Those are the Plant and Mineral Kingdoms.
Joshua:	But they are tied together. Earth energy is strongest in those Kingdoms. Air energies are strongest in lighter spirits. Water energies are of course in the oceans and the waves and the creeks and the rivers. I see them all interchanging and interblending, each representing parts of the whole. Fire energy is a fast energy, not a hot energy. It represents change and forward movement and growth. When fire affects the Earth by volcanoes or forest fires, there is great change. When Man discovers and uses fire, there is great change. So the Fire Elemental is tied to change and growth and expansion.
Howard:	Now we have a representation of the Fire Element of Gaia called the Salamander. Why was the Salamander chosen as the representation for the Fire Element?
Joshua:	Because it is an animal that represents change well. It changes throughout its life and is elementally tied to where it lives. It depends upon its environment and changes the environment that it lives in, and the environment that it lives in changes it as well. Its color depends on where it lives, its size depends, and that's how all of life is, but the Salamander is the best representation to the humans that decided that, of that change itself. The Salamander is there because people chose it to represent that.
Howard:	Well, our representation for the elemental portion of air is a Sprite. What is a Sprite and why was it chosen? How does it function?
Joshua:	Air elemental represents the lightness, the energy field in which we take in energy and move energy out into the world around us. And Sprites are... I see them like light fairies. Sometimes you see the Orbs in photos – those are like Sprites, they're energy 'clumps' and energy beings, so to speak, that are attracted to areas where there is a lot of energy in the air and the energy that is around us that is light and bright and full of energy that is the breath of life, the Om of life, the energy of the air, the oxygen that we breathe that keeps us alive, that is in the air. The Sprites are attracted to, and spend time with, and help with those energies that surround the parts of the Earth that are light and tuned to our inner breath and our outer light.
Howard:	And Orbs are the representation of the Air Element?
Joshua:	They are part of it; they're not Sprites, but they are similar to Sprites. I see Sprites more like little star lights, they are little light creatures that send out light energy, and Orbs are more visibly round energy. Sprites are more like a little star. They give off light and they give off air energy. They work with the air energy. They help us to connect with the air energy by gathering around us and concentrating the air energy into our concentration. They assist with our focus. Their energy assists our energy to help us to focus on that energy that comes in with the breath and goes out with our light.
Howard:	Do the Sprites or the Air Elements interact with the consciousness of humans?

Joshua: They are aware of our energy. They feel our energy. They feel our movement. Say when you meditate and you really get that circle going where you're soaking in energy and putting out energy and you're moving energy within yourself, the Sprites get attracted to that, and they feel that, and they surround you, and the energy moves in and out through them as it moves in and out through you. They give you energy and they gain energy from you, so they assist you. Any time you open yourself up to nature, like when you're in the mountains and the air is very clear, they feel you stronger. In the city, it's hard to feel you because of the denseness of the air. So the more you're in air that's in the open, the more free and closer they can be to you.

Howard: Do the Sprites interact at all with the consciousness of the Earth, with Gaia?

Joshua: They are part of it! We are part of Gaia's consciousness. There's so many different forms... Gaia's consciousness is in and through us, yet separate from us, so we are a part of her, yet separate – just like Creator. It's part of all of us being One, yet being separate, and Sprites are part of that.

Howard: All right. Do the Sprites interact at all with the Earth Element, the Water Element, and the Salamanders?

Joshua: I see them all side by side, they all work together, like when we hold hands and meditate for someone, so we are individually working our energy together and becoming stronger, so each works side by side with the others.

Howard: And when they combine, what is the energy of all four of them together?

Joshua: The energy of Gaia as a whole. The energy of purity and totality.

Howard: What functions or responsibilities does the Water Element representation provide?

Joshua: The connection to Earth as the planet that she is – she's a water planet. I think why I mentioned leaves as part of the water is I saw a leaf dripping water. Water passes through each and all of us, and is crucial for all survival on our Earth, and Mother Earth's survival as well. Water is the element that all things can move into and change within and move back out of and be even better if you allow that energy to get into you. It flows within you, it's what is in each of our cells that allows the movement and the openness of each cell; it's that substance within which all else moves. It provides that medium for transference of energy.

Howard: Now the elemental representation is call an Undine. Is there a form or a characteristic or a shape of an Undine?

Joshua: I'm seeing a shape more of a twisty slug, a very wet animal that depends a lot on the moisture around it to maintain its life. It's very beautiful and colorful and quiet and calm; it's not a creature that pushes itself onto the world, but rather lets the world come into it and absorb into it and be affecting it. And therefore it becomes that creature that's affected by all that's around it.

Howard: OK. Does this Water Element representation interact directly with the Earth Element?

Joshua: More side by side again. They're there together and they share energy together and they work together and water flows throughout the Earth to help the Earth do whatever it needs to do, to move food and organisms and waste out of organisms, yet they stay side by side as they work together.

Howard: All right. Does the Water Element interact directly with the Air Element?

Joshua: It's the same. There is air in water as well in the form of molecules, and they are changed by the water that they are in, and the water is changed by them being there, so they are working side by side, but together.

Howard:	Good. Now what is the interaction like between the Water Element and the Fire Element?
Joshua:	They stand side by side, but when they affect each other, they change each other a lot more greatly than water and the other elements. Fire can boil water or dry water up, and water can extinguish fire or it can move fire, so they affect each other really strongly, but they work side by side, and they both need each other.
Howard:	Their actions have to be maintained in a balance, don't they? Is this balancing done consciously?
Joshua:	It can be done consciously when they are affecting each other. They stay in balance by nature. Gaia's energy keeps all the elements in balance with each other, but sometimes one or the other may overcome, like water may overcome fire and fire may overcome water, but then Earth brings it all back into balance, so there's constant movement and constant change, and always Gaia tries to bring it back into balance, and those Elementals help that to happen. They help Earth keep her balance, and they help us keep our balance upon Earth as part of Gaia. You can tap into their energy and use their energy to help you become balanced as part of Gaia, to communicate with those Elementals. Not many can, but some can, and when they communicate with the Elementals, they gain knowledge from the Elementals.
Howard:	All right. If I were to develop the ability to communicate directly with, say the Earth Element, what other new ability would I have that I do not have now?
Joshua:	You'd have a closer communication with Gaia herself, you might begin to hear her voice better, not just feel her, because she has a voice!
Howard:	And if I learned to communicate with the Air Element, how would I change?
Joshua:	You would feel closer to all the other Elementals, as that lightness helps you move through all the life kingdoms here on Earth. It's a way of touching all the other Elementals in a very light way as if you're Air yourself.
Howard:	Would it be necessary to learn how to communicate with the Air Element before I learned to communicate with any of the others? You mentioned that this communication flows through the Air Element. Is that a necessary....
Joshua:	It's more helpful, it's the easiest point in because the Air Elemental is the lightest Elemental and it's got the biggest spaces for your spirit to move into versus denser space. It's the easiest for you to move into and from there communicate with the rest.
Howard:	And what kind of activities would I participate in to develop that ability to communicate with the Air Element?
Joshua:	Through meditations and through moving into your own spiritual space, you get into a space where you sort of leave the physicality behind and your spirit is free to explore that.
Howard:	Is that similar to the Spiritual Area that Joshua is in now?
Joshua:	Yes. Yes, similar but part of Earth.
Howard:	All right, explain that more.
Joshua:	Joshua... I live in a world of a different dimension; as a spirit I move through different dimensions and different spirit worlds....
Howard:	Is this Anaka talking, or is this Joshua?
Anaka:	I'm moving back and forth; let me become Joshua.
Joshua:	I'm Joshua, I'm spiritual, and I'm on Earth with Anaka, who is also spiritual but is living in Karen, and Karen is a crucial part of Gaia, and the Elementals are a physical and

spiritual part of Gaia. And as Joshua, I can contact the spiritual part of the Elementals, and be aware of and see them, but I can't feel them and I can't feel the effects of what they do as, say, Anaka and the physical beings on the Earth, can. So there's a difference in dimensions, so to speak, that Elementals are part of Earth. They are a dimension of Earth, but they're still all a part of Earth, and Earth is in its own dimensional realms, and there are many other dimensional realms that Earth can reach out and touch and feel and be a part of, but not be a physical part of yet. And as Joshua I can move in and out of this. Anaka can't yet until she becomes completely spiritual. And that would happen either by ascension or death, whichever happens first. Did that help with the difference?

Howard: Yes! Yes it does. Now we haven't really investigated the Earth Element yet. The Earth Element you said was more solid, more dense. The forms of representation that we use know for the Earth Element are little gnomes, elves and fairies. Are these beings real, or are they just representations for those energies?

Joshua: It's funny that you ask it that way because a representation can be real. So it's not a representation OR real, but they're real, but very rarely seen, and they're all basically the same sort of a being, but they look a little different in different forms. Leprechauns are the same, but it's just where you are on Earth when you become aware of this entity that is completely dependent upon the energy of the Earth upon which it lives. Fairies and gnomes and leprechauns are all tied to living in rocks and living in forests so they're all tied to what the physicality of what the Earth is, and that physicality is the representation of Gaia's spirit. So it's very real, but how you perceive it and how sensitive you are to it depends on whether you can see it and feel it, but it's there and they are actual beings that are tied to Earth spirit that we can be sensitive to and become aware of when we can open our spirit enough to be sensitive to Gaia's spirit.

Howard: All right! Good. Now are the different forms of representation such as gnomes and leprechauns, are they culturally dependent? In other words, one part of the world would see that same being as a leprechaun or in another part of the world, that culture would see or feel the representation of a gnome?

Joshua: Yes. Or a fairy or any kind of a.... In a more animal spirit culture like South America and Indonesia, those are represented by animal spirits because those are the spirits that those people see closest to the Earth. But it's all Earth, it's all those kind of creatures who are completely dependent on the spirit of Gaia and are represented by the spirit of Gaia. And humans have put their own exterior things like leprechauns. Humans tend to change their spirit contacts that they get into forms they understand, so they see them as an omen that means something that they can interpret. Sometimes it's just that they become contacted by something that they don't understand. As we all tap into our own abilities to concentrate on love and light, and the positive things in our life, we will become more and more open to all the spirituality that is everything around us, and that spirituality comes through each of those Elementals. So we will all begin to feel and see many more parts of Gaia and parts of the energy of us all as we open ourselves up. And this book and all these beings, not just humans but other beings on Earth that are becoming more open and more clear about all that is going on about Mother Gaia and with the energies together, as all that becomes more available to us the more that we let ourselves open up to the Elementals and everything around us.

Howard: Good! You mentioned all this information becoming available to humans and others. What are the others that this information is being made available to?

Joshua: There are other intelligent species on Earth that humans have not yet opened to. The Cetaceans, we know, are intelligent, but don't know how to communicate with yet, other mammals that we will begin to understand better that live life differently than we live but will still communicate with us. And soon when we begin to contact our Star Brothers and Sisters; that will open up huge new waves of communication between all the energies on Earth and away from Earth. Humans aren't the only beings that can understand this and tap into it and touch it. All can, other animals can, but they don't really need to. They are content in the energies that they live in, and they don't have that curiosity to explore more. They are content to be a part of Gaia's energies in the way that they already are for the most part. There are others with us that we perceive as humans who have more than human in them. Most of us have what we would call extra-terrestrial or beings from places other than earth whose DNA is a part of us, and we haven't recognized that, but those strands of DNA that course through humans, course through many of the creatures that ended up existing on Earth because they were put into our DNA in an early enough part of our development that it spread to other creatures as well. There are more; there are those among us who have... we all have a little bit, there are those who have come in this lifetime because they are needed here who have more ... You and I, Howard, I see that you and I have more of the energy of that DNA in us than some other people do. So there are those with us who don't have very much ET DNA and there are some who have a lot, and there are some with a lot more than us.

Howard: From what world does this other DNA come from?

Joshua: Many. Some Sirian and Pleiadian and others we know, and some we don't know. They are here and they have come as humans, but they are finding it easier to tap into the energies because they have the codes already when they come. We've had to download the codes and receive the codes, but they came with the codes already, like the new Star Children they talk about. They come all ready. They were born as humans, but they had already evolved and moved into a spirit space where they didn't have to return to learn more lessons because they felt they knew what they could learn on Earth. But there was a call for people and beings who already had graduated, who already learned the lessons to move forward spiritually and were very strong therefore in their ability to work with energies and helping others in learning to work with energies. Those needed to come back to Earth to help everyone because now this accelerated growth into ascension is happening, and because of that there were so many souls that needed to come forward that they needed a lot of people to help that to happen. And that's why those people came here now.

Howard: And do these beings come with any other purpose than accelerating our ascension, or do they bring specific information or technology or organizational abilities?

Joshua: Well, each has their own talents to do any of those things, or some of those things, but the main purpose of those who came to assist is to open up energy channels for those who were here and didn't have knowledge yet of how to find their way. So that's why they are called Wayshowers. They are here, like you are Howard, to say, "This is here, this is what's available and this is what you can find." And when they see that and know it's there, they will seek it. And they need help to see that, and that's why the Wayshowers are here – to show that it's there.

Howard: Good. Thank you very much, Joshua. Do you have anything else you'd like to add?

Joshua: No. Just my thanks, that is all. I am here to help.

Howard: All right. Do you have a message for Anaka?

Joshua: Just to stay the course and to keep learning and to go forward. She is!

Howard: Wonderful! Thank you for coming today, Joshua, and with love and gratitude you are released to go about your own activities, and we will meet again. Now Anaka, just take a deep breath, rest and relax. And I want you to record all the impressions, all the images and information that you've received here today. Record it in your own time-line, your own Akashic Record, your own record of growth, as well as that of your physical incarnation at this time. And now, Anaka, let's return to the Spiritual Area where we met, and thank you for coming as well. Now I want you to place your attention on your physical body resting safely and comfortably there in the planes below. And when you're ready, just return to your physical body and your conscious mind, integrating all the information and the images that you've received here today. And when you've fully integrated your spiritual awareness with your physical body and your conscious awareness, just let me know. *(Pause)*

Karen: OK.

Howard: Wonderful! Thank you. Now, when you're ready, emerge yourself from self-hypnosis using the most beneficial method for you at this time. And when you emerge yourself, take a deep breath, open your eyes, emerge yourself from self-hypnosis and return to full consciousness awareness. Go ahead and do that now. *(Pause)* Welcome back!

Karen: Hi!

Spiritual Journey 15 – The Ascension of Gaia.
In this and previous Spiritual Journeys sessions it was learned that "Terra," the initial consciousness of Earth, was purposely limited and could support spiritual growth of evolutionary life forms only up to the Neanderthal stage, 3rd dimensional level of consciousness, that of duality and polarity. At that point, it was determined that the Earth Experiment should be continued with a more evolved planetary consciousness that could support and nurture advanced human life forms capable of an expanded individual spiritual awareness; therefore, the limitations to Terra's consciousness were removed, allowing her to become Gaia, the consciousness that could support life forms up to and including the 5th dimension level of consciousness, and the more advanced human life forms of Homo Sapiens were then subsequently seeded on Earth.

Initially, Gaia was limited to 5th dimensional level consciousness, where the potential for Unity and Oneness of purpose replaced Duality and Polarity, and a few individuals have attained that level of consciousness where cooperation replaced competition and unity replaced duality in all aspects of their thinking and in their life. However, it was a rocky road with very slow progress for the collective human consciousness, and mankind nearly extinguished itself with its nuclear experiments in the last century. However, since the late 1980's, the spiritual awakening in the collective psyche of humanity signaled that additional help and assistance was appropriate and should be provided to Gaia and her inhabitants in the form of additional higher vibrational energies from a variety of extraterrestrial sources, including the Sun.

So Planet Earth has been provided with the expanded consciousness of Gaia, and that consciousness has now been opened to allow continued evolution of Earth life forms, including humanity, up to the twelfth dimensional level of consciousness and awareness. We are told that individual elements of humanity are now at the third, fourth and fifth levels of consciousness, so there's plenty of work to do individually and collectively, and plenty of room to grow. That is the part that is up to us to do, and it's also up to us to choose how long it takes us to do that.

Process:
1. Client moves into her Spiritual Area and does the three things she must always do each time she rises up into her Spiritual Area.
2. Client's Higher Self (CHS) asks her Guide, "Is it permissible to access the Akashic Record for the purpose of understanding the ascension process that Gaia is now in, and that we are also individually and collectively proceeding with?"
3. If not, the client is emerged from self-hypnosis.
4. CHS asks for the specific information or answers to their questions.
5. Client returns to her cocoon and returns to full conscious awareness.

Case Study 1:
SJ-15: The Ascension of Gaia   May 28, 2014 – Directed by Howard Batie
Subject: "Emma"   Subject's Higher Self: "Shirella   Subject's Guide: "Samantha"
      Howard's Higher Self: "Artoomid"   Howard's Guide: "Michael"

In the following session, my hypnotized client (Emma) first contacted her Higher Self (Shirella) and Spirit Guide (Samantha), and then I asked my own Higher Self (Artoomid) and my Spirit Guide (Michael) to come forward as well and provide answers to my questions through Emma. My only direction to each was that, if a being whom I had not been speaking with before wanted to provide additional information, they would first identify who was speaking and from whom the information was coming. All four agreed readily, and the session proceeded quite smoothly with this understanding.

Howard: Thank you. Now, Artoomid, I would like your permission, and Michael, your permission as well, to review the Akashic Record of Gaia, the Akashic Record of Mother Earth, and to understand the means of evolution, the system of ascension, the development of Gaia from third-dimensional consciousness, which I believe has been called Terra, to Gaia. I would like to know more about the Ascension Process that is on-going on Earth within Gaia. If there's anything you could tell me about that, I would be very grateful.

Artoomid: Thank you. It is a long story and process – the development of Terra, now Gaia, and of the beautiful Planet Earth – and we will do our best to explain it. As you know, it was determined that there needed to be a planet dedicated to spiritual ascension. It is a unique experience to have a planet to go from what you would call rock matter to the ephemeral, to the spirit life.

Howard: You say this is a unique experience. Is it unique in this galaxy only?

Artoomid: In your Universe in this manner, yes. Again, delineation of certain types of experiences are difficult, Howard, to explain to you. Please consider nuance, small changes. Other planets may have had pieces of rock matter (rise) to ascension, but without the incorporation of beings as well, or those were done separately. This experience in this universe is of a total ascension of all beings and all life forms simultaneously, growing in spiritual dimension and strength. So it is a unifying experience. If the Hu-Mon can connect with the growth of Gaia, then the two can support (each other) because they are the same process in different experiences. Gaia is an entity unto herself, a planetary consciousness, but her pathway to full ascension is parallel to that of the Hu-Mon, awakening, coming from muck into a fully conscious spiritual being. Is that more clear?

Howard: Yes. Can you compare the nature and characteristics, in terms of consciousness, compare Terra and Gaia.

Shirella: Yes. Howard, this is Shirella. Artoomid requests a break.

Howard: All right. Shirella, can you answer the question?

Shirella: Yes, I can. Gaia started in rock matter and was given what you call Earth, and when she was given consciousness, it was in a base form, limited, as a starting point and as an experiment, test, and was known there as Terra... do you remember in our conversation about plants, that plants have a limited consciousness? It is a similar thing, and so Terra... Artoomid wishes to take over again.

Howard: Please do.

Artoomid: This is Artoomid. Excuse me, Howard, I do not do this often. And while it is a very interesting process, it sometimes confuses me. And so Planet Earth was given the beginning consciousness of Terra. This was her soul consciousness, Terra, and it was during that time that we then allowed and agreed to the formation of the muck (*Note: this is reference to the chemical amino acids that formed the initial building blocks of life that eventually evolved into soulless life forms up through the amoeba on Earth*) and the beginnings of life forms on Earth, now Terra. So Earth is the name we use for the rock planet; Terra is the name for the beginning consciousness, combined with Earth, and she has since evolved into Gaia...

Howard: How did that evolution into Gaia take place? Was there any additional growth required from external sources, or did she do that on her own?

Artoomid: The easiest way to explain it to you is that we removed the sealing from her consciousness when it became apparent that consciousness and rock matter could coexist, continue and grow, and life could be formed in one way or another. And then when we re-seeded with the New Hu-Mon, we could not limit the consciousness of Terra. You see, first of all, Howard, let me explain that The One That Is All experiments, not to the detriment, but to the better. And so it was time to experiment, in your language, with a planet with consciousness and life all ascending at one time. But because it was a new experience for The One That Is All, it needed to be done slowly and with great observation. And so, at the time that the Hu-Mon was determined ready for an expanded consciousness, the meaningless life – meaning that without a soul on Earth – needed not to continue, and that soul life would be given to Earth that automatically meant growth in a spiritual sense. And it would not be possible for that to happen if Terra continued as a limited consciousness.

Howard: The life forms that developed within the limited consciousness of Terra – did that include humanoid life forms?

Artoomid: Yes – the branches that did not develop. Do you understand?

Howard: You mean like Neanderthals?

Artoomid: Yes. It was determined that rock-matter Earth could be a beautiful experience in and of itself with a variety of environments, and that led then to the decision, as well as the other reasons, to have a soul consciousness given to Earth and its beings...

Howard: You mean a higher soul consciousness than Terra?

Artoomid: Yes. Yes. So simultaneously, the soul consciousness of life forms, including Hu-Mons, along with the expansion, that consciousness was limited as Terra. And when it became necessary to raise, and agreed upon, then that limitation was removed and Gaia came forth. And because Gaia was then fully conscious and fully capable of further spiritual growth and development of her own, she could support life to do the same.

Howard: And from that point, did the New Hu-Mon coexist with the previous 'editions' if you will?

Artoomid: For a while. For a... Your time language is so confusing sometimes. How do you do it, Howard? ... For a while. Yes. They were simultaneous, but however, the non-conscious soulless beings were destined not to continue. Once Earth was given Gaia, they necessarily needed to no longer exist, because eventually, all life forms on Earth would have soul consciousness – that is the Law.

Howard: And that veil of forgetting has continued up until very recently, and even including now. So does this veil of forgetting become thinner and thinner, or does it just disappear? How is the limitation going to be removed from our awareness?

Artoomid: Your word "thinner" is in essence appropriate; however, thinner as a dissolving of a mist – that perhaps is a better analogy. It is a dissolving, it is a mist clearing.

Howard: And when this mist clears or begins to dissolve, what are the additional capabilities or characteristics of the human?

Artoomid: Those that you have explored and are beginning to understand in the higher dimensions – telepathic communications, a community sense, a disinterest in the material for material's sake, a different kind of travel and movement from one place to another. Again, understand that some of these I am narrowing a bit to your concepts, because it is not possible, even for one as enlightened as you, to fully understand.

Howard: So it's an expansion of our awareness, of our comprehension and our mental or spiritual abilities, telepathy, teleportation...?

Artoomid: Yes. Howard, this is difficult, but please understand that you are doing your best to move beyond that which, by the nature of your being, a Hu-Mon, is unable to fully comprehend, and so we find ways to try, within your conceptual abilities, to share what is ahead. As you grow in spiritual strength into these dimensions you have defined, and as you are able to spend more time in those dimensions, some of the structure that is required for you to understand will begin to also dissolve, and you will experience rather than define. Does that make sense?

Howard: Perfectly! It's a movement from intellectually conceptualizing something to being it.

Artoomid: Correct! Hu-Mons have limited ability to experience without immediately needing to classify and define. Your linear mind was there for a good purpose, but then became used more like a weapon, a control, and now it is taking extra strength, as you have heard, to break that apart. And I use it that way because the third dimension has become very solid in a sense, wrapped around the soul and the essence of each being, has encapsulated it, and it must be broken open. And so experience without the need to define and classify is a new experience.

Howard: Yes. And that is one of the things that I'm trying to let people become aware of – that they can experience this through at least the methodology that I'm developing now.

Artoomid: Yes. And one reason we are all excited about The Project is that you are moving in that direction of the experience, and then the trickiest part is to find a way to share those experiences without the ego limitations.

Howard: I understand that. Michael, can you assist Artoomid?

Michael: One of the issues of the awakening for the human, as we have said before, is the ability to share its experience in a safe, supportive manner. Perhaps one thing you could ask and discuss with your friends who are helping you is, would such conversations be of benefit? We are at a loss, Howard, in a sense at your level of how best to work with the ego and expansion. We are feeling, again, limitation here in defining for you what we are experiencing and feeling. There is a Oneness that comes with spiritual development that is rarely felt, I believe, by the human. You see, the other is we have been talking about the evolution of Gaia, and as she proceeds, and she is proceeding rapidly as is her nature, there will be energies loosened and the dissolving of mist that may make this sharing more possible in the future. Perhaps, Howard, we have confused... the sharing is to come. But perhaps we have misaligned because we do not work with time often.

Howard: Thank you. Now, I know that it has been a long and very productive conversation, and I want to thank everyone for being here from the bottom of my heart with gratitude for your presence here today Michael, Artoomid, Samantha, Shirella, and Emma and Howard, your conscious aspects as well.

Michael: This is quite the party group, is it not, Howard?

Howard: Yes, it is! Thank you all for coming. And unless someone has something else pertinent, I believe it would be good to let Emma rest and conclude this session. Does anyone else want to say anything else pertinent to the topics that have been raised today?

Samantha:	Samantha is speaking. She only wishes to say to you, Howard, to be patient and continue the work, for it is evolving and going well. And if we have misled you, it is only because it is difficult to communicate what we feel and know to a more limited construct. And if you have questions, Shirella and Emma are available, as am I, Michael, and Artoomid, at any time.
Howard:	Thank you! I'm going to take you up on that!
Samantha:	You are working, whether you are fully consciously aware or not, in a very complicated situation of being given information from a much expanded point of view, and we are asking the nearly impossible task of having you communicate it in a much more limited construct.
Howard:	I do understand that, and I thank you for your continued support, and the support of all the scribes and helpers that are helping to keep me on the straight and narrow, to make that translation as accurate as possible.
Shirella:	It will develop, Howard, and pardon me, but it may not always be so straight.
Howard:	Is this Michael?
Shirella:	No, this is Shirella. I have been asked to speak because I can use humor perhaps more easily. It may not always be so straight and narrow, Howard, but it will be valid.
Howard:	All right! Thank you.
Shirella:	They are laughing! I asked to tell you that because... well, it's fun!
Howard:	Good! Thank you for your presence today, each and every one...
Shirella:	And again, there are many observing who wish to honor you and add their best wishes in the form of positive, supportive energy.
Howard:	Thank you! Always open to positive support! Heaven knows, we need it!
Shirella:	Heaven does know! *(Laughs)* I have learned, Howard, it is fun to play with language with you.
Howard:	Oh, yes! I enjoy words!
Shirella:	Goodbye, Howard.
Howard:	Goodbye for now. Shirella, Samantha, Michael and Artoomid – you're now released to go about your own activities. Thank you so much for coming and sharing today, and we'll be in touch again. Goodbye for now. *(Pause)* Emma, when you're ready, just return to full conscious awareness using the most beneficial method that you know that is appropriate for you, and we can join our friends another day.

* * *

Case Study 2:
SJ-15: The Ascension of Gaia   June 25, 2014 – Directed by Howard Batie
Subject: "Emma"   Subject's Higher Self: "Shirella"   Subject's Guide: "Samantha"
Howard's Higher Self: "Artoomid"   Howard's Guide: "Michael"

Howard:	Thank you, Samantha, for coming today. We value your presence here, too. Now I also call for my Higher Self, Artoomid, to be present, and I invite also my Guide, Michael to join us this afternoon.
Shirella:	Yes. They are welcome.

Howard: Wonderful! I would like to address Michael. Michael, is it appropriate for us to call on
               St. Germain to kind of get an update, a status on the ascension process that we all and
               Gaia are going through?

Michael: Yes, it is.

Howard: Wonderful. I call on St. Germain to be here with us today. Join our Squad!

St. Germain: He is here.

Howard: Good. And who is this speaking?

St. Germain: This is St. Germain.

Howard: Thank you very much for coming, St. Germain.

St. Germain: It is my privilege.

Howard: I would like to ask, what can you tell us about the current state of Gaia's ascension,
               where she is in her progress, and also where humanity in general is in their collective
               ascension process. What can you tell us about that?

St. Germain: Gaia is ascending according to the plan. All is well with Gaia. Hu-Mons are also
               ascending according to plans with some interruptions, some slownesses, but all in all
               are making progress. We are hoping to help that process now that Gaia is at the 12th
               Dimension. We are hoping to help accelerate the Hu-Mon ascension process with sup-
               plemental energies and other kinds of assistance from what you call Galactic Beings.
               The Hu-Mons have reached the necessary level that signifies their intention to con-
               tinue to ascend, and with the removal of the Negative One through the recall of Lucifer,
               the process that was interrupted can now proceed, and hopefully at a more accelerated
               pace.

Howard: And what can we do to accelerate that pace?

St. Germain: To continue to be mindful that, in the ascension journey, the individual is spreading
               energy and light and love, and to stay mindful of that process in your daily life. That
               to the best of your ability, be mindful that each encounter is an opportunity to increase
               vibrations, to send light and love to that space. It is a simple process, we think, but it is
               essential in that it stabilizes the energies in a given area, and to encourage at some level
               others to do the same. Is this clear?

Howard: Yes, thank you. You mentioned also that there would be help from our extra-terrestrial
               brothers and sisters. What may we expect – what form of assistance would that take?

St. Germain: They are also helping to increase and spread the ascension energies for the Hu-Mons,
               and helping to increase to a critical mass. There are additional souls and beings on
               planet Earth and within the realm of Gaia who can add energies at a more localized
               level by just being in the area. In the way that humans are asked in each encounter to
               spread light and love, the additional beings on Earth are also doing the same. The addi-
               tional energy we hope will accelerate the process of ascension for those who are work-
               ing so diligently at their own ascension. This is one way in which they are helping.

Howard: Good. Are there other ways?

St. Germain: They are monitoring incoming positive energies, and they are protecting Gaia and
               Earth from incoming negative energies. They are filtering those energies from beings
               who are not yet ready for the ascension process, and they are filtering out negative
               energies for those on Earth who are not yet ready for the ascension process. Your
               Earth is giving off, losing negative energy at an accelerated rate, and without careful
               management, it could contaminate the process. Those energies must be released so
               they can be reformed and reused in a positive way. Negative or positive, it is energy

which must be managed. Therefore, the other beings are assisting in this filtration, and the turning of the negative to positive.

Howard: You mentioned that there are many extra-terrestrial beings on Earth now, helping to manage this energy. Are they localized, or are they uniformly distributed?

St. Germain: It is like the managing of the negative energy – they are everywhere on Earth, but if one particular area needs additional energy, we will add extra beings to that area. They come in an energetic form that is not yet perceivable by the Hu-Mons, except for some who are in a very advanced state of ascension, may in one way or another be aware of the presence, although it may not be visual. We have to be careful about massing too many beings in one area, in that their energies may impact the ascension energies or create a density that allows certain Hu-Mons to see them, or be aware in some way. So that particular program is managed carefully for several reasons. Does this help? Is this making sense?

Howard: Yes. Thank you. And what is your personal role in this management process?

St. Germain: I am the Overseer, I am the one who approves changes. I see the Project from a whole; therefore, I evaluate any changes in the plan for its effect on the entire Project of Gaia's ascension, as well as human and individual soul ascension. It is easy in a Project such as this to become too focused on an area of great need or demanding of energy, and to lose sight of the whole Project. So my principal role is that of guiding any decisions from a, I believe your term is, global perspective, as opposed to just local. I also am in direct communication with the One That Is All to receive energies and guidance for this Project.

Howard: Does the Angelic Kingdom also support this Project in any particular manner or ways?

St. Germain: All of the Angelic Kingdom is involved with specialized roles, and of course the Elohim are there for evaluation and for information about any changes to the forms. They are not as involved as they were in the earlier parts of the Project. But as Hu-Mon's bodies form and change, they advise us for energy shifts and changes to assist that process.

Howard: Good. What can you tell us about the manner in which the body forms are changing?

St. Germain: As you know, new energies are coming in to change the DNA, and the human body is gradually lightening, strengthening for something that is more durable or flexible for its change into something more of a light body. It is difficult to explain, but the body is evolving along with the consciousness.

Howard: Will these changes be demonstrably obvious to scientists?

St. Germain: Eventually, yes, they cannot help but be, but that is down the road, I believe, if we talk about time in your way. It is a slow, regenerative process. First, there will be some notice of illnesses, diseases, malfunctions repairing, a lessening of certain types of illnesses. The visual form change is the last step in this process. You will begin to notice that for some people on the ascension path, their body seems to heal themselves or certain conditions are no longer as troubling, although in your medical field this may not be obvious. However, the person's individual experience will be different. Is this helpful?

Howard: That's very helpful. You mentioned the medical field. Are there going to be changes in the way medicines and pharmaceuticals are procured, produced and delivered?

St. Germain: Absolutely, yes. It is essential. Your pharmaceutical companies are responsible for prolonging certain types of illnesses in order to sell their drugs or in an effort to make money from some of the drugs – they do harm, rather than good, or along with. As the bodies begin to heal and adjust, those types of drugs will not be needed. It is hoped that, with additional energies and assistance, many of those who are not in the ascension process consciously or are understanding the process will be awakened and triggered into activity. However, we cannot continue that process in an unlimited timeframe. It then becomes something of a punishment for those who are ascending quickly, it becomes a negative experience. To prolong the overall ascension process in hopes of awakening more, can only last for so long.

Howard: We've noticed that things are speeding up.

St. Germain: Not only in the sense of the individual process, but the groups and individuals are beginning to come together and therefore increase the energies. The term 'grass-roots movement' serves well here, I think. It's becoming stronger, and although some may appear on the surface to not be enlightened, they are still helping to trigger change. Am I being clear?

Howard: Yes. My impression is that the grass-roots movement pressure is going to be the catalyst for the change, not the top-down direction...

St. Germain: Correct. And some of these movements may appear to be going backwards; however, they are enhancing the change. Once the movement begins, it is difficult to stop, but it can be guided in a different direction.

Howard: Now, St. Germain, you've given a very rosy picture of our prospects for this ascension process...

St. Germain: I hope that is true. It is my intention from my perspective as the Overseer, we are feeling very good about the process.

Howard: Good. Are you going to be in charge of overseeing that ascension process as humanity continues to ascend all the way to the 12th Dimension, or are you going to be assuming additional functions?

St. Germain: At this point, that is undetermined entirely. I will leave the Project when I am no longer needed, and that is unclear at this point. It may be that the Creator will have other jobs for me to do in this realm. But Earth is my first love, and I intend to stay until I know that the entire process is secure. So therefore, I will be here for the near future, and perhaps indefinitely.

Howard: I understand. Thank you very much for that perspective, and I would ask Michael, do you have any additional information that you would like to share – your perspective of the ascension.

Michael: Only to say that we support in the best way that we can, and are also pleased with the progress made. Because of the difficulties currently being faced in many levels of Hu-Mon life, it is easy I would think to feel discouraged; however, the process is well underway, and those of you who are working steadily and in true desire to ascend, are making headway not only for yourselves, but also for those coming along with you or at a slower pace. Do not lose hope, but stay focused and we are pleased, Howard, with the progress you are making with your Project. I know that it will benefit many.

Howard: Thank you, Michael. Now when the ascension process is finally secure without a doubt, what will be the overall effect or impact of this ascension process here with Gaia, the overall effect on the Galaxy and the Universe?

Michael: A great lifting of the energies, the creative energies, the love energies, however you choose to term them, the energies that are coming from this ascension of Gaia are being spread and will continue to do so throughout the Galaxy and the Universe. It has been a great experiment in the impact of ascending, of developing from a basic form of life into that of multi-dimensions. There is great strength that is gathered in that process. There is a positive power and knowing than comes from going through that experience. That strength and power of positive can be taken as an example, a lesson, to support life in other Universes. This is not just for the Hu-Mons, or for Gaia or for the Solar System, but as a turning point, we hope, in the ascension of the Galaxy and the Universe, the continued awakening and growth.

Howard: Thank you very much, Michael.

Michael: It has been my pleasure, Howard.

Howard: Samantha, would you like to add anything from your perspective regarding the ascension process here on Earth?

Samantha: My comments would be at a more Hu-Mon personal perspective, that we are in great, great awe, support and gratitude for what those who are ascending individually are willing to do to help the process. We are aware that there are great sadnesses on the face of the Earth now; there are dangers to individual humans not just physically but in being pulled off even for a short time from the ascension path by what is happening, and we are continually amazed at times at the strength of the individual to resist these negative forces, these bruising forces, distracting, and to continue with a light heart and awareness of the process. We are here to do the best that we can, all that we can to support those who are working through that process and are spreading the lighter side, the light, the love, but we understand it is difficult at times, and so we work to strengthen human resolve to continue, despite the circumstances surrounding this process that might indicate to the contrary.

Howard: Thank you Samantha, thank you Michael, thank you St. Germain – we love you all, and we need your support, we're grateful for it.

Samantha: Howard, I am asked – this is Samantha – I am asked to say to you that we love you and are overjoyed with the progress with the project that you have so willingly taken on. We are glad to see that you can discern places to keep that project from becoming overwhelming. It is not our intention to burden you, and we ask that you continue that process to remember that we are here to support you and guide you in those decisions, and we do not feel that the changes that you are considering are lessening the value of the Project. We are glad to see that you are realigning to keep balance in your life, to keep the joy of the Project in your heart. Please do not hesitate to ask for whatever kind of support and help you need. We are not always able to discern that – human needs sometimes are not clear to us, especially with one whose spirit is as great as yours. Please do not hesitate to ask for energy, guidance, direction as you may need it.

Howard: Thank you, I do appreciate that! And now, unless anyone has anything further to offer, I think it would be appropriate to close the session for now.

Samantha: We agree.

Howard: Thank you. And St. Germain, you're released to go about your own activities, thanks again. And Michael, Samantha, Shirella, Artoomid – we bring this session to a close. Thank you for your help, guidance, assistance and wisdom. You're all released to go about your own activities with much love and gratitude. *(Pause)* Good. And now, Emma, just relax even deeper, just relax even more, place your awareness on the physical planes below where your physical body is resting there in the safety of your cocoon, and just return to it now, and merge completely and totally. *(Pause)* And when you're ready to return to full conscious awareness, just come on back in the most beneficial way for you. And when you're ready, take a deep breath and open your eyes, and come back to full conscious awareness. *(Pause)* Welcome back!

Emma: I could *feel* St. Germain!

Howard: How did his energies differ from the others?

Emma: They're very light, they're very tingly, very positive, I can still... they're just very tingly!

Howard: Thank you. Thank you so much. I think this will be a good addition to the book. Thanks!

Emma: Oh, yeah! You're welcome! Thank you!

Spiritual Journey 16 – The Golden Age.

My Guide Michael has explained to me that the Akashic Record has within it all that has been, all that is, and all that is likely to be, with a reducing probability of occurrence the farther into the future we look. The Akashic Record, by its very nature, has always been in existence and available to those who can gain access to its information. Further, the ascension process we are in has the effect of 'thinning the veil' and raising the personal vibrations of those who are ready. As evidenced by even this Spiritual Journeys methodology, access is steadily becoming easier. Therefore, a logical step for the curious investigator would be to turn his or her attention away from what has been, and toward what is in the probable future, both for individuals and for Mother Earth and Gaia.

The growing number of individuals who are asking questions and getting answers about the really big issues we face also signals to me that we are being strongly encouraged to expand our awareness and our frame of reference to be able to include this Galactic, Universal and Multi-Universal information and to use that information productively "for the Greater Good of all concerned."

So where are we headed? What do the 'higher dimensions' have in store for us? What will our life and our society be like five years from now, or ten, or twenty? Again – "Ask and ye shall receive!"

Process: 1. Client moves into her Spiritual Area and does the three things she must always do each time she rises up into her Spiritual Area.
2. Client's Higher Self (CHS) asks her Guide if permission is granted to visit the Akashic Record for the purpose of understanding the continuing ascension process of life forms on Planet Earth, and the probable lifestyles, forms of technology and the social, governmental and education institutions that may exist in the near future.
3. If not, the client is emerged from self-hypnosis.
4. CHS asks for the specific information or answers to her questions.
5. Client returns to her cocoon and returns to full conscious awareness.

Case Study 1:
SJ-16: The Golden Age   June 11, 2014 – Directed by Howard Batie
Subject: "Emma"   Subject's Higher Self: "Shirella"   Subject's Guide: "Samantha"

Howard: Shirella, Samantha, today I'd like to do something a little different – I'd like to investigate what's been called The Golden Age. Not Atlantis or Lemuria or times past, but in many cultures around the world there's a myth, a legend, a belief that this is the time of the opening of a Golden Age of lightness and brightness and goodness, and I'd like to explore that to the extent possible and feasible. Samantha, I'd like to know if it's permissible for us to access the Akashic Record to discuss this topic.

Samantha: It is. Where would you like to start? It is a vast subject, the future, the Golden Age.

Howard: Well, we've been told that there's a lot of new, higher frequency energy coming to Earth to birth this new age. Let's start with where does that new energy, those new frequencies, come from and what is their path en route to us?

Samantha:	These energies have existed from the beginning of the Project of Gaia and have all along to be intended to be used at this point in her growth and development, her ascension. As with all Creation, energies come from the One That Is All.
Howard:	Yes. I've seen references about energies coming from the Great Central Sun or other Galaxies....
Samantha:	The source of the energy, once created and designed for the enhancement of the ascension of Gaia was then placed in what you call the Great Central Sun so that it would be available, usable, directable at the time needed.
Howard:	Is the Great Central Sun synonymous with the center of our Galaxy?
Samantha:	It is, but it is also the center of this Universe. It is connected to the center of the Universe, but we allow the information to come from the Great Central Sun. There is an energy path from the center of the Universe to the center of your Galaxy which contains this energy. It is a lesser version of the universal, as it is intended for use only within this Galaxy. So it becomes what you might call a storehouse until specific energies are needed, but it also contains other energies intended for use within the Galaxy.
Howard:	You mentioned an energy link from Source to the center of the Universe to the center of our Galaxy. Does this energy link extend directly to Earth, or does it come via our Sun? How does that work?
Samantha:	Those are energies required for your existence. The energy of your Sun provides life for your planet, and energies from the Great Central Sun assist your Sun in that requirement, that dispersal. The energy from your Sun is more planet-oriented, whereas the energy from the Great Central Sun that has been intended for the ascension of Gaia is more direct. It is very specific, very refined, purposeful energy with specific functions; therefore, it cannot be filtered without disrupting its intended purpose.
Howard:	Good. Now what is the effect of this energy on humans and on Gaia?
Samantha:	Because we are all energetically connected, humans with Gaia, any energy coming in will necessarily affect humans because the energies from the Great Sun have increased, and with specific purpose we have also sent energy to allow humans to assimilate the energy so that they can continue to survive. That is the great awakening of the Human Race, to be able to accommodate new energies. All life forms have been awakened, and it is now a matter of the assimilation and development in the new energies. Gaia's ascension is, as you understand, energy-based, therefore new defined energies are sent. Are you clear on this?
Howard:	Yes. As these higher-frequency energies come to Earth – some directly, some via our Sun – we are changing and evolving, I understand that. Where are we in that evolution, that ascension process?
Samantha:	We would need to define the point at which you think it has begun. In essence, humans have been ascending since the beginning. It is in the plan and program for Gaia and beings on this planet. So great lengths of your time have passed for humans to develop to this point. Please understand that when you speak of consciousness, we are also speaking of a form of energy. So the rising consciousness of the Hu-Mon is due in part to the new energies. It is energy being supported by energy.
Howard:	In the near term, what are the potentials, the likelihood of significant advances in, say, technology?
Samantha:	There is great potential, and we hope that the human race will continue its path with greater speed, now that some elements have been removed that were creating

hindrances. And as the human race begins to demonstrate its ability to use advanced technology appropriately, then these processes will become apparent to them, allowed to be developed. We remain hopeful and positive that this will happen. It is difficult to give time association, but it will be not in the amount of time it has taken... the development is speeding up. The expansion of the human consciousness is developing rapidly. Therefore, we hope it will be soon that we can assist in the development of these technologies, as planet Earth is in great need of them. As the technology is developed, we would like to provide guidance and understanding as to its appropriate use. Some may come from the expanded consciousness and understanding that is becoming more apparent, some may come from off-Earth beings who have had experience, and can assist not only in development, but also in correct use and distribution.

Howard: Good. Now there's been a lot of discussion on our Internet about devices that can provide free energy in a limitless or unending way. Is this technology to be developed and distributed in the near term?

Samantha: It is not possible at this point to give you more than to say it will be much faster than one would think, given current human circumstances and attitudes. Ascension is progressing well, and is speeding up, and in addition planet Earth is in great need of assistance in the form that great numbers of humans are suffering needlessly, and planet Earth needs our attention as soon as possible. However, because of the limited consciousness of the humans still prevalent, we cannot release these assistances until humans demonstrate a more consistent path of positive use. We believe at this point we are looking for a critical mass, and then one day it will appear as if suddenly Earth has awakened. Let me try to be more specific. It may not be a single event such as a free energy device, but the awareness of more people that things are getting better, things should be done, that the common man can make a difference, and in these small things come together in many places around the planet in what seems to be a simultaneous time. There may be a project such as the free energy that will trigger some of this. As you are aware, the ability has always been there, but usage has been blocked by other forces on Earth. The germination of those forces no longer exist. So therefore, the positive has more strength to move forward and fill that hole, the spaces left by the negative. We are hoping for less dictatorial governments. We are hoping for cultures not governed by a single strong ideology, whether it be political or religious, but within those ideologies, a loosening or relaxing happens which accommodates living with other such ideologies without conflict.

Howard: There's a number of political and governmental changes happening around the world. Is this going to increase?

Samantha: Yes, provided those who are awakening in awareness as well as consciousness continue the work of remaining positive and demonstrating positive to others. The positive energies are augmented by those coming from the Central Sun. To make the changes of which you speak there must be a mass agreement of the people affected by them. That will then help to bring about the changes of which you speak. We do not expect or ask for a world government, only that various cultures can accommodate each other in peace. The people within each of those cultures must reach a point where they prefer that type of lifestyle and ask their leaders to accommodate that. That the ego-based, power-based governmental agencies, whether they be political or religious or social, are then moved to change to accommodate the will of the people. Is this better?

Howard: Yes. Now, back to the more technological aspects of what is to come, is there going to be an increased emphasis on the use of alternative fuels, for instance the Sun or the free energy?

Samantha: Yes. It is essential. The use of fossil fuels must end. It is a violation of not only the planet, but of the spirit, the safety of the planet. We see that happening in a relatively short time, very shortly after the introduction of what you call free energy, alternative energy, despite the power and control of the petroleum-based companies. There is a fast-moving... This is very specific, excuse me... We see a great movement that is still quiet for the end of control by fossil fuel companies.

Howard: It seems to me that if free energy were introduced, it would have a major impact on transportation, our ability to move from one place to another. Will there be other advances in our ability to move from Point A to Point B?

Samantha: As the ascension continues and humans grow further into the Light Body, then Yes, they will learn advanced time-travel techniques. This is, however, not in what you would call the near future. There may be exploration with better results than current projects, but ascension must be continued and developed to a point where certain skills can be maintained by a mass public, not just individuals. This opportunity will be available to Hu-Mons, but not until the ascension process and development has reached a cultural acceptance and stability. It is similar to the current attitude about the visitation of aliens. It is only a matter of waiting until Hu-Mons can accept these visitations without fear or negative reactions. To travel without devices is a powerful tool and we must be sure the Hu-Mon race will use it appropriately. Is that better?

Howard: Yes. How much off-world assistance is available right now?

Samantha: A great deal. The human race does not understand the magnitude of the community to which it belongs. Once that information begins to be known, then unlimited amount of assistance is available to assist Earth in healing and to further the ascension and development of the Hu-Mon race. At a point in the growth of your human child, it becomes aware it is part of a community larger than its family, and that this larger community can be of assistance in its own growth, of personality and intellect, et cetera. This is a similar situation. Is that clear?

Howard: Good. Thank you. Now let's kind of shift gears here, and talk about the assistance Gaia and humanity needs to clean up its environment. What kinds of assistance in terms of discoveries or invention or new ideas are going to come about in the very near future?

Samantha: Perhaps I can begin more with a movement or intention. For example, in many countries food is either not available in necessary quantities or as in the larger countries, food itself has been biologically changed to meet needs other than nutrition for which it was intended. One of the primary changes is a need to return to better quality food. Much of what is incorrect about human energy is the incorrect energy it is receiving in its food. Some is from chemical changes, some is from the lack of necessary nutrition. We hope to introduce processes and food strains that will provide great nutrition for those countries that do not have sufficient food, and to encourage the change in those countries that do. But it is essential for the wellbeing of the human body, and therefore spirit connected, that some changes in food intake quality be made. Within the ability to access the necessary food, hopefully you will find some that has not been biologically changed, and will be able to reduce the amount of animal protein, to seek out more balanced diet formation. The amount of negative impact on the human body and therefore mental processes and spirit, the negative impact is not yet understood. Humans will be greatly surprised as a whole, especially in those affluent countries, how the poor nutrition has affected the abilities to think clearly, to learn, stay positive in the face of negative. There is a new awareness of just how extensive this program has become, and those non-affected foods will continue to become more available. It is a matter of finding sources. To some, it is not an economic option. But reducing certain quantities such as animal protein can help.

Howard: How does animal protein slow down those functions, or how does it affect us?

Samantha: It is heavy to digest. It takes great energy to assimilate, it is more complex. A more complex food base requires more energy to assimilate, break down. In addition, despite the heat used in preparation, it carries disease, it carries biological substances not appropriate to the human body. The human has adapted over generations, but with the (recent) biological changes, these adaptations are not sufficient. Is this clear?

Howard: Yes. Samantha, what else can you add about the more important planet-wide changes that are coming about within the next decade?

Samantha: We are hoping to see an end to armed conflict on a massive scale. We are hoping to see more peaceful resolutions and accommodations to disparities in philosophical beliefs. We are hoping, as ascension continues, that the need to be the absolute in any belief will diminish. Is that clear?

Howard: Yes. Thank you, Samantha.

Samantha: You have a term called "grass roots movement" – that is what is happening and what will change, and it is accelerating. There is a definite measurable, meaning noticeable, uneasiness, discomfort among the common citizens of how individual lives are being affected by those in charge. That grass roots movement will accelerate and will be known – its strength will be known – by leaders in the near future. People will stop participating in some of the rules, the processes. And so perhaps, to answer some of your curiosity about the future, watch for continued growth and recognition that the current powers in most governmental areas are not acting in the best interests of the citizens, and in whatever processes the government allows, changes will start to be made by the people. This is a planet-wide movement, so it is difficult to be specific, but unfortunately some will still be violent. But more and more will be simply refusing to participate, not accepting certain guidelines. The success of these movements will be available because much of what has kept them under control is no longer possible. Appropriate changes in government leaders to individuals who are more constructive. For example, Obama came into power as one who would make positive changes. Unfortunately, he could not reach his full potential, but he was able to begin the process by instituting, for example, health care changes and other lesser-known activities that truly benefit the population. This will be seen happening more and more as time progresses, perhaps within a decade significant changes will be seen world-wide – a lessening of the need for violence, uprisings, sooner than that perhaps. The populations, unknown and in some cases even unknown to themselves as a result of the ascension process, are hungry for a different way of living. And that desire will be known in small and in large ways, and once the process is seen as successful even in small areas, it will gain momentum. Have hope, and continue your work, for it contributes greatly to this process.

Howard: Thank you, Samantha. I know this has been a difficult session for you, and I greatly appreciate the information.

Samantha: We all in attendance today would like, as you say, to snap our fingers and give you a new world based on your hopes and dreams, for you are loved. But of course, while we have the power to do so, it is inappropriate. Growth and development is required, and choices must be made to move in that direction. But we see great progress, and we are hopeful, on the verge of being excited! It is difficult to specify because, although things happen at one time, variables can change outcomes. So what we see at this moment may change to one degree or another. However, the larger perspective and pathway is set. It has been agreed upon by humans who wish to ascend, as well as others, that the process will continue and a positive outcome is a matter of time, not will. Gaia has earned her ascension also, and her path is set, therefore human path is set. As you say, the details will be worked out later. So have hope.

Howard: Thank you very much for this time together, Samantha and Shirella. And now, Shirella and Samantha, you are now released to go about your own activities. *(Pause)* Emma, just rest. Good. And when you're ready, in your own time, come on back to full conscious awareness in the most beneficial way for you. *(Pause)* Welcome back! That was a nice message!

* * *

Case Study 2:
SJ-16: The Golden Age   July 12, 2014 – Directed by Howard Batie
Subject: "Karen"   Subject's Higher Self: "Anaka"   Subject's Guide: "Joshua"

Howard: Hello, Anaka. It's good to be with you again. Have you asked that the white light of Creator surround you and protect you always, that a clear channel of communication now be established between yourself and the highest levels of love and wisdom, and that all information you receive be only for the Greater Good of all concerned?

Anaka: Yes.

Howard: Wonderful! Thank you. Now when you're ready, ask Joshua to come forward so we can meet with him and discuss things with him today.

Anaka: He is here.

Howard: Challenge him: Are you in service to the light and love of the One Infinite Creator – Yes or No?

Anaka: Yes.

Howard: Are you in fact Anaka's Guide, Joshua?

Anaka: Yes.

Howard: Good. Welcome, Joshua! And Anaka, just go over to him and give him a big hug. Let him know how glad you are to see him as well. *(Pause)* Good. Now, Anaka, Joshua, today we'd like to explore the Akashic Record for any information that is already recorded there having to do with the next few years of the The Golden Age that we are approaching. And Joshua, is it permissible for us to visit the Akashic Record to learn about the upcoming events in the near future?

Joshua: Yes.

Howard: Good. So, Joshua, I'd like you to examine the Akashic Record for all information that is recorded there now that indicates what may come about as the results of our continued ascension process, humanity's ascension and Gaia's ascension as well. What may we look forward to in the coming months and years in terms of our personal interactions, governmental institutions, or any other facet of Earth life?

Joshua: Earth is ascending, and we are ascending with her; however, not everyone will ascend. Earth is spiritually moving forward, and those humans on her, most humans, will ascend with her. The Old Guard, so to speak, that moved away from Gaia, moved away from Source, are moving on, are dying off, are fighting right now tooth and nail to hold onto the last of the way they have been. It's a major upheaval happening right now, and that will continue for a few years, not many years. It is open now. Things have been opened for information, so you can't take from the people and give nothing back and not be found out any more. Now the fear is going away. People have been held in control by fear, by threats, and even by their own religions.

Howard: And what's going to happen when people find out the truth?

Joshua: They will no longer let themselves be subjected to fear; they will no longer let themselves be controlled by fear; they will learn to understand each individual person, each incarnated being is unique and beautiful each in its own way, so a lot of judgement will fall away. Beings right now have been conditioned to feel separate, to isolate by comparison, they say, "I am better, I am worse, I am different, I am apart from, I am away from." And they will soon begin to realize that's not true. They are already realizing. Young people no longer have the same concepts of what is good and what is beautiful that the old ones do. They accept more in each other, and accept less from those who don't connect with spirit. They become outraged at injustices. So the world will evolve toward a kinder feeling toward everyone else, a knowledge that we are all connected, that we are all important, that we all need each other. Energetics will change very soon. Already those who control with oil and government and money and soldiers, their power is lessening all the time, and they're fighting it, but it's still lessening. So the world will be better for everyone; it'll be better for the people, for the animals, for the plants, for Mother Gaia herself.

Howard: And how long will that change take before we really reach out to each other and realize we are connected, they are extensions of us, and we are extensions of them?

Joshua: Within ten, maybe twenty years. So many people are becoming enlightened now, and it's spreading all over.

Howard: Still, that's a huge change in the psyche of an entire civilization. Are there any external events that will help to accelerate this process that you see very likely happening?

Joshua: There will be physical disasters, there will be humanitarian needs based on those, and there will be a huge shift, the shift that's beginning right now. Let's say the children from Central America – there's becoming a big division of what to do with those children. And that is making people look at it, which is what all of it does. The wars, the disasters, the earthquakes – it's making people pay attention because our communication has reached the point we know what's happening – you can't ignore that there is need. And so we are watching what our leaders are doing, and when they're making wrong choices, we now can say, "They can't lead us anymore" and they know that. So that they're faced with choices: do they want to continue to be greedy or do they want to change the way they work, and I think in twenty years that will change a lot. A lot. And it will take a lot of those who now have the power; it will take the time for them to die, but they will be dying and moving on.

Howard:	People have predicted many things – it's easy to make a prediction. But I'd like to know, in the Akashic Record is there any information as to the, say a generation from now, the total population of the Earth?
Joshua:	It will be many less. Those who will be there will thrive. I'm seeing maybe half.
Howard:	It would take a significant number of major events to cut the population in half within one generation. What types of events do you foresee there in the Akashic Record?
Joshua:	When our ascension is complete, we will know it, and it will be good, and those that didn't ascend will have moved to other places or will have gone back to Spirit World to be reincarnated. And the old Earth will have had some catastrophic events that a lot of those returns to Spirit World by death will have happened through. I see the Earth almost splitting so that the Old Earth as an entity will have major, huge catastrophic events happen, and the New Earth as an ascended, created being will feel that and have some moved and have some changes, but then will be its bright and healthy, ascended self. It happens energetically.
Howard:	Will there be physical changes to our body as we move through this changing process?
Joshua:	Yes, physically – physical energetic changes. You might not be as aware of them until they have already happened and you will realize it's different, but it will change. We'll be light bodies, our inner base, our cell base will be different, the atoms will be changed within us. They will be expanded. They will be much less dense, we'll be aware of them, we'll feel our body, we'll have the body, but it will be... not really ghostly, but much less dense, much easier to carry for the soul, lighter. Your light will shine through better, we'll recognize each other's light more easily because we'll see it in each other more easily.
Howard:	Will we retain a human form, or not?
Joshua:	We can choose. We can choose to look human, we can choose to look other than human. It depends what you call human. If you call Sirians and Pleiadians and Arcturians and humans all humans or Earthlings, we all are human in our own way. Earth beings are Hu-beings, but each of those other incarnations in other places are Hu-ed beings as well. They don't look exactly like us, but they are a physical representation of the soul; that's what any body is. (Note: In the Spirit World, "Hu" is the vibration or name meaning "Divine")
Howard:	Thank you. You mentioned before changes in the way we look at the Petroleum industry. That would have a major impact on our society – the way we heat our homes, the way we move our automobiles. What information is there in the Akashic Record that we might look forward to?
Joshua:	That there will be ways to tap into the energy that doesn't need fossil fuels to happen. We realize already that fossil fuels have served their purpose and have become abusive to the Earth. Abusive in pollution, abusive in the way to control financial resources for the whole globe, a way to control the people of the Earth, a way to gain power; the few people who own that and hold that are receiving a lot of pressure from a lot of people who know what's wrong and know what's hurting Gaia. And it won't maintain. It can't maintain. It would either poison the Earth or stop – that's the choices. So other energy is already being created, already is out there, and it will come forward very soon.
Howard:	What form – is that solar?
Joshua:	Some solar, some might be tapping into Inner Earth energy, and I'm not sure how that will happen, but we'll tap into Inner Earth energy. We will tap into the energy within

the oceans. There's tremendous energy there! We haven't learned how to tap into that. There's chemical energy just within the source of the ocean water, and there's energy within the movement of the ocean, and we need to learn to tap into that energy. And there's even energy in volcanic energy. The Earth is providing energy all around us; we just have to learn how to use it, and people are learning. All around the Earth, I see people working on energy that's not fossil fuel everywhere, but they have to do it on their own and quietly and separately because they're stopped by the money and the power if they become public too soon. But it's there, and it will happen soon!

Howard: And when that happens, what will some of the early changes be to our social structure, to our transportation structure?

Joshua: Transportation will turn more toward electric sources like hydropower and solar and wind. Sources that we learn to charge batteries, and those batteries can become so efficient that you can have vehicles that run on that energy and can maintain longer than just a few miles. Right now, it's only a little ways, but we will learn to take a lot of energy and put it in a small space. Right now, they take a little bit of energy and put it in a big battery, or a big receiver, and it can't hold a lot and runs slow, but there are creators there working who can take a lot of energy and learn how to condense it into a small space that holds and uses and recharges itself as it goes. That comes from electricity – that comes from solar, water and air.

Howard: Wonderful!

Joshua: So that's for vehicles, and that can do your house, too.

Howard: What about governmental changes?

Joshua: The Old Guard that is controlled by those with money will fall by the wayside, but it will be a hard-fought battle. It already is a hard-fought battle. Most elections now are purchased, and the people are seeing that, and the people are raising up against that from the grass-roots. They see, they understand, and they're moving past the ones that have been lying to them. They're starting to see the lies. So the movement will come from below, not above. The change won't come from those who already have it all. The change will come from those who have to change the way it is distributed, and change the way that it is shared.

Howard: We've heard other things from some sources that say that the monetary policy, which is really at the heart of the governmental problems, the monetary policy is about to change into something better.

Joshua: It is. It's a part of the change of the Old Guard, so to speak. The banks won't just automatically change over because they are just not nice guys. They're run by the people who want to put all the money in fewer and fewer places, and so it will come from the people changing the system that the money's filtered through, and that can only be done through election. It's either election or anarchy, and anarchy wouldn't work. So they have to do it in a way that changes the system, and changes from the ground up, the way that it's done. So hard to do, but it can be done.

Howard: So the Akashic Record shows that these changes that are coming about will be the result of governmental elections that elect honest people?

Joshua: People who are from the people, not people who are from the money. Right now, most of those who are in the positions in the government who run things are there from money and by money, and they are controlled by the money and want more money, so they're just part of the Greed Machine. But in every place in the world, the common people, the grass roots, the man on the ground, is standing up and saying, "That's not right! That's not OK!" And their voices will be heard.

Howard: It seems the only way that they can be heard is through the elections, unless you go the anarchy route, which we don't want to. There's a lot of information – I don't know if it's information or dis-information or misinformation – swirling around about some changes that are going to be brought about to the global monetary policies, some efforts that have been undertaken by St. Germain to bring a better balance to everything. Can you talk to what the Akashic Records have to say about that effort, and when, if ever, it may come to fruition?

Joshua: I'm being shown the Vatican and Francis, and that they'll be a key in the change, that the way that the Bank of the Vatican and the control that they have will influence the way that the rest of the banking changes. I see it has to do with Francis. I'm not sure if he works with St. Germain – I think does – and he is one person who has a voice that can help to change an influential financial system. And I see guys like Warren Buffett, there are some people who have lots of money, Bill Gates, people who have lots of money who understand the people, who are willing to help give back, and who can help to make the change. So there are a few in power who aren't the Greedies, who can help from the top, and they will have to. But I'm being pointed toward Europe, so maybe it'll start with Europe.

Howard: All right. Joshua, is it appropriate to call for St. Germain to let him speak of any changes that he is involved with. Is it appropriate to call for him at this time?

Joshua: Yes.

Howard: Thank you. St. Germain, we call you into this conversation as well, please join us, and we ask first, for your presence here, and Anaka, when you can sense or detect St. Germain's presence, please let me know.

Anaka: He is here.

Howard: Good. This being that has presented as St. Germain, are you in service to the love and the light of the One Infinite Creator – Yes or No?

St. Germain: Yes.

Howard: Good. Are you, in fact, St. Germain?

St. Germain: Yes.

Howard: Welcome! Thank you very much, St. Germain! And I would ask you to speak to the last point that I made or question that I asked about any changes that might be impending that you've been working on. And I would ask you to speak directly through our channel today if that's all right.

St. Germain: Yes. Mmmm – ask me more specific questions!

Howard: Yes. We've heard of the revaluation effort that's on-going. What can you tell us about that?

St. Germain: I'm working with some souls on Earth to help change the system, to let the money flow down to the people. I work with the Church and with the World Bank and some in the stock market in places around Earth who have a lot of control with the money and are mixed in with those who control without an agenda to help, and those who have come into this lifetime to bring justice to that job. Francis himself came knowing he would eventually become the Pope and would eventually work with the Church to change the way that the church helps the people, to get back to the basics, to work with the people. For example, the Catholic Church originally was based on the teachings of Jesus/Sananda, and that was to be a lesson for all of Earth, all the world, to share and to love all that are. And the Church was taken over by those who learned that they could control not just a country, but a world, with their religion. And to do that, they began to amass material goods and people they could control. And as the centuries passed, they controlled more and more, and they branched out into other entities they could control, like the British Crown and missionaries in different countries. And all the way until the last Pope, it was all about gathering and hoarding; now it's happening all around the globe, all around the Earth. And so Francis incarnated, knowing he would come, and it would be his mission to change that. And that's what he is doing in the way that he knows how. And he works with me, and he works with others who are seeing the light, and behind the scenes, so to speak, they will be changing the world financially. They will be making huge changes that will surprise the people in good ways for most. Those that are surprised in bad ways will have to choose to change or move on and be an example. None will be treated mean or unkind, but all will be given a choice to help, to change. But there is still work to do, and it will still take us time. What else do you want to know?

Howard: I won't ask questions about the time schedule, I know the sensitivities involved, but thank you very much for sharing what you've told us here today, St. Germain. Thank you very much. And is there anything else that you might like to share on this or any other subject at this time?

St. Germain: I want to say, Howard, to continue to be a scribe, to continue to listen and to share and to continue with your work, and to tell you that you are on your path where you need to be, and to continue with those that you are helping to guide. That is all.

Howard: Thank you. I will continue because they also guide me. Thank you for coming today, St. Germain. And with love and gratitude, we release you now to go about your own activities. Joshua, do you have any comments or observations about what St. Germain has just told us?

Joshua: No. This brings you the truth I could not.

Howard: Thank you. Joshua, do you have anything further to add today to our discussion today of the potential changes that are going to be coming about here in the next generation or so?

Joshua: You will find it wonderful! Continue to stay in the light, and continue to let those things that don't match the light fall by the wayside. The light is growing very strong for us all!

Howard: Good! Thank you. Thank you for coming today, Joshua.

Joshua: You're welcome!

Howard: And again, with much love and gratitude, you are also released to go about your own activities. And now Anaka, just rest, relax, and remember all the conversations here today so that Karen can bring them back to her conscious mind. And when you're ready, just return to your cocoon below, fully integrating your superconscious, your soul awareness, with your physical body and your conscious mind. And when that's complete, and when you're ready, return to full conscious awareness in the most beneficial method for you. Go ahead and do that now. *(Pause)* Hello! Welcome back!

Karen: Whew! That was very strange! When St. Germain came in, he came in from the right. Everything always comes in from the left, and I totally felt the shift to the right! I felt it coming in, and then I kind of trembled and it happened really strange!

Howard: I noticed that you were breathing much deeper when St. Germain was talking.

Karen: I felt like I was way deep inside. Wow! Interesting! Thank you!

Howard: I didn't mean to surprise anything on you, but I do what I'm guided to do as well. Thank you so much! Any questions? *(Note: Prior to the session, we had not planned on inviting St. Germain to join us.)*

Karen: Nope!

Howard: OK!

five

Our Path Ahead

The preceding chapters have provided a practical methodology for discovering and collecting a vast amount of spiritual information on an equally infinite variety of topics. The obvious question is: What do we do with all that information, individually and collectively? How will we share what we have learned? As noted in my Preface, an infinitely large spreadsheet for an infinite amount of information is quite impractical and, in the last analysis, completely unnecessary, since it would be a futile attempt to duplicate what is already recorded in the Akashic Record, which itself continues to grow rapidly with each new daily experience of each individual. However, as humans, we are limited first to the information we can understand, and secondly to our ability to manage the information that we are able to comprehend. Yet as we continue to guide our clients to greater and greater personal discoveries, we also naturally feel the need to share our findings with others who can understand the information.

<u>Spiritual Discussion Groups.</u>

My suggestion is that we start locally. Several years ago, this need to share the information I was receiving urged me to create what I call a "Spiritual Discussion Group" that meets regularly each month in my office. As we became more aware of our spirituality, we needed a safe and friendly environment to discuss and share our experiences with like-minded friends. Each member of our group, which is composed primarily of my clients, students and friends, shares and discusses a very broad variety of spiritual information – personal coincidences, spiritual experiences, channelings from experienced and trusted sources, and more recently, a limited amount of information from their most recent Spiritual Journeys sessions. We have found that this sharing allows us to reinforce the sense that we are collectively on the right path, as well as to add valuable insight and perspectives from others into our own expanding personal experiences. Our individual friendships have become deeper, and our cohesiveness as a group of spiritual explorers has become significantly greater. And, as a growing number of seekers learn about and visit our group, we are all heartened when they say, "I feel like I've come home to my soul family after wandering around on my own!"

<u>Intra-Group Collaboration</u>

However, my Guide Michael has cautioned me that there is a very big difference between sharing *information* about one's individual experience, and sharing the *experience* itself with all its nuances of sensations, images, emotions, and knowings. The difficulty is that when sharing or describing an experience, there is the common failing of the human ego to always compare one thing to another to determine which is 'better'. A great deal of consideration should be given to this 'conundrum,' as Michael calls it, before attempting to share even an intellectual description of one's personal experiences. His exact words are, "But you would have to determine for yourself whether a discussion of your experience is beneficial, or if it would feed the ego and lose the sense of Oneness."

This was carefully considered during the preparation of this manual, and I felt that it would be in the Greater Good of all concerned to illustrate the wide diversity in personal experiences rather than to offer any specific individual experience as something that others should also aspire to. Just as the physical experiences of each person in the world are unique to that individual, so are their spiritual experiences. Therefore, your own Spiritual Journeys will be uniquely what your soul has experienced before, and are usually far outside the limitations of what you think or imagine you are capable of.

As new members are introduced to your Spiritual Discussion Group, it is suggested that this topic be among the first that the Group Leader discusses with them. In my own Spiritual Discussion Group we have agreed that this precaution would provide the best protection against expecting or hoping for similar or 'better' results from their own Spiritual Journeys sessions. Whatever you recall from your own Akashic Record of personal experiences is perfect for you since your subconscious mind will recall only your own truth and your spiritual (or superconscious) mind has no need or reason to relate anything other than your own personal Truth.

My wish is that this or a similar model for small local groups of spiritual explorers will be adopted by other Spiritual Journeys Practitioners who also form their own Spiritual Discussion Groups to meet the needs of their local members and to mentor each individual as appropriate. If you are a Certified Hypnotist or Hypnotherapist and would like to establish your own Spiritual Discussion Group, the first step is to become a Spiritual Journeys Practitioner, then begin to provide and document Spiritual Journeys sessions for your clients, and subsequently to share within your own Spiritual Discussion Group that information that the Leader and the Member mutually determine to be appropriate for sharing The instructions for becoming a Spiritual Journeys Practitioner are available on my website, http://www.howardbatie.com, then click on "Spiritual Journeys" and scroll to the bottom of the page.

At the top of the Spiritual Journeys page on my website, there is a link to download a listing of all the trained Spiritual Journeys Practitioners who have given me permission to publicly list their contact information, and who are ready to attract and assist additional clients to explore their own spiritual experiences. It is intended that, initially, this listing be the only initial centralized management procedure for sharing Spiritual Journeys information, and that each Spiritual Discussion Group Leader conduct their own Group in a manner that best meets the needs of their local members.

Spiritual Discussion Group Organization

The Spiritual Discussion Group (SDG) consists of a mix of individuals: a Leader (a Spiritual Journeys Practitioner and Certified Hypnotherapist who is qualified to coach students on all individual Spiritual Journeys sessions), Members (the core membership who regularly attended our